SQL

PROGRAMMER'S REFERENCE

Kishore Bhamidipati

SQL

PROGRAMMER'S REFERENCE

Kishore Bhamidipati

Osborne/**McGraw-Hill**

Berkeley ▪ New York ▪ St. Louis ▪ San Francisco
Auckland ▪ Bogotá ▪ Hamburg ▪ London
Madrid ▪ Mexico City ▪ Milan ▪ Montreal
New Delhi ▪ Panama City ▪ Paris ▪ São Paulo
Singapore ▪ Sydney ▪ Tokyo ▪ Toronto

Osborne/**McGraw-Hill**
2600 Tenth Street
Berkeley, California 94710
U.S.A.

For information on translations or book distributors outside the U.S.A., or to
arrange bulk purchase discounts for sales promotions, premiums, or
fund-raisers, please contact Osborne/**McGraw-Hill** at the above address.

SQL Programmer's Reference

Publisher   Brandon A. Nordin
Editor-in-Chief   Scott Rogers
Acquisitions Editor   Megg Bonar
Project Editor   Mark Karmendy
Technical Editor   Scott Urman
Proofreader   Pat Mannion
Indexer   Richard Shrout
Computer Designers   Michelle Galicia and Jean Butterfield
Illustrator   Sue Albert

1234567890 DOC DOC 901987654321098

ISBN 0-07-882460-5

This book is dedicated to my parents for all their love and encouragement. -KB

ABOUT THE AUTHOR

Kishore Bhamidipati is a senior member of Oracle's Worldwide Support organization. Since 1995 he has worked in the Programming Languages Group and is currently with the Center of Expertise department of Oracle's Premium Customer Support Services.

CONTENTS @ A GLANCE

CONTENTS

x Contents

II Syntax Flowcharts 135

III   Keywords and Parameters   217

ACKNOWLEDGMENTS

First and foremost thanks go to my wife Sirisha for her constant love and understanding, especially given that I embarked on this project right during our wedding period and was busy through the first few months of our marriage. I am positive that the book could not have been possible without her support. I also thank Scott Urman for recommending me to Osborne/McGraw-Hill for this project and for his technical reviews. I cannot forget to thank my family and friends (too numerous to name; you know who you are) for their words of encouragement when I was feeling overwhelmed. Thanks are also due to the folks at Osborne/McGraw-Hill, especially Megg Bonar and Mark Karmendy for their patience. I am also grateful to the management in the Oracle Support and Legal organizations for their encouragement and help.

I have used various sources of reference to build this manual including *Oracle8 SQL Reference*, *Oracle8 Pro*C/C++ Precompiler Programmer's Guide*, *Oracle8 PL/SQL User's Guide and Reference*, and *SQL*Plus User's Guide and Reference*.

I hope you shall enjoy using this book as much as I did writing it. I apologize for any errors or omissions. Please do send your comments to kbhamidi@us.oracle.com.

-KB

Structured Query Language (SQL, pronounced "sequel") is a nonprocedural language that is used to handle data in the modern-day relational database systems (RDBMS). It is a set of commands used by all programmers and application developers to access data stored in any database. SQL was developed by IBM in the 1970s with the intention of using E. F. Codd's model of storing data in relational databases. The relational model itself was proposed in a paper titled, "A Relational Model of Data for Large Shared Data Banks." Oracle was the first company to develop the commercially available implementation of SQL. Other companies such as IBM, Microsoft, Informix, and Sybase have their own implementations.

Currently, SQL is the first language of choice to access and manipulate data stored in relational databases.

Since the time of its design, SQL has been enhanced to include many new features. The American National Standards Institute (ANSI) defines certain standards to which all the commercially available implementations must adhere. There are three levels of compliance: Entry, Intermediate, and Full. Most of the major database companies' SQL offerings comply with the Entry level at the very minimum. Oracle, for example, has many additional features that are defined in the Intermediate or Full compliance model. There are different standards that are specified also. The current implementation of SQL is called the SQL92 standard, and ANSI is working on the SQL3 framework.

The SQL3 standard has several new object-oriented extensions, created basically to address the need for object-oriented application development.

How SQL Works

Perhaps the single most important reason for the high popularity of SQL among database programmers is its ease of use. It is a very straightforward language whose biggest factor in its ease of use is that it is nonprocedural. When we say that SQL is nonprocedural we mean that the programmer does not have to tell the database how to perform a certain task in SQL. He or she just specifies what the task is and the SQL engine in the database does its operations behind the scenes. SQL is a fourth-generation language (4GL) as opposed to languages such as C, Pascal, COBOL, Ada, etc., which are third-generation languages. The third-generation languages require you to specify not only which tasks to perform but also how to perform them. Oracle's PL/SQL combines the best of both worlds in that it provides procedural extensions to SQL— which makes it a very good database programming language.

The design goal behind SQL was to keep it simple so that the application developer would not get bogged down with the details of the implementation of the logic itself but instead spend his or her time and efforts on understanding the problem domain. Some of the salient features of SQL are as follows:

- It processes sets of data as groups rather than as individual elements.

- It provides automatic navigation to the data.

- It uses statements that are complex and powerful individually.

Essentially, SQL lets you work with data at the logical level without having to worry about the details of data retrieval or manipulation.

SQL provides commands to perform a variety of tasks, including the following:

- Querying data

- Inserting, updating, and deleting rows in a table

- Creating, replacing, altering, and dropping objects

- Controlling access to the database and its objects

- Guaranteeing database consistency and integrity

Perhaps the biggest plus point of SQL is its portability. As a result, all programs written in SQL can be moved from one database to another with very little modification.

Embedded SQL

Embedded SQL refers to the use of standard SQL commands embedded within a procedural programming language. The SQL commands are embedded in third-generation languages like C, COBOL, FORTRAN, and Ada. Different vendors provide tools to convert the embedded SQL commands in these 3GL programs to the host language (the language in which the SQL commands are embedded). These tools are the precompilers that operate on the embedded SQL commands and generate the equivalent host language code.

Classification of SQL Commands

As explained in the previous section, SQL provides commands for different types of functions within a database. The following is a brief description of each of the categories into which SQL commands can be divided.

Data Definition Language (DDL)

Data Definition Language commands are those commands that allow you to create, alter, and drop objects. They allow you to grant and revoke privileges and roles. They establish auditing options and add comments to the data dictionary. These commands perform an implicit commit when they are executed.

Data Manipulation Language (DML)

Data Manipulation Language commands allow you to query and manipulate data in existing database objects such as tables, views, etc. These commands do not implicitly commit the transaction of which they are a part.

Transaction Control (TCL)

Transaction Control commands manage changes made by the DML statements. These are statements such as COMMIT, ROLLBACK, etc.

Session Control

Session Control commands dynamically manage the properties of a user session. These commands do not implicitly commit a transaction of which they are a part.

System Control

System Control commands dynamically manage the properties of the instance of the server. These commands do not implicitly commit the current transaction.

Structure of this Book

This book is divided into three parts. Each part contains a listing of every command, and the commands are laid out alphabetically according to type into these sections:

DDL Commands
DML Commands
Transaction Control Commands
Session and System Control Commands
Embedded SQL Commands
Object-Related SQL Commands

Part I lists each command with an explanation of its purpose and prerequisites, followed by an example or examples of its usage. This part also contains a brief overview of Oracle's PL/SQL, which is Oracle's procedural extension; a discussion of SQLJ and JDBC, along with descriptions of the various types of JDBC drivers; a listing of all the ANSI keywords and reserved words; and a brief description of Oracle's reporting tool SQL Plus, the most common environment in which to write and execute SQL and PL/SQL scripts.

Part II shows the syntax, explained via flow diagrams, for each command. Part III lists all the keywords and parameters for each command.

Tables Used in the Book

The schema used in this book consists of two tables: *emp* and *dept*. We initially create these tables in user *scott's* schema and populate them as shown later. We then use these tables and the data within them to demonstrate the various SQL commands' syntax.

The *emp* table has the following columns:

Column Name	Null?	Type
EMPNO	NOT NULL	NUMBER(4)
ENAME		VARCHAR2(10)
JOB		VARCHAR2(9)
MGR		NUMBER(4)
HIREDATE		DATE
SAL		NUMBER(7,2)
COMM		NUMBER(7,2)
DEPTNO		NUMBER(2)

The *dept* table has the following columns:

Column Name	Null?	Type
DEPTNO	NOT NULL	NUMBER(2)
DNAME		VARCHAR2(14)
LOC		VARCHAR2(13)

The following are the SQL commands used (in Oracle SQL) to create these tables and to insert rows into them:

```
CREATE TABLE emp
       (empno number(4) not null,
        ename varchar2(10),
        job varchar2(9),
```

```
        mgr number(4),
        hiredate date,
        sal number(7,2),
        comm number(7,2),
        deptno number(2));

INSERT into emp values
        (7369,'Smith','Clerk',7902,'17-Dec-
-80',800,null,20);
INSERT into emp values
        (7499,'Allen','Salesman',7698,'20-Feb-
-81',1600,300,30);
INSERT into emp values

(7521,'Ward','Salesman',7698,'22-Feb-81',1250,500,30);
INSERT into emp values
        (7566,'Jones','Manager',7839,'2-Apr-
-81',2975,null,20);
INSERT into emp values
        (7654,'Martin','Salesman',7698,'28-Sep-
-81',1250,1400,30);
INSERT into emp values

(7698,'Blake','Manager',7839,'1-May-81',2850,null,30);
INSERT into emp values
        (7782,'Clark','Manager',7839,'9-Jun-
-81',2450,null,10);
INSERT into emp values
        (7788,'Scott','Analyst',7566,'09-Dec-
-82',3000,null,20);
INSERT into emp values

(7839,'King','President',null,'17-Nov-81',5000,null,10);
INSERT into emp values
        (7844,'Turner','Salesman',7698,'8-Sep-
-81',1500,0,30);
INSERT into emp values
        (7876,'Adams','Clerk',7788,'12-Jan-
-83',1100,null,20);
INSERT into emp values

(7900,'James','Clerk',7698,'3-Dec-81',950,null,30);
INSERT into emp values
        (7902,'Ford','Analyst',7566,'3-Dec-
-81',3000,null,20);
```

```
INSERT into emp values
        (7934,'Miller','Clerk',7782,'23-Jan-
-82',1300,null,10);

CREATE TABLE dept
        (deptno number(2),
         dname varchar2(14),
         loc varchar2(13) );

INSERT into dept values
        (10,'Accounting','New York');
INSERT into dept values (20,'Research','Dallas');
INSERT into dept values
        (30,'Sales','Chicago');
INSERT into dept values
        (40,'Operations','Boston');
```

Part I
SQL Commands

DDL Commands

In this section, we shall discuss the Data Definition Language (DDL) commands in alphabetical order. DDL commands can be described as those SQL commands that allow a user to perform the following tasks:

- Create, alter, and drop database objects such as tables, views, sequences, etc.
- Provide access to database objects through granting and revoking roles.
- Analysis of information on a table, index, or a cluster.
- Control auditing options.
- Adding comments to data dictionary.

In order for any of the DDL operations to succeed, the privileges to perform the specific operation must be granted to the user either directly or via a role. An important point to bear in mind about all DDL commands is that they perform and implicitly COMMIT the transaction in which they are invoked. Therefore, you must be very careful about invoking these commands in the middle of transactions that are likely to be rolled back due to some business logic.

The following is an alphabetical listing of DDL commands supported by Oracle, Informix, and SQL Server.

ALTER CLUSTER

Purpose
To redefine storage and parallelism characteristics for a cluster.

Prerequisite

The cluster must be in your own schema or you must have the
ALTER ANY CLUSTER system privilege.

Example

The following example alters the *customer* cluster in the user
scott's schema:

```
ALTER CLUSTER scott.customer
SIZE 512
STORAGE (MAXEXTENTS 25);
```

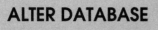

ALTER DATABASE

Purpose

To alter an existing database in one of the several ways
given below:

- Mount the database or standby database.

- Convert an Oracle version 7 data dictionary when migrating
  to Oracle8.

- Open the database.

- Choose archivelog or noarchivelog mode for redo log
  file groups.

- Perform media recovery.

- Add or drop a redo log file group or a member of a redo log
  file group.

- Clear and initialize an online redo log file.

- Rename a redo log file member or a data file.

- Back up the current control file.

- Back up SQL commands (that can be used to re-create the
  database) to the database's trace file.

- Take a data file online or offline.

- Enable or disable a thread of redo log file groups.

- Change the database's global name.

- Prepare to downgrade to an earlier release of Oracle.
- Resize one or more data files.
- Create a new data file in place of an old one for recovery purposes.
- Enable or disable the autoextending of the size of data files (Oracle8).

NOTE: The ALTER DATABASE command is specific to Oracle.

Prerequisites
You must have the ALTER DATABASE system privilege.

Examples
Here are a few examples of the use of the ALTER DATABASE command. Note that not all of the operations mentioned above have been demonstrated. The first is an example of a command that mounts the database called *stocks* exclusively:

```
ALTER DATABASE stocks
MOUNT EXCLUSIVE;
```

The following command drops all members of the redo log file *group 3*:

```
ALTER DATABASE stocks DROP LOGFILE GROUP 3;
```

The following command changes the size of a data file called *mydb.dat*:

```
ALTER DATABASE DATAFILE 'mydb.dat' RESIZE 10 M;
```

The following statement clears a log file called *mylog.dbf*:

```
ALTER DATABASE CLEAR LOGFILE 'mylog.dbf';
```

ALTER FUNCTION

Purpose
To recompile a stand-alone stored function.

Prerequisites

You must be the owner of the function or you must have the
ALTER ANY PROCEDURE system privilege.

Example

You would execute the following command to explicitly recompile
the function *hire_emp*:

```
ALTER FUNCTION hire_emp RECOMPILE;
```

ALTER INDEX

Purpose

To change storage allocation for an index or to rebuild an index.

Prerequisites

The index must be in your own schema or you should have the
ALTER ANY INDEX system privilege.

Example

The following example alters scott's *customer* index so that future
data blocks within this index use five initial transaction entries and
an incremental extent of 100K:

```
ALTER INDEX scott.customer
INITRANS     5
STORAGE (NEXT 100K);
```

ALTER PACKAGE

Purpose

To recompile a stored package or package body.

Prerequisites

The package must be in your own schema or you must have the
ALTER ANY PROCEDURE system privilege.

Examples

Here is an example that recompiles the specification of the package called *hire_fire*:

```
ALTER PACKAGE hire_fire
COMPILE;
```

The next example compiles the body of the same package:

```
ALTER PACKAGE hire_fire
COMPILE BODY;
```

ALTER PROCEDURE

Purpose

To recompile a stand-alone procedure.

Prerequisites

The procedure must be in your own schema or you must have the ALTER ANY PROCEDURE system privilege. The ALTER PROCEDURE and ALTER FUNCTION commands are used to explicitly recompile a procedure or function (respectively) that is invalid. When you explicitly recompile a stored procedure or function, you eliminate the need for runtime recompilation, thereby preventing associated runtime compilation errors and performance degradation. You can use this command only to explicitly recompile stand-alone procedures, not packaged procedures. Recompiling a procedure automatically causes the recompilation of objects upon which the procedure is dependent.

NOTE: Oracle invalidates any local objects that are dependent upon the procedure, such as procedures, functions, or triggers that call the procedure that was recompiled.

Example

To explicitly recompile a procedure called *employee_status*, you would use the following command:

```
ALTER PROCEDURE employee_status COMPILE;
```

ALTER PROFILE

Purpose
To add, modify, or remove a resource limit in a profile.

Prerequisites
You must have the ALTER PROFILE system privilege.

Examples
The following statement is an example that defines a new limit of five concurrent sessions for the profile called *engineer*:

```
ALTER PROFILE engineer LIMIT SESSIONS_PER_USER 5;
```

The following command defines unlimited idle time for the *engineer* profile:

```
ALTER PROFILE engineer LIMIT IDLE_TIME UNLIMITED;
```

ALTER RESOURCE COST

Purpose
To specify a formula to calculate the total resource cost used in a session. For any session, this cost is limited by the value of the COMPOSITE_LIMIT parameter in the user's profile.

Prerequisites
You must have the ALTER RESOURCE system privilege.

Example
The following statement assigns weights to the two resources CPU_PER_SESSION and CONNECT_TIME:

```
ALTER RESOURCE COST
CPU_PER_SESSION 50
CONNECT_TIME    1;
```

The above command establishes the following cost formula for a session:

$$T = 100 * CPU + CON$$

where

T is the total resource cost for the session in service units;
CPU is the CPU time used by the session, measured in hundredths of seconds;
CON is the elapsed time of a session, measured in minutes.

ALTER ROLE

Purpose
To change the authorization needed to enable a role.

Prerequisites
Either you must have the ALTER ANY ROLE system privilege or you must have been granted the role with ADMIN OPTION. (ADMIN OPTION is specific to the GRANT command, which is discussed later in this section.)

Example
The following statement changes the password of the role *temp_emp* to '*temporary*':

```
ALTER ROLE  temp_emp IDENTIFIED BY 'temporary';
```

ALTER ROLLBACK SEGMENT

Purpose
To alter a rollback segment in one of the following ways:

- By bringing it online
- By taking it offline

- By changing its storage characteristics
- By shrinking it to an optimal or given size

Prerequisites

You must have the ALTER ROLLBACK SEGMENT system privilege.

Examples

The following statement brings the rollback segment called *rb1* online:

```
ALTER ROLLBACK SEGMENT rb1 ONLINE;
```

The following statement changes the storage parameters for *rb2*:

```
ALTER ROLLBACK SEGMENT rb2 STORAGE (NEXT 1000 MAXEXTENTS
20);
```

The following statement attempts to resize a rollback segment to an optimum size of 50 megabytes:

```
ALTER ROLLBACK SEGMENT rb2 SHRINK TO 50M;
```

ALTER SEQUENCE

Purpose

To change the sequence in one of the following ways:

- Changing the increment between future sequence values
- Setting or eliminating the minimum or maximum value
- Changing the number of cached sequence numbers
- Specifying whether sequence numbers should be ordered

Prerequisites

The sequence must be in your own schema or you must have the ALTER ANY SEQUENCE system privilege, or you must have the ALTER SEQUENCE privilege on the specific sequence you are trying to alter.

Examples

The following example sets a maximum value for the sequence called *myseq* to 100:

```
ALTER SEQUENCE myseq MAXVALUE 100;
```

The following command turns on cycling (numbers are reused after the maximum value is reached) for the sequence called *myseq*:

```
ALTER SEQUENCE myseq CYCLE;
```

ALTER SNAPSHOT

Purpose

To alter a snapshot in one of the following ways:

- Changing its storage characteristics
- Changing its AUTOMATIC REFRESH mode and times

Prerequisites

The snapshot must be in your own schema or you must have the ALTER ANY SNAPSHOT system privilege.

Examples

There are many different parameters that determine how a snapshot can be altered. Here are a couple of examples. The first statement changes the automatic refresh mode of the snapshot called *new_emps*:

```
ALTER SNAPSHOT new_emps REFRESH FAST;
```

The following statement stores a new interval between automatic refreshes for the snapshot called *new_emps*:

```
ALTER SNAPSHOT hq_emp REFRESH NEXT SYSDATE+7;
```

The following statement specifies a new refresh mode, next refresh time, and a new interval between automatic refreshes of the *new_emps* snapshot:

```
ALTER SNAPSHOT new_emps
REFRESH COMPLETE
START WITH TRUNC(SYSDATE + 1) + 9/24
NEXT SYSDATE+7;
```

The following example changes the remote master rollback segment used during a snapshot refresh to *remote_seg*:

```
ALTER SNAPSHOT new_emps
REFRESH USING MASTER ROLLBACK SEGMENT remote_seg;
```

ALTER SNAPSHOT LOG

Purpose
To change the storage characteristics of a snapshot log.

Prerequisites
The snapshot log is nothing but a table; therefore, the privileges that authorize operations on it are the same as those for the table. To change the storage characteristics of the underlying table, you should have the ALTER TABLE privilege.

Example
The following statement changes the MAXEXTENTS value of the snapshot log called *hq_emp_log* to 50:

```
ALTER SNAPSHOT LOG hq_emp_log STORAGE MAXEXTENTS 50;
```

ALTER TABLE

Purpose
To alter the definition of the table in one of the following ways:

- To add a column
- To add an integrity constraint
- To redefine a column (change its datatype, size, default value)

- To modify storage characteristics or other parameters (extents, tablespace, etc.)
- To enable, disable, or drop an integrity constraint or trigger
- To explicitly allocate an extent
- To explicitly deallocate the unused space of a table
- To allow or disallow writing to a table
- To modify the degree of parallelism

Prerequisites

The table must be in your own schema or you must have the ALTER TABLE privilege on the given table, or you must have the ALTER ANY TABLE system privilege.

Examples

Here are a few examples of the ways in which you can modify a table. The first example adds a column called *tempcol* to the *emp* table. The datatype of the column is NUMBER.

```
ALTER TABLE emp
ADD (tempcol        NUMBER);
```

The following example allocates an extent of 5K for the *emp* table:

```
ALTER TABLE emp
ALLOCATE EXTENT (SIZE 5K);
```

The following example modifies the column called *sal* in the *emp* table by giving it a default value of 500:

```
ALTER TABLE emp
MODIFY (sal    DEFAULT 500);
```

The following example modifies the INITRANS parameter for the index segment of the index-organized table *myindex*:

```
ALTER TABLE myindex INITRANS 4;
```

The following example adds a partition called *new_emps* to the *emp* table in the *users* tablespace:

```
ALTER TABLE emp
ADD PARTITION new_emps VALUES GREATER THAN (2000)
TABLESPACE users;
```

The following example drops the *new_emps* partition:

```
ALTER TABLE emp DROP PARTITION new_emps;
```

The following example converts the partition *new_emps* to *newbies*:

```
ALTER TABLE emp EXCHANGE PARTITION new_emps WITH TABLE
newbies WITHOUT VALIDATION;
```

The following example changes MAXEXTENTS for PARTITION *new_emps*:

```
ALTER TABLE emp MODIFY PARTITION new_emps STORAGE
(MAXEXTENTS 50) LOGGING;
```

The following example renames the *emp* table to *emp_renamed*:

```
ALTER TABLE emp RENAME TO emp_renamed;
```

ALTER TABLESPACE

Purpose
To alter an existing tablespace in one of the following ways:

- To add data file(s)
- To rename data files
- To change default storage parameters
- To take the tablespace online or offline
- To begin or end backup
- To allow or disallow writing to a tablespace
- To change the default logging attribute of a tablespace (Oracle8)
- To change the minimum tablespace extent length (Oracle8)

Prerequisites
In order to execute this command, you need to have the ALTER TABLESPACE system privilege. You can only perform the following tasks if you have the MANAGE TABLESPACE privilege:

- Take the tablespace online or offline
- Begin or end backup
- Make the tablespace read-only or read-write

Before a tablespace can be made read-only, the following conditions must be met:

- The tablespace must be online.
- There must not be any active transactions in the entire database (so as to avoid having any undo information applied to the tablespace).
- The tablespace must not contain any active rollback segments.
- The tablespace must not be involved in an open backup, since the end of a backup updates the header file of all data files in the tablespace.
- The COMPATIBLE initialization parameter must be set to 7.1 or higher.

Examples

The following statement tells the database that the tablespace called *tbsp1* is about to be backed up:

```
ALTER TABLESPACE tbsp1 BEGIN BACKUP;
```

The following command brings the tablespace *tbsp1* back online:

```
ALTER TABLESPACE tbsp1 ONLINE;
```

The following command takes the tablespace *tbsp1* offline:

```
ALTER TABLESPACE tbsp1 OFFLINE NORMAL;
```

The following statement adds a data file to tablespace *tbsp1* and changes the default logging attribute to NOLOGGING; when more space is needed, a new extent of size 20K will be added—to a maximum of 100K:

```
ALTER TABLESPACE tbsp1 NOLOGGING ADD DATAFILE '/usr
/oracle/tbsp1.dat'
AUTOEXTEND ON
NEXT 20K
MAXSIZE 100K;
```

ALTER TRIGGER

Purpose

To enable, disable, or compile a database trigger.

Prerequisites

The trigger must be in your own schema or you must have the ALTER ANY TRIGGER system privilege. You can use the ALTER TRIGGER command to explicitly recompile a trigger that is invalid. Explicit recompilation eliminates the need for runtime recompilation, thereby improving performance and reducing the number of runtime compilation errors. Just as in the case of stored objects recompilation, objects upon which the trigger is dependent are also recompiled (prior to the trigger itself), and if there are compilation errors that arise, then the trigger itself remains invalid.

Enabling and Disabling Triggers

A trigger is always in one of two states: ENABLED or DISABLED. If the trigger is enabled, Oracle fires the trigger when a triggering statement is issued. If the trigger is disabled, then the trigger doesn't get fired when a triggering statement is executed. Oracle enables a trigger automatically at the time of creation. An ALTER TRIGGER statement does not change the definition of a trigger. That is done by dropping and re-creating the trigger.

Examples

The following command compiles the trigger called *raise_sal*:

```
ALTER TRIGGER raise_sal COMPILE;
```

The following command disables the trigger called *raise_sal*:

```
ALTER TRIGGER raise_sal DISABLE;
```

ALTER USER

1

Purpose

To change one or more of the following characteristics of a
database user:

- Authentication mechanism of the user
- Password
- Default tablespace for object creation
- Tablespace for temporary segments created for the user
- Tablespace access and tablespace quotas
- Limits on database resources
- Default roles

Prerequisites

You must have the ALTER USER privilege; however, you can
change your own password without this privilege.

Examples

The following statement changes the password of user *scott* from
tiger to *scott* and the default tablespace to *users*:

```
ALTER USER scott
IDENTIFIED BY scott
DEFAULT TABLESPACE users;
```

The following command assigns a default role *admin* to user *scott*:

```
ALTER USER scott DEFAULT ROLE admin;
```

NOTE: The changes take effect at the beginning of the
next session.

ALTER VIEW

Purpose
To recompile a view.

Prerequisites
The view must be in your own schema or you must have the
ALTER ANY TABLE system privilege.

Example
The following command compiles the view called SAL_VIEW:

```
ALTER VIEW sal_view COMPILE;
```

ANALYZE

Purpose
To perform one of the following functions on an index, table,
or cluster:

- To collect statistics about the objects used by the optimizer
  and store them in the data dictionary
- To delete statistics about the object from the data dictionary
- To validate the structure of the object
- To identify migrated and chained rows of the table or cluster
- To collect statistics on scalar object attributes (Oracle8)
- To validate and update object references (REFs) (Oracle8)

Prerequisites
The objects to be analyzed must be in your own schema or you
must have the ANALYZE ANY system privilege.

Examples
The following command estimates statistics for the *emp* table and
all its indexes:

```
ANALYZE TABLE emp ESTIMATE STATISTICS;
```

The following command deletes statistics about the *emp* table and all its indexes from the data dictionary:

```
ANALYZE TABLE emp DELETE STATISTICS;
```

The following command collects information about the chained rows of the table *emp*:

```
ANALYZE TABLE emp
LIST CHAINED ROWS;
```

AUDIT

Purpose
To choose specific SQL statements or a schema object for auditing in subsequent user sessions.

Prerequisites
You must have the AUDIT SYSTEM system privilege. Auditing keeps track of operations performed by database users. The audit record contains information such as the user performing the operation, the type of operation, the object involved in the operation, and the date and time of the operation.

Examples
The following statement audits every SQL statement that creates, alters, drops, or sets a role, regardless of whether the statement is successful or not:

```
AUDIT ROLE;
```

The above statement can be modified to audit only when a SQL statement is successful:

```
AUDIT ROLE WHENEVER SUCCESSFUL;
```

The following command audits statements issued using CREATE ANY TABLE system privilege:

```
AUDIT CREATE ANY TABLE;
```

The following command audits all queries on the *emp* table:

```
AUDIT SELECT ON emp;
```

The following command audits all successful queries on the *emp* table:

```
AUDIT SELECT ON emp WHENEVER SUCCESSFUL;
```

The following command audits all the INSERT, UPDATE, and DELETE operations on *scott's emp* table:

```
AUDIT INSERT, UPDATE, DELETE ON scott.emp;
```

COMMENT

Purpose
To add a comment about a table, view, snapshot, or column into the data dictionary.

Prerequisites
The table, view, or snapshot must be in your schema or you must have the COMMENT ANY TABLE system privilege.

Examples
The following statement adds a comment about the *comm* column in the *emp* table:

```
COMMENT ON COLUMN comm
IS 'Commission as a percentage of base salary';
```

The following statement drops the comment added by the above command:

```
COMMENT ON COLUMN comm IS '';
```

CONSTRAINT

Purpose
To define an integrity constraint. An *integrity constraint* is a rule
that restricts the values of one or more columns in a table or an
index-organized table.

Prerequisites
Since the CONSTRAINT clause appears in a CREATE TABLE or
ALTER TABLE statement, in order to create the constraint, you
must have the privilege to either create the table or alter it.

Examples
The following command alters the *emp* table and defines a NOT
NULL constraint on the *sal* column:

```
ALTER TABLE emp
MODIFY (sal NUMBER CONSTRAINT not_null_sal NOT NULL);
```

The following command creates and enables a unique key on the
dname column:

```
CREATE TABLE dept
(deptno        NUMBER(2),
dname          VARCHAR2(9)      CONSTRAINT unique_name
                                UNIQUE,
loc            VARCHAR2(10));
```

The following command defines a composite unique key on the
combination of the *dname* and *loc* columns of the *dept* table:

```
ALTER TABLE dept
ADD CONSTRAINT unq_dname_loc
UNIQUE (dname, loc);
```

The following command creates the *dept* table and defines and enables a primary key on the *deptno* column:

```
CREATE TABLE dept(
deptno          NUMBER(2)      CONSTRAINT pk_dept PRIMARY
                               KEY,
dname           VARCHAR2(9),
loc             VARCHAR2(10));
```

The following command defines a referential integrity constraint with *table_constraint* syntax:

```
CREATE TABLE emp(
empno           NUMBER(4),
ename           VARCHAR2(10),
job     VARCHAR2(9),
mgr     NUMBER(4),
hiredate DATE,
sal     NUMBER(7,2)
comm            NUMBER(7,2),
deptno          CONSTRAINT fk_deptno FOREIGN KEY (deptno)
REFERENCES dept(deptno);
```

The following command imposes the CHECK constraint on the *emp* table by ensuring that the sum of an employee's salary and commission is less than $5,000:

```
CREATE TABLE emp(
empno           NUMBER(4),
ename           VARCHAR2(10),
job     VARCHAR2(9),
mgr     NUMBER(4),
hiredate DATE,
sal     NUMBER(7,2)
comm            NUMBER(7,2),
deptno  NUMBER(2),
CHECK    (sal + comm <= 5000));
```

CREATE CLUSTER

1

Purpose

To create a cluster. A cluster is a schema object that contains one or more tables that all have one or more columns in common. There are two types of clusters: indexed clusters and hashed clusters.

Prerequisites

To create a cluster in your own schema, you need to have the CREATE CLUSTER system privilege. To create a cluster in another user's schema, you must have the CREATE ANY CLUSTER system privilege.

Example

The following example creates an indexed cluster named *personnel* with the cluster key column *department_number*, a cluster size of 512 bytes, and storage parameter values:

```
CREATE CLUSTER personnel
(department_number    NUMBER(2))
SIZE 512
STORAGE (INITIAL 100K NEXT 50K PCTINCREASE 10);
```

CREATE CONTROLFILE

Purpose

To re-create a control file in one of the following cases:

- All copies of your existing control files have been lost through media failure.

- You want to change the name of the database.
- You want to change the maximum number of redo log files.

NOTE: You should perform a full backup of your database before executing this command.

Prerequisites

You must have the OSDBA role enabled. The database must not have been mounted by any instance.

Example

Look at the examples of usage of this command in documentation specific to your database.

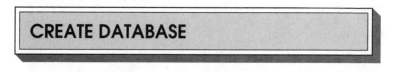

CREATE DATABASE

Purpose

To create a database, making it available for general use with the following options:

- To establish a maximum number of instances, data files, redo log files groups, or redo log file members
- To specify names and sizes of data files and redo log files
- To choose a mode of use for the redo log

NOTE: This command prepares a database for initial use and erases any data currently in the specified files. You must use this command with great caution.

Prerequisites

You must have the OSDBA role enabled.

Example

The following command creates a small database using default values for all options:

```
CREATE DATABASE.
```

You should look at the documentation specific to your database for the exact syntax and options for this command on your database.

CREATE DATABASE LINK

Purpose

To create a database link. A database link is an object in the local database that allows you to access objects on a remote database. The remote database could be either an Oracle or a non-Oracle database. If it is a non-Oracle database, then you would need to use a gateway to access data.

Prerequisites

To create a private database link, you must have the CREATE DATABASE LINK system privilege. To create a public database link, you must have CREATE PUBLIC DATABASE LINK system privilege. (A public database link is available to all users, whereas a private database link is only available to the creator.) Also, you must have the CREATE SESSION privilege on the remote database. In order to access the remote database, SQL*Net must be installed on both the databases.

Examples

The following statement defines a database link named *boston* that refers to user *scott* on the database specified by the connect string *boston-db*:

```
CREATE DATABASE LINK boston
CONNECT TO USER scott
IDENTIFIED BY tiger
USING 'boston-db';
```

The following example shows how you can execute a query on a table (*emp*) residing on the remote database:

```
SELECT * FROM emp@boston;
```

CREATE FUNCTION

Purpose

To create a stored function. A stored function is very similar to a stored procedure, the only difference being that a function returns a value to the calling environment whereas a procedure does not. These functions can be called in SQL expressions.

Prerequisites

To create a stored function in your own schema, you need to have the CREATE PROCEDURE system privilege. To create a function in another user's schema, you must have CREATE ANY PROCEDURE system privilege. To create a stored function, you must have the procedural option installed.

Example

The following is an example of the creation of a function called *get_sal* which takes an employee number as a parameter and returns the salary for that employee:

```
CREATE FUNCTION get_sal(emp_no    NUMBER)
RETURN NUMBER IS
emp_sal NUMBER;
BEGIN
   SELECT sal
     INTO emp_sal
     FROM emp
     WHERE empno = emp_no;
     RETURN (emp_sal);
END;
```

When you want to execute this function, you must specify a value for the parameter and also a variable for the value returned by the function.

CREATE INDEX

Purpose

To create an index on one or more columns of a table or a cluster. An *index* is a database object that contains an entry for each value that appears in the indexed column(s) of the table or cluster and provides direct, fast access to rows.

Prerequisites

To create an index in your own schema, you must have the table or cluster in your own schema, you must have the INDEX privilege on the table to be indexed, and you must have the CREATE INDEX privilege. To create an index in another user's schema, you must have the CREATE ANY INDEX system privilege. Also, the owner of the schema, to contain the index, must have a space quota on the tablespace to contain the index.

Example

The following command creates an index called *emp_idx1* on the *emp* table on the *empno* and *ename* columns:

```
CREATE INDEX emp_idx1 ON emp(empno, ename);
```

You cannot create two different indexes that reference the same column in a table.

NOTE: Adding indexes causes the overhead in the maintenance of tables to increase when the table is updated, but it does improve query performance.

CREATE PACKAGE

Purpose

To create the specification for a stored package. A package is an encapsulated collection of relation functions and procedures and other program variables stored together in the database. The package specification declares these objects. A package specification is really like a named DECLARE section. Everything that can go into a DECLARE section of a PL/SQL block can go into a package specification.

Prerequisites

To create a package in your own schema, you need to have the CREATE PROCEDURE system privilege. To create a package in another user's schema, you must have the CREATE ANY PROCEDURE system privilege.

Example

The following example shows the creation of a package called *hire_fire*:

```
CREATE OR REPLACE PACKAGE hire_fire AS
  local_var NUMBER;
    FUNCTION hire_emp(ename VARCHAR2, deptno NUMBER, sal
    NUMBER)
      RETURN NUMBER;
    PROCEDURE fire_emp(empno NUMBER);
END hire_fire;
```

CREATE PACKAGE BODY

Purpose

To create the body of a stored package. A package is an encapsulated collection of related procedures, stored functions, and other program objects stored in the database. The body defines these objects.

Prerequisites

To create a package in your own schema, you need to have the CREATE PROCEDURE system privilege. To create a package in a different user's schema, you need to have the CREATE ANY PROCEDURE system privilege.

Example

The following example creates the body of the package *hire_fire* created previously:

```
CREATE OR REPLACE PACKAGE BODY hire_fire AS
  FUNCTION hire_emp(empname VARCHAR2, deptnum NUMBER
  sal NUMBER)
    RETURN NUMBER IS
      new_empno NUMBER;
  BEGIN
    SELECT empseq.NEXTVAL INTO new_empno FROM dual;
      INSERT INTO emp(empno, ename, deptno) VALUES
      (new_empno, empname, deptnum);
      RETURN new_empno;
  END;
PROCEDURE fire_emp(emp_num NUMBER)IS
  BEGIN
    DELETE FROM emp WHERE empno = emp_num;
  END;
END hire_fire;
```

CREATE PROCEDURE

Purpose

To create a stand-alone procedure. A procedure is a group of PL/SQL statements that can be called by a name.

Prerequisites

To create a procedure in your own schema, you must have the CREATE PROCEDURE system privilege. To create a procedure in another schema, you must have the CREATE ANY PROCEDURE system privilege. To replace a procedure in another schema, you should have the REPLACE ANY PROCEDURE system privilege.

Example

The following example creates the procedure *fire_emp*:

```
CREATE OR REPLACE PROCEDURE fire_emp(emp_num NUMBER)IS
  BEGIN
    DELETE FROM emp WHERE empno = emp_num;
  END;
```

CREATE PROFILE

Purpose

To create a profile. A profile is a set of limits on database resources. If you assign a profile to a user, that user cannot exceed these limits. The various parameters that you can specify are as follows:

- Sessions per user
- CPUS per sessions
- CPUS per call
- Connect time
- Idle time
- Logical reads per session
- Logical reads per call
- Composite limit
- Private SGA

Prerequisites

You must have the CREATE PROFILE system privilege.

Example

The following command creates a profile called *engineer*:

```
CREATE PROFILE engineer
LIMIT SESSIONS_PER_USER            5
CPU_PER_SESSION                    UNLIMITED
CPU_PER_CALL                       3000
CONNECT_TIME                       UNLIMITED
LOGICAL_READS_PER_SESSION          1000
PRIVATE SGA                        15K
COMPOSITE_LIMIT                    500000
```

CREATE ROLE

Purpose

To create a role. A role is a set of privileges that can be granted to users or to other roles.

Prerequisites

You must have the CREATE ROLE system privilege.

Examples

The following command creates a role called *teller*:

```
CREATE ROLE teller.
```

The following command creates a role called *teller* that has a password *letter*:

```
CREATE ROLE teller IDENTIFIED BY letter.
```

NOTE: A very important point to remember about privileges in relation to roles is that privileges granted through roles are disabled inside stored procedures, functions, and packages.

CREATE ROLLBACK SEGMENT

Purpose

To create a rollback segment. A *rollback segment* is an object that Oracle uses to store data necessary to reverse or undo changes made by transactions.

Prerequisites

You must have the CREATE ROLLBACK SEGMENT system privilege. In addition, you should also have either the space quota on the tablespace to contain the rollback segment or the UNLIMITED TABLESPACE system privilege.

Example

The following statement creates a rollback segment called *rbs1* in the system tablespace:

```
CREATE ROLLBACK SEGMENT rbs1 TABLESPACE system;
```

CREATE SCHEMA

Purpose

To create multiple tables and views in a single transaction. It is also used to perform multiple grants in a single transaction.

Prerequisites

Since this command can include CREATE TABLE, CREATE VIEW, and GRANT commands, privileges necessary to issue the included statements must be given to the user executing this command.

Example

The following example demonstrates the creation of a schema called TEST_SCHEMA for user *scott*:

```
CREATE SCHEMA TEST_SCHEMA scott;
CREATE TABLE  schem_tab(name    varchar2(20), age
number);
CREATE VIEW age_view AS SELECT age FROM schem_tab WHERE
name like 'JOHN';
GRANT select ON age_view to JOHN;
```

CREATE SEQUENCE

Purpose

To create a sequence that can be used to generate unique integers.

Prerequisites

You must have the CREATE SEQUENCE privilege to create a sequence on your own schema. To create a sequence in another user's schema, you should have the CREATE ANY SEQUENCE system privilege.

Example

The following command creates a sequence called *myseq*, which starts from 10, increments by 1, goes up to 20, and then recycles the numbers:

```
CREATE SEQUENCE myseq START WITH 10
    INCREMENT BY 1
MAXVALUE 20
CYCLE;
```

CREATE SNAPSHOT

Purpose

To create a snapshot. A *snapshot* is a table containing the results of a query of one or more tables or views.

Prerequisites

You must have the distributed option installed (in Oracle). To create a snapshot in your own schema, you must have the CREATE SNAPSHOT, CREATE TABLE, and CREATE VIEW system privileges and the SELECT privilege on the master tables. To create a snapshot in another user's schema, you must have the CREATE ANY SNAPSHOT system privilege and also the SELECT privilege on the master table. The owner of the snapshot must be able to create the snapshot. Before a snapshot can be created, the user sys must run DBMSSNAP.SQL and PRVTSNAP.PLB on both the database to contain the snapshot and the database(s) containing the tables and views of the snapshot query.

Example

The following example demonstrates the creation of a snapshot called *mysnap* that contains data from *scott's emp* table in a remote database:

```
CREATE SNAPSHOT mysnap
TABLESPACE users
REFRESH FAST NEXT sysdate + 7
AS
SELECT * FROM scott.emp@NY;
```

CREATE SNAPSHOT LOG

Purpose

To create a snapshot log. A *snapshot log* is a table associated with the master table of a snapshot.

Prerequisites

The privileges required to create a snapshot log directly relate to the privileges necessary to create the underlying objects associated with a snapshot log. If you own the master table, you can create an associated snapshot log if you have the CREATE TABLE and CREATE TRIGGER system privileges. If you are creating a snapshot log for a table in another user's schema, you must have the CREATE ANY TABLE and CREATE ANY TRIGGER system privileges. Before a snapshot log can be created, the user sys must run DBMSSNAP.SQL and PRVTSNAP.PLB on the database containing the master table.

Example

The following statement creates a snapshot log on the *emp* table:

```
CREATE SNAPSHOT LOG ON emp
TABLESPACE users;
```

CREATE SYNONYM

Purpose

To create a synonym. A *synonym* is an alternative name for a table, view sequence, procedure, stored function, package, snapshot, or another synonym.

Prerequisites

To create a private synonym in your own schema, you need the CREATE SYNONYM system privilege. To create a private synonym in another user's schema, you must have the CREATE ANY SYNONYM system privilege. To create a PUBLIC synonym, you must have the CREATE PUBLIC SYNONYM system privilege. A private synonym name must be different from all other objects in the schema.

Examples

To create a private synonym called *scott_emp* for the *emp* table in scott's schema, the following command is used:

```
CREATE SYNONYM scott_emp FOR scott.emp;
```

To create a PUBLIC synonym *scott_emp* for the *emp* table in scott's
schema at a remote location NY, the following command is used:

```
CREATE PUBLIC SYNONYM scott_emp FOR scott.emp@NY;
```

CREATE TABLE

Purpose
To create a table specifying information such as column definition,
including column width (where appropriate) and datatypes, integrity
constraints, table's tablespace, storage characteristics, etc.

Prerequisites
To create a table in your own schema, you must have the
CREATE TABLE system privilege. To create a table in another
user's schema, you must have the CREATE ANY TABLE system
privilege. Also, the owner of the schema to contain the table must
have either the SPACE QUOTA or UNLIMITED TABLESPACE
system privilege.

Example
The following command defines the *emp* table in scott's schema:

```
CREATE TABLE scott.EMP
        (empno NUMBER NOT NULL,
ENAME VARCHAR2(10),
JOB VARCHAR2(9),
MGR NUMBER(4) CONSTRAINT fk_mgr REFERENCES
scott.emp(empno),
HIREDATE DATE   DEFAULT sysdate,
SAL NUMBER(7,2)        CONSTRAINT ck_sal CHECK(sal > 500),
COMM NUMBER(7,2) DEFAULT NULL,
DEPTNO NUMBER(2)        CONSTRAINT nn_deptno NOT NULL
CONSTRAINT fk_deptno REFERENCES scott.dept(deptno));
```

CREATE TABLESPACE

Purpose

To create a tablespace. A tablespace is an allocation of space in the database that can contain objects.

Prerequisites

You must have the CREATE TABLESPACE system privilege. The SYSTEM tablespace must contain at least two rollback segments, including the SYSTEM rollback segment.

Example

The following command creates a tablespace called *ts2* with one data file, *ts2.dat*, and makes it online:

```
CREATE TABLESPACE ts2 DATAFILE 'ts2.dat' SIZE 20M
DEFAULT STORAGE (INITIAL 10K NEXT 10K
MINEXTENTS 1 MAXEXTENTS 500
PCTINCREASE 10)
ONLINE;
```

CREATE TRIGGER

Purpose

To create and enable a database trigger. A database trigger is a stored PL/SQL block that is associated with a table. The trigger block gets executed automatically whenever the triggering action takes place (i.e., a specific SQL statement is issued against the table).

Prerequisites

To create a trigger in your own schema, you must have the CREATE TRIGGER system privilege, and to create a trigger in another user's schema, you must have the CREATE ANY TRIGGER system privilege. If the trigger calls stored procedures or functions, or performs DML operations, then the owner of the schema must have adequate privileges to perform these actions.

NOTE: The privileges should be granted directly to the user rather than through roles. No DDL operations and TCL commands (COMMIT, ROLLBACK, etc.) are permitted within the body of a trigger. This is because the trigger is fired as part of the SQL statement itself, and this is committed or rolled back along with it.

NOTE: Triggers can be in one of two states, enabled or disabled. When a trigger is created, it is automatically enabled. You can subsequently enable or disable a trigger by using the ALTER TRIGGER or ALTER TABLE command with the ENABLE and DISABLE options.

Example

There are 12 different types of triggers, based on the time when the trigger is fired (BEFORE or AFTER), the number of times the trigger should execute when the triggering event occurs (FOR EACH ROW), and the actual statement that causes the trigger to fire (INSERT, UPDATE, DELETE).

The following example creates a trigger called *after_hire_emp* on the *emp* table in scott's schema, which gets executed after an employee gets hired:

```
CREATE OR REPLACE TRIGGER after_hire_emp
   AFTER INSERT ON emp
DECLARE
   test     NUMBER;
BEGIN
   SELECT count(*) FROM emp INTO test;
   INSERT INTO emp_count VALUES test;
END;
```

CREATE USER

Purpose

To create a database user, or an account through which you can log on to the database, and establish the means by which the database permits access by the user.

Prerequisites

You must have the CREATE USER system privilege.

Examples

The following command creates user *scott* with a password *tiger*:

```
CREATE USER scott
IDENTIFIED BY tiger
DEFAULT TABLESPACE users;
```

The following command creates a user who can log on to the database through the operating system username and password. The operating system username in this example is *scott*:

```
CREATE USER ops$scott
IDENTIFIED EXTERNALLY
DEFAULT TABLESPACE users;
```

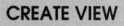

CREATE VIEW

Purpose

To define a view—a logical table that is based on one or more tables or views.

Prerequisites

To create a view in your own schema, you must have the CREATE VIEW system privilege. To create a view in another user's schema, you must have the CREATE ANY VIEW system privilege. The owner of the schema containing the view must have the privileges to perform DML operations from all the tables and views on which the view is based.

Example

The following statement creates a view of the *emp* table named *emp_sal*, which shows the employees from the *emp* table whose salary is > $1,000:

```
CREATE VIEW emp_sal
AS SELECT ename, empno
FROM emp
WHERE sal>1000;
```

DROP

Purpose

To remove an integrity constraint from the database.

Prerequisites

The DROP clause can appear in an ALTER TABLE statement. To drop an integrity constraint, you must have the privilege to issue an ALTER TABLE command.

Examples

The following statement drops the primary key of the *dept* table.

```
ALTER TABLE dept
DROP PRIMARY KEY CASCADE;
```

The following statement drops the primary key constraint whose name is *pk_dept*.

```
ALTER TABLE dept
DROP CONSTRAINT pk_dept CASCADE;
```

DROP CLUSTER

Purpose

To remove a cluster from the database.

Prerequisites

The cluster must be in your own schema or you must have the DROP ANY CLUSTER system privilege.

Example

The following example drops a cluster named *emp_cluster*, all its tables, and integrity constraints:

```
DROP CLUSTER emp_cluster
    INCLUDING TABLES
        CASCADE CONSTRAINTS;
```

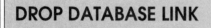

DROP DATABASE LINK

Purpose
To remove a database link from the database.

Prerequisites
The database link must be in your own schema if it is a private database link. If the database link is PUBLIC, you must have the DROP PUBLIC DATABASE LINK system privilege.

Example
The following statement drops the database link called *boston*:

```
DROP DATABASE LINK boston;
```

DROP FUNCTION

Purpose
To remove a stand-alone function from the database.

Prerequisites
You must be the owner of the function or you must have the DROP ANY PROCEDURE system privilege.

Example
The following statement drops the function called *hire_emp*:

```
DROP FUNCTION hire_emp;
```

DROP INDEX

Purpose
To drop an index from the database.

Prerequisites
The index must be in your own schema or you must have the DROP ANY INDEX system privilege.

Example
The following statement drops an index called *empsal*:

```
DROP INDEX empsal;
```

DROP PACKAGE

Purpose
To remove a stored package from the database.

Prerequisites
The package must be in your own schema or you must have the DROP ANY PROCEDURE privilege.

Example
The following command drops the package called *hire_fire*:

```
DROP PACKAGE hire_fire;
```

DROP PROCEDURE

Purpose
To remove a stand-alone stored procedure from the database.

Prerequisites

The procedure must be in your own schema or you must have the DROP ANY PROCEDURE system privilege.

Example

The following command drops the procedure called *raise_sal*:

```
DROP PROCEDURE raise_sal;
```

DROP PROFILE

Purpose

To remove a profile from the database.

Prerequisites

You must have the DROP PROFILE system privilege.

Example

The following example drops the profile called *engineer*:

```
DROP PROFILE engineer CASCADE;
```

DROP ROLE

Purpose

To remove a role from the database.

Prerequisites

You need to have been granted the role with the ADMIN OPTION or you should have the DROP ANY ROLE system privilege.

NOTE: When a role is dropped, the role is automatically revoked from all the users and roles to whom it has been granted.

Example

The following command drops the role called *temp_emp*:

```
DROP ROLE temp_emp;
```

DROP ROLLBACK SEGMENT

Purpose
To remove a rollback segment from the database.

Prerequisites
You must have the DROP ROLLBACK SEGMENT system privilege.

Example
The following command drops the rollback segment called *rb1*:

```
DROP ROLLBACK SEGMENT rb1;
```

DROP SEQUENCE

Purpose
To drop a sequence from the database.

Prerequisites
The sequence must be in your own schema or you must have the
DROP ANY SEQUENCE system privilege.

Example
The following command drops the sequence called *myseq*:

```
DROP SEQUENCE myseq;
```

DROP SNAPSHOT

Purpose
To remove a snapshot from the database.

Prerequisites
The snapshot must be in your own schema or you must have the
DROP ANY SNAPSHOT system privilege. You must also have the

privileges to drop the internal tables, views, and indexes that are used to maintain the snapshot data.

Example

The following command drops the snapshot called *hq_emp*:

```
DROP SNAPSHOT hq_emp;
```

DROP SNAPSHOT LOG

Purpose

To remove a snapshot log from the database.

Prerequisites

Since the snapshot log consists of a table and a trigger, you must have the privileges to drop the corresponding table and the trigger.

Example

The following command drops the snapshot log called *hq_emp_log* on the *emp* table:

```
DROP SNAPSHOT LOG ON emp;
```

DROP SYNONYM

Purpose

To remove a synonym from the database.

Prerequisites

To drop a private synonym, you should have the synonym in your own schema or you must have the DROP ANY SYNONYM system privilege. If you want to drop a public synonym, you should either have the synonym in your own schema or you should have the DROP ANY PUBLIC SYNONYM system privilege.

Example

The following command drops the synonym called *emp_syn*:

```
DROP SYNONYM emp_syn;
```

DROP TABLE

Purpose
To remove a table and all its data from the database.

Prerequisites
The table must be in your own schema or you must have the DROP ANY TABLE system privilege.

Example
The following command drops the *emp* table:

```
DROP TABLE emp;
```

DROP TABLESPACE

Purpose
To remove a tablespace from the database.

Prerequisites
You must have the DROP TABLESPACE system privilege. No rollback segments in the tablespace can be assigned active transactions.

Example
The following command drops the tablespace called *tbsp1*:

```
DROP TABLESPACE tbsp1
INCLUDING CONTENTS
CASCADE CONSTRAINTS;
```

DROP TRIGGER

Purpose
To remove a database trigger from the database.

Prerequisites

The trigger must be in your own schema or you must have the DROP ANY TRIGGER system privilege.

Example

The following command drops the trigger called *raise_sal*:

```
DROP TRIGGER raise_sal;
```

DROP USER

Purpose

To remove a database user and, optionally, remove the user's objects.

Prerequisites

You must have the DROP USER system privilege.

Example

The following command drops user *scott* and all the objects in scott's schema:

```
DROP USER scott CASCADE;
```

DROP VIEW

Purpose

To remove a view from the database.

Prerequisites

The view must be in your own schema or you must have the DROP ANY VIEW system privilege.

Example

The following command drops the view called *sal_view*:

```
DROP VIEW sal_view;
```

GRANT

Purpose
To grant system/object privileges and roles to users and roles.

Prerequisites
To grant a system privilege, you must either have been granted the system privilege with the ADMIN OPTION or have been granted GRANT ANY PRIVILEGE system privilege. To grant a role, you must have either been granted the role with ADMIN OPTION, have been granted the GRANT ANY ROLE system privilege, or have created the role. To grant a privilege for a particular object, you must own the object or the owner of the object should have granted you the object privileges with the GRANT OPTION.

Examples
The following command allows user *scott* to log on to the database:

```
GRANT CREATE SESSION TO scott;
```

The following command grants the role *resource* to user *scott*:

```
GRANT resource TO scott;
```

The following command grants SELECT privilege on the *emp* table in scott's schema to user *john*:

```
GRANT SELECT ON emp to john;
```

NOTE: The above command is executed in scott's schema.

NOAUDIT

Purpose
To stop the auditing chosen by the AUDIT command.

Prerequisites
The object on which you stop the auditing must be in your own schema or you must have the AUDIT ANY system privilege.

Example

The following command stops the audit on SELECTs on scott's
emp table:

```
NOAUDIT SELECT ON scott.emp;
```

RENAME

Purpose
To rename a table, view, sequence, or private synonym.

Prerequisites
The object must be in your own schema.

Example
The following statement renames the *dept* table to *new_dept*:

```
RENAME dept TO temp_dept;
```

REVOKE

Purpose
To revoke system/object privileges and roles from users and roles.

Prerequisites
You must have been granted the system privilege or role with the
ADMIN OPTION. Also, you can revoke any role if you have the
GRANT ANY ROLE system privilege.

Examples
The following command revokes the *resource* role from user *scott*:

```
REVOKE resource FROM scott;
```

The following command revokes the SELECT privileges on scott's
emp table from user *john*:

```
REVOKE SELECT ON emp FROM john;
```

NOTE: The above statement is executed in scott's schema.

STORAGE

Purpose
To specify storage characteristics for tables, indexes, clusters, and rollback segments, and the default storage characteristics for tablespaces.

Prerequisites
The STORAGE clause can appear in commands that create or alter schema objects such as tables, indexes, clusters, rollback segments, snapshots, snapshot logs, and tablespaces. You must have the privilege to use the appropriate CREATE or ALTER command in order to execute the STORAGE option.

Example
The following command creates a table called test with storage parameters assigned:

```
CREATE TABLE test (
col1      NUMBER,
col2      DATE,
col3      VARCHAR2(20))
STORAGE (INITIAL 100K      NEXT 50K
MINEXTENTS   1   MAXEXTENTS   50   PCTINCREASE   5);
```

TRUNCATE

Purpose
To remove all rows from a table or cluster and reset the STORAGE parameters to the values when the table or cluster was created.

Prerequisites
The table or cluster must be in your own schema or you must have the DELETE TABLE system privilege.

Example

The following command deletes all rows from the *emp* table in scott's schema:

```
TRUNCATE TABLE emp;
```

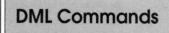

DML Commands

In this section, we shall discuss the Data Manipulation Language (DML) commands in alphabetical order. DML commands can be described as those SQL commands that allow a user to perform operations on the data and return the execution plan of a SQL statement. These commands do not perform an implicit commit of the transaction in which they are invoked.

The following is an alphabetical listing of DML commands supported by Oracle.

DELETE

Purpose

The purpose of the DELETE command is to delete rows from a table or from the base table on which a view is built.

Prerequisites

The privilege to delete rows from the table should be granted to the user either directly or through a role.

Examples

There are various ways in which a DELETE statement can be invoked. To delete all the rows from the *emp* table, the statement would be

```
DELETE FROM emp;
SQL> DELETE FROM emp;
10 rows deleted.
```

To delete all the employees who are in department 20, the statement would be

```
DELETE FROM emp WHERE deptno = 20;
SQL> DELETE FROM emp WHERE deptno = 20;
5 rows deleted.
```

For user *scott* to delete all the employees who are in department 20 from a table owned by user *john*, the statement would be

```
DELETE FROM john.emp WHERE deptno = 20;
SQL> DELETE FROM john.emp WHERE deptno = 20;
0 rows deleted.
```

NOTE: In example 3 above, the owner name of the *emp* table is prefixed to tell SQL that the rows are to be deleted not from scott's *emp* table but from john's *emp* table. For this statement to execute successfully, *scott* must have been granted DELETE privileges on john's *emp* table.

EXPLAIN PLAN

Purpose
The EXPLAIN PLAN command is used to determine the execution plan the database server follows to execute a specified SQL statement. This command inserts a row describing each step of the execution plan into a specified table.

Prerequisites
You need to have the privileges to insert rows into the specified table. You must also have the privilege (including the privileges to access the database tables and views) to execute the SQL statement whose execution plan you are interested in.

Examples
```
EXPLAIN PLAN
SET STATEMENT_ID = 'Raise in Chicago'
          INTO plan_table FOR
          UPDATE emp SET sal = sal * 1.05
WHERE deptno = (SELECT deptno from dept WHERE loc = 'CHICAGO'
```

```
SQL> EXPLAIN PLAN
2 SET STATEMENT_ID = 'Raise in Chicago'
3 INTO plan_table FOR
4 UPDATE emp SET sal = sal * 1.05
5 WHERE deptno = (SELECT deptno from dept WHERE loc = 'CHICAGO');

Explained.
```

Purpose

This is used to add rows to the specified table.

Prerequisites

Privileges to insert into a table or a table underlying a view must
be granted to the user who is executing the INSERT statement.
This may be granted either explicitly to the user or via a role.

Examples

The following statement inserts a row into the *emp* table. Notice
that we do not specify the column names when we specify values
for all the columns in the VALUES clause.

```
INSERT INTO emp values(7369, 'Smith', 'clerk', 7902,
14-SEP-97,
800,NULL, 20);

SQL> INSERT INTO emp VALUES
2                  (7369,'SMITH','CLERK',7902,'14-SEP-97',
800,NULL,20);

1 row created.
```

The following statement inserts a row into the *emp* table, with
values for the rest of the columns being NULL:

```
INSERT INTO emp(empno, ename) VALUES(2000, 'joe');

SQL> INSERT INTO emp(empno, ename) VALUES
2                  (2000, 'joe');

1 row created.
```

The following statement copies managers and presidents or employees whose commissions exceed 25 percent of their salary into the bonus table. The description of the bonus table is given below:

```
SQL> desc bonus

Name                    Null?            Type
-------------------- --------       --------------
ENAME                                   VARCHAR2(10)
JOB                                     VARCHAR2(9)
SAL                                     NUMBER
COMM                                    NUMBER

SQL> insert into bonus select ename, job, sal, comm from emp
2   where comm > .25 * sal or job in ('PRESIDENT', 'MANAGER');

6 rows created.

SQL>
```

LOCK TABLE

Purpose

This is used to lock one or more tables in a specified mode. The following are the modes that are possible in Oracle:

- ROW SHARE   Allow concurrent access to the locked table.
- ROW EXCLUSIVE   Same as row share but prohibits locking in SHARE mode.
- SHARE UPDATE   Exactly same as ROW SHARE.
- SHARE   Multiple users can place this lock on the same table simultaneously.
- SHARE ROW EXCLUSIVE   This is for row-level locking.
- EXCLUSIVE   Locks table in EXCLUSIVE mode so another user cannot acquire any kind of lock on the table.
- NOWAIT   Specifies that Oracle returns control to you immediately if the specified table cannot be locked by you because some other user has it locked.

Prerequisites

If a user has been given privileges to perform any DML operation on a certain table, then the user automatically is able to lock the table in any mode with this command. Therefore, the user must have been granted privileges to perform some DML operations on the table.

Examples

The following statement locks the *emp* table in exclusive mode. However, if some other user has already locked the table, then the statement waits for the table to be unlocked.

```
LOCK TABLE emp IN EXCLUSIVE MODE
SQL> LOCK TABLE emp IN EXCLUSIVE MODE;
Table(s) Locked.
```

The following statement accomplishes the same thing, but it does not wait if the table is locked by a different user:

```
LOCK TABLE emp in EXCLUSIVE MODE NOWAIT
SQL> LOCK TABLE emp in EXCLUSIVE MODE NOWAIT;
Table(s) Locked.
```

The rest of the commands are specific to Oracle.

SELECT

Purpose

This is used to query tables for rows that meet certain criteria. The simplest form of a query is one that returns all the rows and all the columns in a table. To obtain all the columns, instead of specifying each column name separately, you should use the *, as shown below in the examples. There are different types of queries, such as hierarchical queries, Cartesian products, inner joins, outer joins, subqueries, correlated subqueries, and distributed queries. We shall go through each one of them in this section. In addition to the several types of queries, there are also a few clauses that go in the WHERE condition of the query that determine how the results are returned. We shall also look at these clauses in this section.

Prerequisites

To perform a query from a table, the user executing the query must have the table in his or her own schema, or have been granted privileges to perform the query on the table(s) explicitly. The privileges could be granted via a role, too. To select rows from a view, the user must have been granted SELECT privilege on the base tables. The SELECT ANY TABLE system privilege allows a user to query any table or any view's base table.

Examples

To select all rows and columns from the *emp* table:

```
SELECT * FROM emp
SQL> SELECT * FROM emp;
```

EMPNO	ENAME	JOB	MGR	HIREDATE	SAL	COMM	DEPTNO
7369	SMITH	CLERK	7902	17-DEC-80	800		20
7499	ALLEN	SALESMAN	7698	20-FEB-81	1600	300	30
7521	WARD	SALESMAN	7698	22-FEB-81	1250	500	30
7566	JONES	MANAGER	7839	02-APR-81	2975		20
7654	MARTIN	SALESMAN	7698	28-SEP-81	1250	1400	30
7698	BLAKE	MANAGER	7839	01-MAY-81	2850		30
7782	CLARK	MANAGER	7839	09-JUN-81	2450		10
7788	SCOTT	ANALYST	7566	09-DEC-82	3000		20
7839	KING	PRESIDENT		17-NOV-81	5000		10
7844	TURNER	SALESMAN	7698	08-SEP-81	1500		30
7876	ADAMS	CLERK	7788	12-JAN-83	1100		20
7900	JAMES	CLERK	7698	03-DEC-81	950		30
7902	FORD	ANALYST	7566	03-DEC-81	3000		20
7934	MILLER	CLERK	7782	23-JAN-82	1300		10

14 rows selected.

To select the employee number and employee name for all the employees in department number 20 whose salary is greater than $2,000:

```
SELECT empno, ename
FROM emp
WHERE deptno=20 AND sal > 2000
```

```
SQL> SELECT empno, ename FROM emp WHERE deptno=20 AND
sal > 2000;
```

EMPNO	ENAME
7566	JONES
7788	SCOTT
7902	FORD

Now let us look at an example of a *hierarchical* query. If a table contains hierarchical data, you can select rows in a hierarchical order using the following clauses:

START WITH	To specify the root row(s) of the hierarchy. This condition can contain a subquery.
CONNECT BY	To specify the relationship between parent rows and child rows of the hierarchy.
PRIOR	To evaluate the following expression for the parent row of the current row in a hierarchical query.
WHERE	To restrict rows returned by the query.

Here is an example that returns all the employees in hierarchical order starting with *job = 'PRESIDENT'*.

```
SELECT ename, empno, mgr, job
FROM emp
START WITH job = 'PRESIDENT'
CONNECT BY PRIOR empno = mgr.
```

```
SQL> SELECT ename, empno, mgr, job FROM emp START WITH
2   job = 'PRESIDENT' CONNECT BY PRIOR empno = mgr;
```

ENAME	EMPNO	MGR	JOB
KING	7839		PRESIDENT
JONES	7566	7839	MANAGER
SCOTT	7788	7566	ANALYST
ADAMS	7876	7788	CLERK
FORD	7902	7566	ANALYST
SMITH	7369	7902	CLERK
BLAKE	7698	7839	MANAGER
ALLEN	7499	7698	SALESMAN
WARD	7521	7698	SALESMAN

MARTIN	7654	7698	SALESMAN
TURNER	7844	7698	SALESMAN
JAMES	7900	7698	CLERK
CLARK	7782	7839	MANAGER
MILLER	7934	7782	CLERK

14 rows selected.

Another type of a query is one that involves a *join* operation. A join is a query that combines rows from two or more tables, views, or snapshots. A join is performed whenever multiple tables appear in the FROM clause. The query can select any columns from any of the tables involved in the join. An important point to remember is that if the query involves selecting two columns having the same name from two different tables, then you must qualify all references to these columns to avoid ambiguity.

Here is an example of an *equijoin* (which has an equality operator in the join condition) that returns the name and job of each employee and the number and name of the department in which the employee works:

```
SELECT ename, job, dept.deptno, dname FROM emp, dept
WHERE emp.deptno = dept.deptno

SQL> SELECT ename, job, dept.deptno, dname FROM emp,
dept
2   WHERE emp.deptno = dept.deptno;
```

ENAME	JOB	DEPTNO	DNAME
CLARK	MANAGER	10	ACCOUNTING
KING	PRESIDENT	10	ACCOUNTING
MILLER	CLERK	10	ACCOUNTING
SMITH	CLERK	20	RESEARCH
ADAMS	CLERK	20	RESEARCH
FORD	ANALYST	20	RESEARCH
SCOTT	ANALYST	20	RESEARCH
JONES	MANAGER	20	RESEARCH
ALLEN	SALESMAN	30	SALES
BLAKE	MANAGER	30	SALES
MARTIN	SALESMAN	30	SALES
JAMES	CLERK	30	SALES
TURNER	SALESMAN	30	SALES
WARD	SALESMAN	30	SALES

14 rows selected.

A *self join* is a join of the table to itself. The name of the table appears twice in the FROM clause and is followed by table aliases that are used to qualify column names in the join condition. The following example demonstrates a self join to return the name of each employee and his manager:

```
SELECT e1.ename||'    '||e2.ename FROM emp e1, emp e2
WHERE e1.mgr = e2.empno

SQL> SELECT e1.ename||'         '||e2.ename FROM emp e1, emp e2
2   WHERE e1.mgr = e2.empno;

E1.ENAME||''||E2.ENAME
-------  ---------------
SCOTT            JONES
FORD             JONES
ALLEN            BLAKE
WARD             BLAKE
JAMES            BLAKE
TURNER           BLAKE
MARTIN           BLAKE
MILLER           CLARK
ADAMS            SCOTT
JONES            KING
CLARK            KING
BLAKE            KING
SMITH            FORD
13 rows selected.
```

The above example illustrates one important feature, known as an alias. An *alias* is another name that we give a table when there is a reason to believe that there would be ambiguity. This helps the database in its name resolution process.

The next type of query that we look at is called the *Cartesian product*. If two tables in a join query have no join condition, their Cartesian product is returned. If there are m rows in table A and there are n rows in table B, then a Cartesian product of A and B generates $m * n$ rows.

Another type of query is an *outer join*. The outer join extends the result of a simple join. It returns all the rows that satisfy the join condition and those rows from one table for which no rows from the other satisfy the join condition. There is a special operator to force the outer join to be performed, which is the '+' sign. This sign can appear only in the WHERE clause, not in the SELECT list, and can only be applied to a column of a table or a view.

The following example demonstrates the use of an outer join to return all the employees in each department, and in addition it also returns the name of departments in which no employee works. In this particular example, there is one such department (OPERATIONS).

```
SELECT ename, job, dept.deptno, dname FROM emp, dept
WHERE emp.deptno (+) = dept.deptno

SQL> SELECT ename, job, dept.deptno, dname FROM emp, dept
2   WHERE emp.deptno (+) = dept.deptno;
```

ENAME	JOB	DEPTNO	DNAME
CLARK	MANAGER	10	ACCOUNTING
KING	PRESIDENT	10	ACCOUNTING
MILLER	CLERK	10	ACCOUNTING
SMITH	CLERK	20	RESEARCH
ADAMS	CLERK	20	RESEARCH
FORD	ANALYST	20	RESEARCH
SCOTT	ANALYST	20	RESEARCH
JONES	MANAGER	20	RESEARCH
ALLEN	SALESMAN	30	SALES
BLAKE	MANAGER	30	SALES
MARTIN	SALESMAN	30	SALES
JAMES	CLERK	30	SALES
TURNER	SALESMAN	30	SALES
WARD	SALESMAN	30	SALES
		40	OPERATIONS

```
15 rows selected.
```

A *subquery* is a form of a SELECT command that appears inside another SQL statement. It is also known as a *nested query*.

The following example creates a very simple statement by selecting its column names from a different table via a subquery:

```
CREATE TABLE newemp(empno, ename)
AS SELECT empno, ename FROM emp

SQL> CREATE TABLE newemp(empno, ename)
2   AS SELECT empno, ename FROM emp;

Table created.
```

A *correlated subquery* is a subquery that is evaluated once for each row processed by the outer statement, or the *parent statement*.

The following example returns data about employees whose salaries exceed the averages for their departments:

```
SELECT deptno, ename, sal FROM emp x
WHERE sal > (SELECT AVG(sal) FROM emp WHERE x.deptno =
deptno)
ORDER BY deptno
```

NOTE: MIN, MAX, AVG, SUM, COUNT, etc., are group functions that are supported by most databases.

```
SQL> SELECT deptno, ename, sal FROM emp x
2  WHERE sal > (SELECT AVG(sal) FROM emp WHERE x.deptno
= deptno)
3  ORDER BY deptno;
```

DEPTNO	ENAME	SAL
10	KING	5000
20	JONES	2975
20	SCOTT	3000
20	FORD	3000
30	ALLEN	1600
30	BLAKE	2850

6 rows selected.

A distributed query is one that performs a query from tables on different databases. You would use the appropriate syntax (via database links) to access remote data.

Now we shall look at the various clauses that can be used to decide how the data is sorted or displayed.

GROUP BY

The GROUP BY clause is used to group selected rows and return a single row of summary information.

Here is an example that returns the minimum and maximum salaries for each department in the company and groups them by department number.

```
SELECT deptno, MIN(sal), MAX(sal) FROM emp GROUP BY deptno
```

```
SQL> SELECT deptno, MIN(sal), MAX(sal) FROM emp GROUP BY deptno;
```

DEPTNO	MIN(SAL)	MAX(SAL)
10	1300	5000
20	800	3000
30	950	2850

HAVING

The HAVING clause is used to restrict which groups of rows defined by the GROUP BY clause are returned by the query.

The following example returns the minimum and maximum salaries for the clerks in each department whose lowest salary is below $1,000.

```
SELECT deptno, MIN(sal), MAX(sal) FROM emp
WHERE job='CLERK' GROUP BY deptno
HAVING MIN(sal) < 1000
```

```
SQL> SELECT deptno, MIN(sal), MAX(sal) FROM emp
2   WHERE job='CLERK' GROUP BY deptno
3   HAVING MIN(sal) < 1000;
```

DEPTNO	MIN(SAL)	MAX(SAL)
20	800	1100
30	950	950

ORDER BY

The ORDER BY clause guarantees that the data returned by a query will be retrieved in a certain order. In the absence of an ORDER BY clause, there is no guarantee that the same query when executed at different times will return the results in the same order.

Here is a simple query that retrieves the names and employee numbers from the *emp* table and orders them in descending order of employee numbers:

```
SELECT empno, ename FROM emp ORDER BY empno DESC.
```

```
SQL> SELECT empno, ename FROM emp ORDER BY empno DESC;
```

```
EMPNO           ENAME
---------       --------
7934            MILLER
7902            FORD
7900            JAMES
7876            ADAMS
7844            TURNER
7839            KING
7788            SCOTT
7782            CLARK
7698            BLAKE
7654            MARTIN
7566            JONES
7521            WARD
7499            ALLEN
7369            SMITH
14 rows selected.
```

FOR UPDATE

The FOR UPDATE clause is used to lock the rows selected by the query. Once a row has been selected for update, other users cannot lock or update it until it has been unlocked.

The following example shows the use of the FOR UPDATE clause:

SELECT empno, ename FROM emp WHERE job='CLERK' FOR UP-DATE.

SQL> SELECT empno, ename FROM emp WHERE job='CLERK' FOR UPDATE;

```
EMPNO           ENAME
--------        -----------
7369            SMITH
7876            ADAMS
7900            JAMES
7934            MILLER
```

SET OPERATORS

There are certain operators such as INTERSECT, MINUS, UNION, and UNION ALL that combine the results of two queries into a single result. The number and datatypes of the columns selected by each component must be the same, but the column lengths can be different.

Here is a brief explanation of the SET operators:

INTERSECT	Returns all distinct rows selected by both queries
MINUS	Returns all distinct rows selected by the first query, but not the second
UNION	Returns all rows selected by either query
UNION ALL	Returns all rows selected by either query, including duplicates

UPDATE

Purpose

This is used to change existing data in a table or in a view's base table.

Prerequisites

The table must be owned by the user executing the update or the user must have been granted privileges to update a different user's table. If it is a view that a user wants to update, then the privileges must be granted on the underlying table(s).

Examples

Here is an example of a very simple UPDATE statement that increases the salaries of all the employees in the *emp* table by 10 percent:

```
UPDATE emp SET sal = sal * 1.10.

SQL> UPDATE emp SET sal = sal * 1.10;

14 rows updated.
```

The following UPDATE statement increases the salary of all employees who are in the department which has *deptno=20* by 10 percent.

```
UPDATE emp SET sal = sal * 1.10 WHERE deptno=20

SQL> UPDATE emp SET sal = sal * 1.10 WHERE deptno=20;

5 rows updated.
```

In order to perform an update on a table in a remote database, you need to specify the database link in the table name as shown in the next example. Here, the same operation is performed as in the previous example but this time on a remote database called NY.

```
UPDATE emp@NY SET sal = sal * 1.10 WHERE deptno=20;
```

The '@' sign is used to signify that the table being updated is on a remote database that is accessed via a database link. In this example, the name of the database link is 'NY'.

Transaction Control Commands

A *transaction* is a sequence of SQL statements that comprises a unit of work that is performed atomically, i.e., either all the steps in the transaction are performed and committed to the database or none are. For example, consider a scenario in which you want to transfer an employee named JOHN from the FINANCE department to the MARKETING department, and similarly you want to transfer an employee named TOM from the MARKETING department to the FINANCE department. It is a business requirement that either both the transfers happen or neither of them happens. So you would have them as a part of a single transaction. Transaction control commands manage changes made to the database by the DML commands.

Since the transaction control commands are interdependent, we'll use one example at the end of this section to demonstrate the effect of each of these commands, in addition to the smaller examples in each section.

COMMIT

Purpose

This command is used to end the current transaction and make permanent all changes made by statements in the transaction. It also erases all savepoints in the transaction.

In Microsoft SQL Server, the equivalent command is COMMIT TRANSACTION, which could also be written as COMMIT TRAN. Transactions in Microsoft SQL Server are started implicitly by DML commands. However, there is a way to start a user-defined transaction through the BEGIN TRANSACTION (or BEGIN TRAN) statement. The transaction is ended by COMMIT TRANSACTION (or COMMIT TRAN) if the transaction is to be committed to the database.

In Informix, the equivalent command is COMMIT WORK.

Prerequisites

No privileges are required to commit a transaction.

Example

The following statement performs an INSERT into the *emp* table and then the transaction is committed by the COMMIT statement:

```
INSERT INTO emp(empno, ename) VALUES (2500, 'james');
COMMIT;
```

Instead of COMMIT, you could also say COMMIT WORK, which does the exact same thing.

NOTE: A DDL command automatically performs a COMMIT. Therefore, be careful when performing a DDL operation if there is a possibility of the transaction being rolled back.

ROLLBACK

Purpose

This is used to undo all the changes since the beginning of the transaction or since a savepoint.

Prerequisites

No special privileges are needed to roll back a transaction.

Example

The following statement updates the *emp* table and then does a ROLLBACK.

```
UPDATE emp SET ename='John' WHERE empno=2500;
ROLLBACK;
```

Performing a ROLLBACK without a TO SAVEPOINT clause performs the following operations:

- Ends the transaction
- Undoes all the changes in the current transaction
- Erases all the savepoints in the transaction
- Releases the transaction's locks

When you roll back with a TO SAVEPOINT clause, the following operations occur:

- The portion of the transaction after the savepoint is rolled back
- All savepoints are lost after the specified savepoint
- All locks obtained after the specified savepoint are released

SAVEPOINT

Purpose

This is used to identify a point in a transaction to which you can later roll back. In Microsoft SQL Server, the equivalent command is SAVE TRANSACTION.

Prerequisites

There are no prerequisites for this command.

Example

The following piece of code performs an insert, establishes a savepoint, does an update, establishes another savepoint, and then after a subsequent delete, rolls back to the last savepoint:

```
INSERT INTO emp(empno) VALUES(3000);
SAVEPOINT sp1;
UPDATE emp SET ename='TOM' WHERE empno=3000;
SAVEPOINT sp2;
```

```
DELETE FROM emp where empno=3000;
ROLLBACK TO SAVEPOINT sp2;
```

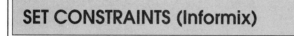

```
/* The last DELETE is rolled back which means that the employee
tom is not deleted from the emp table.*/
```

SET CONSTRAINTS (Informix)

Purpose
This is used to turn effective checking off and on in database
with logging.

Prerequisites
You should have the privilege to modify the constraints on the
tables or views.

Example
The following example sets the constraint called *test_constraint* to
deferred mode.

```
SET CONSTRAINTS test_constraint DEFERRED;
```

SET ISOLATION (Informix)

Purpose
This is used to define the degree of concurrency among processes
that attempt to access the same rows simultaneously.

Prerequisites
The isolation level must be defined before a transaction is started.

Example
The following command sets the isolation to DIRTY READ:

```
SET ISOLATION TO DIRTY READ;
```

SET TRANSACTION

Purpose
The purpose of this statement is one of the following:

- Establish the current transaction as either read-only or read-write
- Establish the isolation level
- Assign a transaction to a specific rollback segment

Prerequisites
If the SET TRANSACTION statement is being used, it should be the first one in the transaction. Every transaction, however, need not have a SET TRANSACTION statement.

NOTE: The transaction is read-consistent from the start of the transaction, rather than within each statement.

Examples
The following example demonstrates the use of the SET TRANSACTION to a READ ONLY mode.

```
COMMIT;
SET TRANSACTION READ ONLY;
SELECT COUNT(*) FROM emp;
COMMIT;
```

The last COMMIT does not make any permanent changes to the database. It just ends the read-only transaction.

Here is the example that demonstrates the usage of all the transaction control commands mentioned in this section.

```
SQL> INSERT INTO emp(empno) VALUES(3000);
1 row created.
SQL> SAVEPOINT sp1;
Savepoint created.
SQL> UPDATE emp SET ename='TOM' WHERE empno=3000;
2 rows updated.
SQL> SAVEPOINT sp2;
Savepoint created.
```

```
SQL> DELETE FROM emp where empno=3000;
2 rows deleted.
SQL> ROLLBACK TO SAVEPOINT sp2;
Rollback complete. /* The DELETE operation is rolled back. */
SQL> COMMIT;
Commit complete.
SQL> SET TRANSACTION READ ONLY;
Transaction set. /* You cannot perform an update after
this statement */
SQL> SELECT COUNT(*) FROM EMP;
COUNT(*)
----------
17
SQL> COMMIT;
Commit complete.
```

Session and System Control Statements

Session control commands are defined as those commands that dynamically manage the properties of the current user session. There are two session control commands, namely, ALTER SESSION and SET ROLE. These commands do not implicitly commit a transaction in which they are called. *System control commands*, on the other hand, dynamically manage the properties of the server instance. In Oracle, there is only one command, called ALTER SYSTEM, which does not implicitly commit the transaction in which it is called. The SET command in Microsoft SQL Server is discussed. These commands are given below.

ALTER SESSION

Purpose
This is used to alter your current session in one of many possible ways, as follows:

- To enable or disable SQL trace
- To enable or disable global name resolution
- To change the value of an NLS (National Language Support) parameter
- To specify the size of the cache used to hold frequently used cursors
- To enable or disable the closing of cached cursors on COMMIT or ROLLBACK
- To change the handling of remote procedure call dependencies
- To change a transaction level handling (specifies how transactions containing database modification are handled)
- To close a database link
- To send advice to remote databases for forcing an in-doubt distributed transaction
- To permit or prohibit stored procedures from issuing COMMIT or ROLLBACK
- To change the goal of the optimizer
- In a parallel server, to enable DML statements to be considered for parallel execution
- To allow deferrable constraints to be checked either immediately following every DML statement or at the end of a transaction

Prerequisites

To enable and disable the SQL trace facility, you need to have the ALTER SESSION privilege. To perform other operations, you do not need any privileges.

Examples

We present some examples of the usage of the ALTER SESSION command. To enable the SQL_TRACE facility, you would issue the following statement:

```
ALTER SESSION SET SQL_TRACE = TRUE;
```

The following example sets the NLS_CURRENCY to Deutschemark:

```
ALTER SESSION SET NLS_CURRENCY = 'DM';
```

The following example enables parallel DML:

```
ALTER SESSION ENABLE PARALLEL DML;
```

The following example enables committing in stored procedures:

```
ALTER SESSION ENABLE COMMIT IN PROCEDURE;
```

Look up your server-specific documentation for setting other server-specific session parameters.

ALTER SYSTEM

Purpose
The purpose of the ALTER SYSTEM command is to dynamically alter the server instance in one of the following ways:

- To restrict logons to the server to only those users with RESTRICTED SESSION system privileges
- To clear all data from the shared pool in the SGA (System Global Area)
- To explicitly perform a checkpoint
- To verify access to data files
- To enable or disable resource limits
- To enable or disable global name resolution
- To dynamically change or disable threshold limits for concurrent usage licensing and named user licensing
- To terminate a session

Prerequisites
You must have ALTER SYSTEM system privilege.

Examples
Here are a couple of examples of how you can use the ALTER SYSTEM command to enable and disable a restricted session:

```
ALTER SYSTEM ENABLE RESTRICTED SESSION;
ALTER SYSTEM DISABLE RESTRICTED SESSION;
```

Here is an example that sets the MTS_SERVERS value to 20:

```
ALTER SYSTEM SET MTS_SERVERS = 20;
```

For commands specific to your system, look in the corresponding manual.

SET (Microsoft SQL Server)

Purpose
This is used to set the various database parameters such as

- Query processing options
- Exception handling options
- Displaying performance statistics
- Options for application program use to interpret results
- Options relating to language and date formats

Prerequisites
You must have the privileges to set the options that you want to set.

Examples
The following example sets the date format to '*ddmmyy*':

```
SET DATEFORMAT 'ddmmyy';
```

The following example sets the SQL Server PARSEONLY option to ON:

```
SET PARSEONLY ON;
```

The following example sets the NOEXEC option to ON:

```
SET NOEXEC ON;
```

SET ROLE

Purpose
The purpose of this command is to enable and disable roles for the current user session.

Prerequisites

The user must have been granted the roles that are being named in
the SET ROLE command.

Examples

The following command enables the role called *resource* in the
current session:

```
SET ROLE resource.
SQL> set role resource;
Role set.
SQL>
```

The following command, in contrast, enables all the roles except
manager.

```
SET ROLE ALL EXCEPT manager;
```

The following command enables the *resource* role by
authentication through the password *resource*:

```
SET ROLE resource IDENTIFIED BY resource;
```

Embedded SQL Statements

Embedded SQL commands place Data Definition Language (DDL),
Data Manipulation Language (DML), transaction control
statements, and session control statements within a procedural
language program. In order to introduce embedded SQL commands
in 3GL programs (such as C, COBOL, etc.), you need to use a
precompiler to process the embedded SQL statements and
generate the equivalent statements in the host language (that is,
the language in which the program is written). There are different
types of embedded SQL statements that you can include in your
3GL program, such as declarative statements, PL/SQL blocks,
cursor manipulation statements, etc. When going against the
Oracle database, you should prefix the actual command by the
keywords EXEC SQL. The following commands are specific to
Oracle, and are used in programs meant to be precompiled using
the Oracle precompilers.

If you are using other databases, such as Informix, you should use the relevant precompilers.

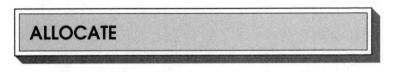

ALLOCATE

Purpose

You use this command to allocate a cursor variable to be referenced in a PL/SQL block. The difference between a static cursor and a cursor variable is that whereas a cursor is static, a cursor variable is dynamic because it is not tied to a specific query. You can open a cursor variable for a variety of queries, the important point being that the return results are type compatible. Note that cursor variables are available starting with version 2.1 of Pro*C, which is supported against Oracle Server release 7.2 and higher.

Prerequisites

You should define the cursor variable as a SQL_CURSOR pseudotype before allocating the cursor variable. An important point to remember is that you cannot fetch rows from a closed cursor.

NOTE: When you precompile your program with the MODE option set to ANSI, a commit will close the cursor automatically.

Example

Here is a simple example of the usage of the ALLOCATE command:

```
EXEC SQL BEGIN DECLARE SECTION;
SQL_CURSOR       emp_cv;
struct{ename_var      emp.ename%type, hiredate_var
emp.hiredate%type}          emp_rec;
EXEC SQL END DECLARE SECTION;

EXEC SQL ALLOCATE emp_cursor;
EXEC SQL EXECUTE
     BEGIN
          OPEN emp_cursor FOR SELECT ename, hiredate
          FROM emp;
     END;
```

```
END-EXEC;
for(;;)
    EXEC SQL FETCH :emp_cv INTO emp_rec;
    ...
    printf("Employee name is %s and his hiring date is
    %s\n", ename_var, hiredate_var);
```

CLOSE

Purpose
This is used to disable a cursor, releasing the resources (such as parse locks and temporary space) that it holds.

Prerequisites
Before you allocate a cursor variable, you should ensure that the cursor is open by using the OPEN statement.

Example
Continuing from the previous example, you would close the *emp_cv* cursor variable as follows:

```
EXEC SQL CLOSE emp_cv;
```

COMMIT

Purpose
This command is used to end your current transaction, making all changes permanent to the database.

Prerequisites
To commit your current transaction, no privileges are necessary. To manually commit a distributed in-doubt transaction that you originally committed, you must have FORCE TRANSACTION system privilege. To manually commit a distributed in-doubt transaction that was originally committed by another user, you must have FORCE ANY TRANSACTION system privilege.

Example

This example illustrates the use of the embedded SQL COMMIT command:

```
EXEC SQL AT sales_db COMMIT RELEASE;
```

CONNECT

Purpose

The CONNECT statement is used to log on to a server instance.

Prerequisites

You must have the CREATE SESSION privilege granted to you to execute this command successfully.

Examples

There are different ways that you can execute the CONNECT command depending on whether you are making a single connection from an application or concurrent logons, or you are connecting to remote databases.

The first example demonstrates a very simple connect statement where database user *scott*, having password *tiger*, connects to a local instance. Note that the username and password to be used to log on to the database have to be passed via host variables declared previously. All the variables required by the examples given below are declared in the declare section. Also note that you don't need a declare section in Pro*C 2.0 and higher releases.

```
EXEC SQL BEGIN DECLARE SECTION;
...
char*   username = "scott";
char*   password="tiger";
char*   uname_pass="scott/tiger";
char*   conn_str="alias_name";
...
EXEC SQL END DECLARE SECTION;

EXEC SQL CONNECT :username IDENTIFIED BY :password;
```

The next example demonstrates a CONNECT statement wherein the username and password are combined together by a slash:

```
EXEC SQL CONNECT :uname_pass;
```

If you are connecting to a remote database, then the syntax would be as follows:

```
EXEC SQL DECLARE DATABASE dbname;
```

NOTE: This statement must appear in the Declare Section.

```
EXEC SQL CONNECT :uname IDENTIFIED BY :passwd AT dbname
USING :conn_str;
```

The AT clause specifies a logical name for the connection. It is not necessarily a variable name. Its purpose is to identify the database connection against which a certain SQL operation is to be performed, and *conn_str* is the connect string to be used to connect to the instance.

There are other forms of CONNECT, as shown below:

```
EXEC SQL CONNECT :uname IDENTIFIED BY :passwd AT :dbname
USING :conn_str;
```

NOTE: This example uses a host variable for the database name, unlike the previous example.

Remember that when you use the AT clause to connect to the database, you need to specify the database name in every subsequent SQL statement so as to identify the connection on which it will be executed. See the example in the DECLARE DATABASE section in this section.

If you are making multiple connections from the same program, then you need to use different database names for each connection, as shown below:

```
EXEC SQL DECLARE DATABASE dbname1;
EXEC SQL DECLARE DATABASE dbname2;
```

```
EXEC SQL BEGIN DECLARE SECTION;
...
char*   username = "scott";
char*   password="tiger";
char*   uname_pass="scott/tiger";
```

```
char*   conn_str1="alias_name1";
char*   conn_str2="alias_name2";
...
EXEC SQL END DECLARE SECTION;

EXEC SQL CONNECT :username IDENTIFIED BY :password AT
     dbname1 USING:conn_str1;
EXEC SQL CONNECT :username IDENTIFIED BY :password AT
     dbname2 USING:conn_str2;
```

CONTEXT ALLOCATE

Purpose
To initialize a SQLLIB runtime context that is referenced in an
EXEC SQL CONTEXT USE statement.

Prerequisites
The runtime context must be declared of type *sql_context.*

Example
This example illustrates the use of a CONTEXT ALLOCATE
command in a Pro*C/C++ embedded SQL program:

```
EXEC SQL CONTEXT ALLOCATE :ctx1;
```

CONTEXT USE

Purpose
To direct the precompiler to use the specified SQLLIB runtime
context on subsequent executable SQL statements.

Prerequisites
The runtime context specified by the CONTEXT USE directive must
be previously allocated using the CONTEXT ALLOCATE command.

Example
This example illustrates the use of a CONTEXT USE directive in a
Pro*C/C++ embedded SQL program:

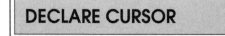

```
EXEC SQL CONTEXT USE :ctx1;
```

DECLARE CURSOR

Purpose
This is used to declare a cursor, giving it a name and associating it with a SQL statement or a PL/SQL block. A cursor is required to execute a query that returns more than one row.

Prerequisites
The variable to be associated with a cursor must have been declared previously.

Examples
If you would like to fetch the names and employee IDs of all the employees who are in the department whose number is 20, you would declare the cursor for that query as follows:

```
EXEC SQL DECLARE CURSOR c1
    FOR SELECT empno, ename FROM emp
        WHERE deptno = 20;
```

You could modify the above cursor to fetch records to update their salaries. You would do that as shown here:

```
EXEC SQL DECLARE CURSOR c1
    FOR SELECT empno, ename FROM emp
    WHERE deptno = 20 FOR UPDATE OF sal;
```

DECLARE DATABASE

Purpose
This is used to declare an identifier for a nondefault database to be accessed in subsequent SQL statements.

Prerequisites
You need to be able to log on to the nondefault database; that is, you need an account on that database.

Examples

From our example for the CONNECT statement, here is a
DECLARE DATABASE example:

```
EXEC SQL DECLARE dbname DATABASE;
```

In order to execute SQL statements on this database, you need to
use the AT clause in your SQL statements, as shown here:

```
EXEC SQL AT dbname SELECT * FROM emp INTO :emp_rec;
WHERE empno = 7698;
```

where *emp_rec* is a struct defined that has members corresponding
to the column values in the *emp* table.

DECLARE STATEMENT

Purpose

This is used to declare an identifier for a SQL statement or PL/SQL
block to be used in other embedded (dynamic) SQL statements.

Prerequisites

There are no prerequisites to execute this statement.

Examples

The most popular place to use the DECLARE STATEMENT would
be in dynamic SQL programming when the actual SQL statement
that is going to be executed (or part thereof) is not known. The
style of usage can be demonstrated as follows:

```
...
char*        my_string="UPDATE emp SET deptno=20";
...

EXEC SQL DECLARE my_statement STATEMENT;
EXEC SQL PREPARE my_statement FROM :my_string;
EXEC SQL EXECUTE my_statement;
...
```

DECLARE TABLE

Purpose
This is used to define the structure of a table, including all the columns in the table, their datatypes, default values, NULL specifications, etc. The purpose of doing this is to facilitate the semantic check that the precompilers do when there is an embedded PL/SQL block in the precompiler program, or if you force a semantic check by specifying SQLCHECK=semantics.

Prerequisites
There are no prerequisites to execute this statement.

Examples
To declare a table called *temp* with two columns of type NUMBER and VARCHAR2(10) respectively, we would use the following syntax:

```
EXEC SQL DECLARE temp TABLE
      (col1          NUMBER,        col2      VARCHAR2(10));
```

DECLARE TYPE

Purpose
To define the attributes of a type for a semantics check by the precompiler.

Prerequisites
No prerequisites.

Example
The following example creates a TYPE called *project_type* with three attributes:

```
EXEC SQL DECLARE project_type TYPE (
pno             CHAR(5),
pname           CHAR(20),
budget          NUMBER);
```

DESCRIBE

Purpose

The DESCRIBE statement is used in dynamic SQL programming to initialize a descriptor to hold descriptions of host variables. By description of the host variables, we mean the datatype, length, etc. When using the DESCRIBE statement to get information about SELECT list items, the SELECT descriptor gets populated by similar information that is gathered from the database.

Prerequisites

You must have prepared the SQL statement or PL/SQL block previously via a PREPARE statement. The DESCRIBE command gives more information about the query that you are executing, such as the column types, widths, etc.

Example

The following example illustrates the use of the DESCRIBE statement in a program segment written in Pro*C (which is Oracle's precompiler for C). Note that there are two different DESCRIBE statements—one each for the SELECT descriptor and the BIND descriptor.

```
...
char*      my_string="SELECT * FROM emp";
...

EXEC SQL PREPARE my_statement FROM :my_string;

EXEC SQL DECLARE emp_cursor
    FOR SELECT empno, ename
    FROM emp
    WHERE deptno := dept_number;

EXEC SQL DESCRIBE BIND VARIABLES FOR my_statement INTO
bind_descriptor;
```

```
EXEC SQL OPEN emp_cursor USING bind_descriptor;

EXEC SQL DESCRIBE SELECT LIST FOR my_statement INTO
select_descriptor;
...
```

ENABLE THREADS

Purpose
To initialize a process that supports multiple threads.

Prerequisites
You must be developing a precompiler application for and
compiling it on a platform that supports multi-threaded
applications, and THREADS=YES must be specified on the
command line or in the appropriate makefile.

Example
This example illustrates the use of the ENABLE THREADS
command in a Pro*C/C++ embedded SQL program:

```
EXEC SQL ENABLE THREADS;
```

EXECUTE...END-EXEC

Purpose
To embed an anonymous PL/SQL block into an Oracle Precompiler
program.

Prerequisites
None.

Example
The following section of code illustrates the embedding of a
PL/SQL block in a precompiler application.

```
EXEC SQL EXECUTE
BEGIN
  SELECT ename, job, sal
  INTO :emp_name:ind_name, :job_title, :salary
  FROM emp
  WHERE empno = :emp_number;
    IF :emp_name:ind_name IS NULL
    THEN RAISE name_missing;
    END IF;
  END;
END-EXEC;
```

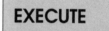

EXECUTE

Purpose

In Oracle, there are two different scenarios in which an EXECUTE statement is used. One of them is to execute PL/SQL blocks and the other is to execute previously PREPAREd dynamic SQL statements. We shall first look at the one for PL/SQL blocks, followed by the one for dynamic SQL statements.

Prerequisites

In case of a PL/SQL block, in order to precompile the program successfully, you should be sure to set the Precompiler options properly. You need to specify the Userid option and also set the Sqlcheck option to Semantics or Full.

If it is a dynamic SQL statement, you must first PREPARE the statement.

Examples

An example of the use of EXECUTE to embed a PL/SQL block is shown below. The purpose of the PL/SQL block is to invoke a very simple stored procedure that does not take any parameters. You could have a more elaborate PL/SQL block with a DECLARE section and parameter passing between PL/SQL and C host variables.

```
EXEC SQL EXECUTE
    BEGIN
        my_proc;
```

```
      END;
END-EXEC;
```

The following example demonstrates the use of EXECUTE to execute a dynamic SQL statement that has been previously PREPAREd:

```
EXEC SQL PREPARE my_statement FROM :my_string;
EXEC SQL EXECUTE my_statement USING :my_var;
```

EXECUTE IMMEDIATE

Purpose
This is used to prepare and execute a DML/DDL statement or a PL/SQL block that has no host variables. Also, the DML statement cannot be a query.

Prerequisites
There are no prerequisites for this command.

Examples
The following example illustrates the usage of EXECUTE IMMEDIATE by creating a table called *mytab* with a single column *col1* of type *number*:

```
...
char*     sql_stmt = "CREATE TABLE mytab(col1 number)";
...

EXEC SQL EXECUTE IMMEDIATE :sql_stmt;
```

FETCH

Purpose
This is used to retrieve one or more rows returned by a query. The retrieval of data is performed from a cursor.

Prerequisites

The cursor must have been opened before the FETCH operation is performed.

Example

The following example demonstrates the use of a cursor to execute and fetch results from a query that returns more than one row of data. Here, we are executing a query that returns the employee numbers and names of all employees who are in department number 20:

```
...
int     employee_id;
char    employee_name[30];
...

EXEC SQL DECLARE emp_cur CURSOR
FOR SELECT empno, ename
FROM emp
WHERE deptno = 20;
...

EXEC SQL OPEN emp_cur;
...
EXEC SQL FETCH emp_cur
    INTO :employee_id, :employee_name;
...
```

Typically, since the cursor usually has more than one row, you would execute the FETCH in a loop. Therefore, you should have a condition to check for availability of data and exit from the loop whenever there is no more data to be retrieved. See the description of the WHENEVER statement later in this section for more information.

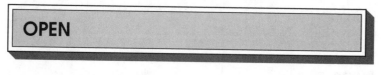

OPEN

Purpose

This is used to open a cursor. There are two different types of cursors, one that retrieves multiple rows of data as a result of the execution of a query and the other that is used to execute a query in dynamic SQL.

Prerequisites

The cursor must have been declared before it can be opened.

Examples

The following example demonstrates the opening of a cursor to retrieve multiple rows from the *emp* table:

```
...
int     employee_id;
char    employee_name[30];
...

EXEC SQL DECLARE emp_cur CURSOR
FOR SELECT empno, ename
FROM emp
WHERE deptno = 20;
...

EXEC SQL OPEN emp_cur;
...
```

The following example demonstrates the use of OPEN to open a cursor to execute a SQL statement dynamically:

```
...
EXEC SQL DECLARE emp_cursor
     FOR SELECT empno, ename
     FROM emp
     WHERE deptno := dept_number;

EXEC SQL DESCRIBE BIND VARIABLES FOR my_statement INTO
bind_descriptor;
EXEC SQL OPEN emp_cursor USING bind_descriptor;

...
```

PREPARE

Purpose

This is used to parse a SQL statement or PL/SQL block specified by a host variable and associate it with an identifier.

Prerequisites

There are no prerequisites to execute this statement.

Examples

The follow example demonstrates the use of the PREPARE statement in a Pro*C program:

```
...
char* my_string="SELECT * FROM emp";
...
EXEC SQL PREPARE my_statement FROM :my_string;
```

ROLLBACK

Purpose

To undo work done in the current transaction. You can also use this command to manually undo the work done by an in-doubt distributed transaction.

Prerequisites

To roll back your current transaction, no privileges are necessary. To manually roll back an in-doubt distributed transaction that you originally committed, you must have FORCE TRANSACTION system privilege. To manually roll back an in-doubt distributed transaction originally committed by another user, you must have FORCE ANY TRANSACTION system privilege.

Examples

The following statement rolls back your entire current transaction:

```
EXEC SQL ROLLBACK;
```

The following statement rolls back your current transaction to savepoint *sp5*:

```
EXEC SQL ROLLBACK TO SAVEPOINT sp5;
```

SAVEPOINT

Purpose
To identify a point in a transaction to which you can later roll back.

Prerequisites
None.

Example
This example illustrates the use of the embedded SQL SAVEPOINT command to create a savepoint called *sp5*:

```
EXEC SQL SAVEPOINT sp5;
```

TYPE

Purpose
This is used to perform user-defined type equivalencing or to assign an Oracle external datatype to a class of host variables by equivalencing the external datatype to a user-defined datatype.

Prerequisites
The user-defined datatype must be previously declared in an embedded SQL program.

Example
Let us assume that you want to declare a datatype called *photos* and declare variables of that type. Using Pro*C, you can do it as follows:

```
struct    picture    {short    length;
                      char data[200000];};
typedef struct picture photos;
```

```
EXEC SQL BEGIN DECLARE SECTION;
...
EXEC SQL TYPE photos is VARRAW(20000);
photos      my_var;
...
EXEC SQL END DECLARE SECTION;
```

You would use type equivalencing to accomplish one of the following:

- Null-terminate a character host variable
- Store program data as binary data in the database
- Override default datatype conversion

The main advantage of the TYPE statement is to convert between the internal datatypes (types of columns in the database such as LONG RAW, etc.) and the external datatypes (host variable types such as *char*).

VAR

Purpose
This is used to perform host variable equivalencing or to assign an Oracle-specific external datatype to a host variable, overriding the default datatype assignment.

Prerequisites
The host variable must have been previously declared.

Example
The following example illustrates the equivalencing of the host variable *dept_name* to datatype STRING:

```
EXEC SQL BEGIN DECLARE SECTION;
...

char dept_name[15];

EXEC SQL VAR dept_name IS STRING;
```

```
dept_name my_dept;
...

EXEC SQL END DECLARE SECTION;
```

You would use type equivalencing to accomplish one of the following:

- Null-terminate a character host variable
- Store program data as binary data in the database
- Override default datatype conversion

The difference between the EXEC SQL VAR and EXEC SQL TYPE statements is that the former is used for individual variables, whereas the latter is used for all variables of a given type.

WHENEVER

Purpose

This is used to specify an action to be performed whenever an error or warning results from the execution of a SQL program.

Prerequisites

There are no prerequisites to execute this command.

Example

The following Pro*C program segment demonstrates the use of the WHENEVER command:

```
EXEC SQL WHENEVER SQLERROR  myerror();
...
EXEC SQL SELECT ename INTO :my_ename FROM emp
WHERE empno = :my_empno;
...

myerror() {
    ...
    printf("The error code was %d\n", sqlca.sqlcode);
```

```
EXEC SQL ROLLBACK WORK RELEASE;
...
}
```

The WHENEVER clause forces Pro*C to generate the SQL codes corresponding to errors reported by the database. These error messages are passed into the *sqlca* structure. The *sqlcode* field in the *sqlca* structure has the return code after execution of a SQL statement.

SQL Commands Related to Object Extensions

In this section, we will discuss the SQL commands corresponding to object extensions that are specific to Oracle8. These commands are classified into Data Definition Language (DDL) and Data Manipulation Language (DML) categories for clarity. Note that the commands described in this section will be executed only if the Oracle objects option is installed on your database server.

DDL Commands

The following are the DDL commands in alpabetical order.

ALTER TYPE

Purpose
This command is used to recompile the specification and or body, or to change the specification of an object type by adding new object member subprogram specifications.

Prerequisites

The object type must be in your own schema and you must have CREATE TYPE or CREATE ANY TYPE system privileges, or you must have ALTER ANY TYPE system privileges.

Examples

Here is an example of the alteration of a user-defined type in which a member function is added to the type definition of *data_t*:

```
CREATE TYPE data_t AS OBJECT (
year      NUMBER,
MEMBER FUNCTION prod(invent NUMBER, prodcode CHAR)
RETURN NUMBER);

CREATE TYPE BODY data_t IS
    MEMBER FUNCTION prod(invent NUMBER, prodcode CHAR)
    RETURN NUMBER IS
      BEGIN
RETURN (year + invent);
      END;
END;

ALTER TYPE data_t REPLACE AS OBJECT (
    MEMBER FUNCTION prod(invent NUMBER, prodcode CHAR)
RETURN NUMBER,

MEMBER FUNCTION qtr(der_qtr DATE) RETURN CHAR);

CREATE OR REPLACE TYPE BODY data_t IS

    MEMBER FUNCTION prod(invent NUMBER, prodcode CHAR)
    RETURN NUMBER IS

        BEGIN
            RETURN (year + invent);
        END;

    MEMBER FUNCTION qtr(der_qtr DATE)
RETURN CHAR IS
```

```
          BEGIN
               RETURN 'FIRST';
          END;
END;
```

Another example that compiles the user-defined object is shown below:

```
CREATE TYPE loan_t AS OBJECT (
    loan_num      INTEGER,
    interest_rate    FLOAT,
    amount      FLOAT,
    start_date      DATE,
    end_date      DATE);

ALTER TYPE loan_t COMPILE;
```

NOTE: In order to compile a type specification, you would add the keyword SPECIFICATION to the ALTER TYPE statement.

CREATE DIRECTORY

Purpose

This command is used to create a directory object, which represents an operating system directory in which BFILEs resides. A directory is an alias for the full (actual) path name on the server's file system where the files are actually located.

Prerequisites

You must have the CREATE ANY DIRECTORY privilege to create directories. You should also have the operating system privilege to create the file in the specified location. The system administrator should also ensure that the operating system directory has the correct read permissions for Oracle processes.

Example

Here is a simple example to create a directory alias called *my_dir* that points to */usr/files/bfiles*:

```
CREATE OR REPLACE DIRECTORY my_dir AS
'/usr/files/bfiles';
```

CREATE LIBRARY

Purpose
This is used to create a schema object (library), which represents an operating-system shared library, from which SQL and PL/SQL can call external 3GL functions and procedures. Currently in Oracle, these functions can be written only in C. This is a part of the new functionality called "external procedures" that is available in Oracle8.

NOTE: An important point to remember is that this functionality is valid only on operating systems that support shared libraries and dynamic linking.

Prerequisites
You must have the CREATE ANY LIBRARY system privilege granted to you. To use the procedures and functions in the library, you must have EXECUTE object privileges on the library.

Examples
The following example demonstrates the creation of a library called *my_lib*:

```
CREATE LIBRARY my_lib AS '/home/users/scott/my_lib.so';
```

NOTE: The complete path name of the library has to be specified. Only when you execute a procedure that is in the shared library will the PL/SQL run time check to see if the function that is being called is in the shared library.

The following example replaces the library *my_lib.so* if it already exists:

```
CREATE OR REPLACE my_lib AS '/home/users
/scott/my_lib.so';
```

CREATE TABLE

Purpose

In order to have an object identifier assigned to an object, the object must reside in an object table. This command is used to create an object table. The columns of an object table correspond to the top-level attributes of the object type.

Prerequisites

To create an object table in your own schema, you need to have the CREATE TABLE privilege and also you should either own the object type or have the EXECUTE ANY TYPE system privilege. These privileges must be granted to the user explicitly, not through a role.

Examples

Here is an example of an object table creation. First an object type called *person_t* is created, and then an object table is created.

```
CREATE TYPE person_t AS OBJECT (
          name                VARCHAR2(20),
          age                 NUMBER(2),
          sex                 CHAR);

CREATE TABLE persons OF person_t;
```

NESTED TABLES

Nested tables are created as a column in a relational table. Creating a table with columns of type TABLE implicitly creates a storage table for each nested table column. The storage table is created in the same tablespace as the parent table and stores the nested table values of the column for which it was created. Here is an example:

```
CREATE TYPE project AS OBJECT(
projname   varchar2(20),
projno          number(3));
CREATE TABLE projects of project;
CREATE TABLE employee(
empno NUMBER,
name VARCHAR2(30),
```

```
projects PROJ_TABLE_TYPE)
NESTED TABLE projects STORE AS nested_proj_table;
```

CREATE TYPE

Purpose

This command is used to create a user-defined object type, which could be a varying array (called VARRAY), a nested table type, or an incomplete object type. An incomplete object type is one that is created by a forward type definition. It is called "incomplete" because it has a name but no attributes or methods.

Prerequisites

In order to create a type in your own schema, you need the CREATE TYPE system privilege; to create a type in a different user's schema, you need to have the CREATE ANY TYPE system privilege. These privileges could be granted to the user directly or via a role.

NOTE: Just as in the case of stand-alone stored procedures, privileges granted via a role are disabled inside a type. This implies that either the owner of the type must be granted the EXECUTE object privilege in order to access all other types referenced within the definition of the type, or the type owner must have been granted the EXECUTE ANY TYPE system privilege. If the owner of the type intends to grant other users access to the type, the owner must be granted the EXECUTE privilege with GRANT OPTION or the EXECUTE ANY TYPE privilege with the ADMIN OPTION. Without these privileges, the type owner cannot grant access on the type to other users.

Examples

The following example creates an object type called *person_t*:

```
CREATE TYPE person_t AS OBJECT (
          name               VARCHAR2(20),
          age                NUMBER(2),
          sex                CHAR);
```

The above example demonstrates the creation of a simple object type that has no methods associated with it. The following example demonstrates the creation of an object type called *emp_db* that also has a couple of methods:

```
CREATE TYPE emp_db AS OBJECT (
        empno           NUMBER(5),
        ename           VARCHAR2(20),
        deptno          NUMBER(2),

        MEMBER PROCEDURE hire_emp(empno, ename, deptno),
        MEMBER PROCEDURE fire_emp(empno));
```

A member function is a function that is defined as a part of the object specification. The actual function itself is in the TYPE BODY, which is created by the CREATE TYPE BODY command described next.

CREATE TYPE BODY

Purpose
The purpose of this statement is to implement the member methods defined in the object type specification.

Prerequisites
Every function that has a declaration in the object specification must have the corresponding function definition in the CREATE TYPE BODY statement. To create a type body in your own schema, you need the CREATE TYPE or CREATE ANY TYPE privilege granted to you. In order for you to be able to create an object type in another user's schema, you must have the CREATE ANY TYPE system privilege. To replace any object type (via the CREATE OR REPLACE command) in another user's schema, you must have the DROP ANY TYPE privilege.

Example
Continuing on our example from the CREATE TYPE command, we create the TYPE BODY to include the appropriate methods, as follows:

```
CREATE TYPE BODY emp_db AS OBJECT (

    MEMBER PROCEDURE hire_emp(v_empno, v_ename,
    v_deptno) IS
```

```
        BEGIN
             INSERT INTO emp(empno, ename, deptno)
    VALUES (v_empno, v_ename, v_deptno)
             END;

        MEMBER PROCEDURE fire_emp(v_empno) IS

BEGIN
  DELETE  FROM emp WHERE
  empno = empno;
END;
    END;
```

DROP DIRECTORY

Purpose
This is used to drop a directory object from the database.

Prerequisites
You must have the DROP ANY DIRECTORY privilege to execute
this command.

Example
To drop the directory called *my_dir*, you would execute the
following command:

```
DROP DIRECTORY my_dir;
```

DROP LIBRARY

Purpose
This is used to remove an external procedure library from
the database.

Prerequisites
You must have the DROP LIBRARY system privilege.

Example

To drop a library called my_procs, you would execute the following command:

```
DROP LIBRARY my_procs;
```

DROP TYPE

Purpose

This is used to drop the specification and the body of an object, a VARRAY, or a nested table type.

Prerequisites

You should either be the owner of the type that you are dropping or have been granted the DROP ANY TYPE system privilege.

Examples

To drop the type called *person_t*, you would execute the following command:

```
DROP TYPE person_t;
```

If the *person_t* object type has any dependencies, you should use the FORCE option as shown below:

```
DROP TYPE person_t FORCE;
```

NOTE: You need to be careful about using the FORCE option. If there is data in dependent tables, that data could become inaccessible because the DROP operation is irrecoverable. Unless the FORCE option is specified, you can only drop object, nested table, or VARRAY types that are stand-alone schema objects with no dependencies.

DROP TYPE BODY

Purpose
You would use the DROP TYPE BODY command to drop the body of an object, a VARRAY, or a nested table type.

Prerequisites
The object body must be in your own schema or you must have the DROP ANY TYPE privilege.

Example
The following statement drops the *emp_db* object type body:

```
DROP TYPE BODY emp_db;
```

DML Commands

The following are the DML commands in alphabetical order.

DELETE

Purpose
This is used to remove rows from a nested table.

Prerequisites
The prerequisites for this command are exactly identical to the ones for the DELETE statement mentioned earlier.

Example

The following example deletes rows of a nested table called *projs* in department 123:

```
DELETE THE (SELECT projs
FROM dept d WHERE d.dno = 123);
```

INSERT

Purpose

This is used to add rows to an object table or an object view's base table.

Prerequisites

The privileges to INSERT rows into an object table are exactly identical to the ones required to insert into a normal relational table (described earlier under "INSERT" in the DML commands section).

Examples

The following command inserts an object of type *person* into the object table *persons*:

```
INSERT INTO persons VALUES('John Doe', 25, 'M');
```

The following command also does the same job:

```
INSERT INTO persons VALUES(person_t('John Doe', 25,
'M'));
```

The following command inserts a value of type *person* into a relational table *rel_dept* that has a column of type *person_t* (shown first is the description of the *rel_dept* table):

```
Name                   Type
--------------         ------------
deptno                 NUMBER
employee               person
location               varchar2(20)
```

```
INSERT INTO rel_dept(deptno, employee, loc) VALUES
(25, person('John Doe', 25, 'M'), 'San Francisco');
```

SELECT

Purpose
This is used to retrieve data from object tables or object views, or relational tables having object type columns.

Prerequisites
The prerequisites for this command are exactly identical to the ones for the SELECT command described earlier in the DML commands section.

Examples
The following command returns rows from an object table *persons*:

```
SQL> desc persons
 Name                              Null?    Type
 ------------------------------    -------- ----
 NAME                                       VARCHAR2(20)
 AGE                                        NUMBER(2)
 SEX                                        CHAR(1)

SQL>

SQL> select * from persons;

NAME                      AGE S
--------------------  ---------- -
John Doe                   20 M
Mary Doe                   30 F
```

The following command returns rows from a relational table *rel_persons* containing a column that holds objects of type *person*:

```
SQL> desc rel_persons
 Name                              Null?    Type
 ------------------------------    -------- ----
 PEOPLE                                     PERSON_T
 ID                                         NUMBER

SQL> select * from rel_persons;
```

```
PEOPLE(NAME, AGE, SEX)                      ID
------------------------------------------------
PERSON_T('John Doe', 35, 'F')               100

SQL>
```

Results of queries that use the THE or MULTISET keyword cannot be combined with SET operators such as UNION, UNION ALL, INTERSECT, and MINUS.

When you perform a SELECT FOR UPDATE, the rows returned from subqueries whose column values are nested tables or VARRAYs, not scalar values, are not locked.

NOTE: You must lock the row containing a LOB before updating it.

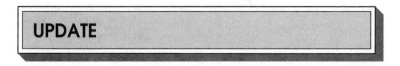

UPDATE

Purpose
This is used to change the existing values in a table or in a view's base table.

Prerequisites
The prerequisites are exactly the same as those for the UPDATE command explained earlier in the DML commands section.

Examples
The following command updates particular rows in a table:

```
UPDATE THE(SELECT projects
FROM employee e
WHERE e.empno = 1000) x
SET x.projname = 'SQL Book'
WHERE x.projno IN (123, 456);
```

Embedded SQL Commands

CACHE FREE ALL

Purpose
To free all memory in the object cache.

Prerequisites
An active database connection must exist.

Example
The following command demonstrates the usage of the CACHE FREE ALL command:

```
EXEC SQL AT mydb CACHE FREE ALL;
```

CONTEXT OBJECT OPTION GET

Purpose
To determine the values of options set by CONTEXT OBJECT OPTION SET for the context in use.

Prerequisites
Precompiler option OBJECTS must be set to YES.

Example
The following example demonstrates the usage of the CONTEXT OBJECT OPTION GET:

```
char EuroFormat[50];
...
EXEC SQL CONTEXT OPTION GET DATEFORMAT INTO :EuroFormat ;
printf("Date format is ", %s\n");
```

CONTEXT OBJECT OPTION SET

Purpose
To set options to specified values of Date attributes:
DATEFORMAT, DATELANG for the context in use.

Prerequisites
Precompiler option OBJECTS must be set to YES.

Example
The following example demonstrates the use of the CONTEXT
OBJECT OPTION SET command:

```
char *new_format = "DD-MM-YYYY";
char *new_lang = "Dutch";
...
EXEC SQL CONTEXT OBJECT SET DATEFORMAT, DATELANG to
:new_format, :new_lang;
```

FREE

Purpose
To free memory in the object cache.

Prerequisites
The memory must have been already allocated. An active database
connection must exist.

Example
The following statement frees the memory pointed to by *ptr*:

```
EXEC SQL FREE :ptr;
```

OBJECT CREATE

Purpose
To create a referenceable object in the object cache.

Prerequisites
Precompiler option OBJECTS must be set to YES. The INTYPE option must specify the OTT-generated type files and the OTT-generated header files must be included in your program.

Example
The following piece of code demonstrates the usage of the OBJECT CREATE command:

```
person *pers_p;
person_ind *pers_ind;
person_ref *pers_ref;
...
EXEC SQL CREATE :pers_p:pers_ind TABLE PERSON_TAB
RETURNING REF INTO :pers_ref;
```

OBJECT DELETE

Purpose
To mark a persistent object or array of objects as deleted in the object cache.

Prerequisites
Precompiler option OBJECTS must be set to YES. The INTYPE option must specify the OTT-generated type files and the OTT-generated header files must be included in your program.

Example

The following piece of code demonstrates the usage of the OBJECT
DELETE command:

```
customer *cust_p;
...
EXEC SQL OBJECT DELETE :cust_p;
```

OBJECT DEREF

Purpose

To pin an object or array of objects in the object cache.

Prerequisites

Precompiler option OBJECTS must be set to YES. The INTYPE
option must specify the OTT-generated type files and the
OTT-generated header files must be included in your program.

Example

The following code segment demonstrates the use of the OBJECT
DEREF command:

```
person *pers_p;
person_ref *pers_ref;
...
/* Pin the person REF, returning a pointer to the person
 object */
EXEC SQL OBJECT DEREF :pers_ref INTO :pers_p;
```

OBJECT FLUSH

Purpose

To flush persistent objects that have been marked as updated,
deleted, or created, to the server.

Prerequisites

Precompiler option OBJECTS must be set to YES. The INTYPE option must specify the OTT-generated type files and the OTT-generated header files must be included in your program.

Example

The following piece of code demonstrates the usage of the OBJECT DELETE command and the OBJECT FLUSH command:

```
person *pers_p;
...
EXEC SQL OBJECT DELETE :pers_p;
/* Flush the changes, effectively deleting the person
object */
EXEC SQL OBJECT FLUSH :pers_p;
/* Finally, free all object cache memory and logoff */
EXEC SQL OBJECT CACHE FREE ALL;
EXEC SQL COMMIT WORK RELEASE;
```

OBJECT GET

Purpose

To convert attributes of an object type to native C types.

Prerequisites

Precompiler option OBJECTS must be set to YES. The INTYPE option must specify the OTT-generated type files and the OTT-generated header files must be included in your program.

Example

This example gets the attributes of the *pers_p* object type into the C struct *pers*.

```
person *pers_p;
struct { char lname[21], fname[21]; int age; } pers;
...
/* Convert object types to native C types */
EXEC SQL OBJECT GET lastname, firstname, age FROM
:pers_p INTO :pers;
```

```
printf("Last Name: %s\nFirstName: %s\nAge: %d\n",
       pers.lname, pers.fname, pers.age );
```

OBJECT RELEASE

Purpose
To unpin an object in the object cache. When an object is not pinned and not updated, it is eligible for implicit freeing.

Prerequisites
Precompiler option OBJECTS must be set to YES. The INTYPE option must specify the OTT-generated type files and the OTT-generated header files must be included in your program.

Example
The following command releases the object type pointed to by *pers_p*

```
person *pers_p;
...
EXEC SQL OBJECT RELEASE :pers_p;
```

OBJECT SET

Purpose
To update attributes of persistent objects, marking them eligible for writing to the server when the object is flushed or the cache is flushed. To update the attributes of a transient object.

Prerequisites
Precompiler option OBJECTS must be set to YES. The INTYPE option must specify the OTT-generated type files and the OTT-generated header files must be included in your program.

Example
The following example sets the attributes of the object pointed to by *pers_p* to the values in the client-side struc called *addr1.*

```
person *pers_p;
struct {int num; char street[61], city[31], state[3],
zip[11];} addr1;
...
addr1.num = 500;
strcpy((char *)addr1.street , (char *)"Oracle Parkway");
strcpy((char *)addr1.city,    (char *)"Redwood Shores");
strcpy((char *)addr1.state,   (char *)"CA");
strcpy((char *)addr1.zip,     (char *)"94065");
/* Convert native C types to object types */
EXEC SQL OBJECT SET :pers_p->addr TO :addr1;
```

OBJECT UPDATE

Purpose
To mark persistent objects as updated in the object cache. The
changes are written to the server when the object is flushed or
when the cache is flushed. For transient objects, this statement
is a no-op.

Prerequisites
Precompiler option OBJECTS must be set to YES. The INTYPE
option must specify the OTT-generated type files and the
OTT-generated header files must be included in your program.

Example
In this example, the pers_p object is marked as updated.

```
person *pers_p;
...
/* Mark as updated */
EXEC SQL OBJECT UPDATE :pers_p;
```

PL/SQL Overview/Syntax

PL/SQL is Oracle's procedural extension to SQL. As we know, SQL
is a nonprocedural language, which means that you cannot control
how a statement gets executed. PL/SQL offers several features

such as encapsulation, exception handling, ease of use, portability, data hiding, and object orientation.

The goal of this section is to highlight the main features of PL/SQL and explain its syntax. The main features are explained here.

Structured Language

PL/SQL is a structured programming language. That is, the basic units that make up a PL/SQL program are logical blocks, which can contain any number of nested sub-blocks. A block lets you group logically related declarations and statements. A PL/SQL block has three main parts: the DECLARE section, the EXECUTABLE section (demarcated by a BEGIN-END pair), and the EXCEPTION section. The EXCEPTION section is not mandatory, nor is the DECLARE section. The nesting of PL/SQL blocks takes place in the EXECUTABLE section typically, but it could also be in the exception-handling block.

Variables and Constants

Variables and constants must be declared in the DECLARE section before they are used. Once they have been declared, they can be used anywhere an expression can be used. The variables declared in PL/SQL can have any SQL datatype such as DATE, CHAR, NUMBER, etc., or any PL/SQL datatypes such as BOOLEAN and so forth.

Cursors

Cursors are pointers into specific areas of memory used by Oracle during SQL statement execution. There are two types of cursors: *implicit* and *explicit*. An explicit cursor has to be declared for queries that return more than one row. Implicit cursors are declared by PL/SQL automatically for every SQL statement, even if it is not a query. Cursors basically let you manipulate multiple rows of data one at a time. As an enhancement to the cursor, there is a variable cursor. The relationship between a cursor and a variable cursor is exactly the same as that between a constant and a variable. The variable cursor can be opened for any type compatible query.

1

Attributes

PL/SQL variables and cursors have *attributes*, which are properties that let you reference the datatype and structure of an item without repeating its definition. There are two main attribute types: %TYPE and %ROWTYPE. The former provides the datatype of a database column or a datatype of a variable. The latter provides a record type that represents a row in a table. The row could be fetched from a table, a cursor, or a cursor variable.

Control Structures

Perhaps the most important distinguishing factors between PL/SQL and SQL are the control structures. There are five different control statements: IF-THEN-ELSE, FOR-LOOP, WHILE-LOOP, EXIT-WHEN, and GOTO.

Modularity

PL/SQL allows you to write modular programs by dividing your applications into logically grouped packages. Each package could then contain several procedures or functions, variables, cursors, etc. These packages can be stored in the Oracle database and executed repeatedly. In Oracle8, the procedures and functions could also be written in the C language and are known as *external procedures*. These essentially allow the delegation of operations that are beyond the scope of PL/SQL to a 3GL.

Data Abstraction

Data abstraction allows you to extract the essential properties of the data without getting bogged down by the details. PL/SQL supports object-oriented programming through object types. An *object type* contains the data and the procedures and functions that operate on it. The variables comprising the object are its *attributes*, and the functions and procedures that characterize its behavior are its *methods*. PL/SQL also provides two collection types called VARRAY (varying array) and TABLE (nested table). Collections work like the arrays found in most third-generation programming languages. *Records* are like structures in the C language that allow you to group logically related data into one entity. The record can have multiple members of either native PL/SQL datatypes or a nested record type.

Advantages of PL/SQL

Some of the advantages of PL/SQL are explained here:

Support for SQL   PL/SQL lets you write SQL statements for easy data manipulation within PL/SQL programs.

Support for Object-oriented Programming   PL/SQL does this through support for object types.

Better Performance   PL/SQL allows you to bundle several statements into a PL/SQL block and send that block to the server for execution. This saves several potential network round trips. PL/SQL also helps increase performance through stored program units such as procedures, functions, and packages.

Portability   PL/SQL runs on any platform that Oracle supports, therefore programs written in PL/SQL can run without any modification when they are moved from one platform to another.

Bundled with the Server   PL/SQL is a part of the Oracle server, and through the support for %TYPE and %ROWTYPE it has a strong link with the data dictionary, too.

PL/SQL Syntax

The following is an explanation of the various PL/SQL constructs such as structure, cursors, conditional statements, iterative control, exceptions, packages, procedures, and functions.

Basic PL/SQL Block Structure

The basis structure of a PL/SQL block is as follows:

```
[DECLARE]
...
BEGIN
...
    [BEGIN
      ...
      EXCEPTION
      ...
      END;]
```

```
[EXCEPTION]
...
END;
```

The part within the square brackets is optional—that is, a PL/SQL block can be built without them. As you can see, PL/SQL blocks can be nested within themselves up to any depth. The DECLARE section and the EXCEPTION block are optional.

Cursor

A cursor is always declared in the DECLARE section as follows:

```
DECLARE CURSOR cur_name
IS SELECT col1, col2
FROM tablename
WHERE condition1 = TRUE;
```

In this statement, *cur_name* is the cursor identifier and *condition1* is some criterion that the rows selected must satisfy. In a later example, the condition is for the *empno* to be > 7900.

Conditional Control

A conditional statement is one that allows the execution of a certain set of statements if a certain condition is true and a different set of statements if the condition is false. In PL/SQL, this is accomplished through the IF-THEN-ELSE construct. The basic structure is as follows:

```
IF (condition) THEN
statements
ELSE statements;
```

The example given below demonstrates the use of the conditional flow of control of program execution:

```
DECLARE
     v_empno number;
     v_ename varchar2(20);
     v_hiredate date;

BEGIN
     CURSOR C1 IS SELECT empno, hiredate FROM emp WHERE
     empno > 7900;
     OPEN C1;
     IF C1%ROWCOUNT <1 THEN
          dbms_output.put_line('Did not find a row
```

```
                satisfying the search condition');
       ELSE
                FOR i IN 1..C1%ROWCOUNT LOOP
                FETCH C1 INTO v_empno;
```

Iterative Control

The LOOP statement lets you execute a sequence of statements multiple times. It is the simplest kind of iterative statement in PL/SQL. The syntax for LOOP is as follows:

```
LOOP
...--sequence of statements
END LOOP;
```

In order to exit the loop, there has to be an exit condition that will cause control to break out of the loop.

The FOR LOOP lets you specify a range of integers, then execute a sequence of statements once for each integer in the range. The syntax for the FOR LOOP is as follows:

```
FOR i IN 1..N LOOP
...--some SQL or other statements
END LOOP;
```

The WHILE-LOOP statement relates a condition with a set of statements. As long as (WHILE) the condition is true, the statements are executed. The condition is tested before each execution of the set of statements. If the condition yields FALSE or NULL, then the set of statements is not executed and the statements following the LOOP are executed. The structure of the WHILE LOOP is as follows:

```
WHILE (condition)  LOOP
...--some statements (SQL or otherwise)
END LOOP;
--control resumes here
```

The EXIT-WHEN statement lets you complete a loop if further processing is impossible or undesirable. When the EXIT statement is encountered, the condition in the WHEN clause is evaluated. If the condition is true, the loop completes and control passes to the next statement. Here's a simple code segment demonstrating this:

```
LOOP
...
```

```
x := x + y;
EXIT WHEN x > 1000;
END LOOP;
--control goes here
```

The GOTO statement lets you branch to a label unconditionally.
The label is denoted by a name (identifier) enclosed in double
angle brackets. For example, *<<more_than_a_k>>* is a label. Here
is an example of its usage:

```
BEGIN
...
IF x > 1000 THEN
GOTO <<more_than_a_k>>;
END IF;
...
<<more_than_a_k>>
...--do some processing
END;
```

Exceptions

PL/SQL has the concept of exception handling. A warning or an
error message returned by the Oracle server is called an *exception*.
There are two types of exceptions supported in PL/SQL: predefined
or user defined. Some of the common predefined exceptions are
NO_DATA_FOUND, VALUE_ERROR, etc. A user can define his or
her own exception anywhere in the declarative part of a PL/SQL
program. Having exceptions helps to manage error handling in a
clean manner. Depending on the nature of the application code
being executed, exceptions can be handled so that the program
executes smoothly without irritating error messages being thrown
on the screen every once in a while. Exceptions also improve
readability of the application.

Standard scoping rules apply for PL/SQL exceptions like for PL/SQL
blocks. Just as PL/SQL blocks can be nested within one another,
exceptions can also be nested. They are nested by virtue of the fact
that PL/SQL blocks are nested. If an exception is redeclared within
a nested block, this innermost exception prevails over the
exception declared in the outer block(s), even if they have the same
name. The outer exception could also be a global exception.

There are two functions specific to exception handling in PL/SQL:
RAISE and RAISE_APPLICATION_ERROR. RAISE raises either a
user-defined exception or a predefined exception. The syntax is

RAISE *exception_name*. RAISE_APPLICATION_ERROR is a procedure in the package STANDARD provided by Oracle. This procedure is used to issue user-defined error messages that might be more meaningful to the end user. They can be used to tailor an application and its exceptions to the specific domain. The following is an example of a PL/SQL block with an exception and an exception handler:

```
DECLARE
hiring_exception      EXCEPTION;
  BEGIN
    IF SELECT hiredate FROM emp < SYSDATE THEN
    RAISE hiring_exception;
    END IF;
  SELECT empno FROM emp WHERE ename LIKE '%SMITH%';
  EXCEPTION
  WHEN hiring_exception THEN
  DBMS_OUTPUT.PUT_LINE( "Employee was hired prior to
  today");
  WHEN OTHERS THEN
  err_num := SQLCODE;
  err_msg := SUBSTR(SQLERRM, 1, 100);
  DBMS_OUTPUT.PUTL_LINE('Error message is'||err_msg);
  END;
```

Packages, Procedures, and Functions

PL/SQL supports modular programming through packages, procedures, and functions. Developing packages, procedures, and functions also helps to achieve very good performance by reducing the number of network round trips. *Procedures* and *functions* are named PL/SQL blocks that can take parameters and be invoked from a large number of environments. Procedures do not return values, they perform tasks. Functions also perform tasks, but they return values. The following are examples of a stored procedure that removes an employee from a job, a function that adds an employee to the database, and a package that combines the procedure and function into a logical entity. The following is the example of a procedure:

```
CREATE OR REPLACE PROCEDURE fire_emp(emp_num NUMBER)IS
BEGIN
DELETE FROM emp WHERE empno = emp_num;
END fire_emp;
```

A *package* has two parts to it: a specification and the body. The specification has all the package variables, cursors, procedures, and functions declarations in it. The package body has the bodies of the procedures and functions. The following is an example of a package called *hire_fire*. We have the package specification followed by the package body.

```
CREATE OR REPLACE PACKAGE hire_fire AS
  local_var NUMBER;

  FUNCTION hire_emp(ename VARCHAR2, deptno NUMBER, sal
  NUMBER)
    RETURN NUMBER;
  PROCEDURE fire_emp(empno NUMBER);
END hire_fire;

CREATE OR REPLACE PACKAGE BODY hire_fire AS
  FUNCTION hire_emp(empname VARCHAR2, deptnum NUMBER,
  sal NUMBER)
  RETURN NUMBER IS
  new_empno NUMBER;
  BEGIN
    SELECT empseq.NEXTVAL INTO new_empno FROM dual;
    INSERT INTO emp(empno, ename, deptno) VALUES
    (new_empno, empname, deptnum);
    RETURN new_empno;
  END;

  PROCEDURE fire_emp(emp_num NUMBER) IS
  BEGIN
    DELETE FROM emp WHERE empno = emp_num;
  END;
END hire_fire;
```

JDBC and SQLJ Tools

This section addresses the support for JDBC and SQLJ standards by Oracle. It also explains the role of Java Stored Procedures in

Oracle 8.0.4. Java has become an extremely popular language in a very short time. Perhaps the two biggest reasons for that are its ease of use and its portability. Thanks to its tremendous popularity, most database application developers are looking to use Java as a language to access data in relational databases. The two main tools that are being (and have been) built by database vendors are JDBC drivers and the SQLJ precompiler. JDBC (Java Database Connectivity) is a Java class library for accessing relational data. It is an API modeled by Javasoft based on open database connectivity (ODBC). By using JDBC, Java programs can query and modify data in relational databases. Just like ODBC, a class library is supplied by Javasoft that facilitates database operations. JDBC supports SQL92 syntax and types, supports data streaming to and from the database, and allows for vendor-specific extensions. The JDBC class library is a vendor-independent layer. Individual vendors are expected to provide drivers that implement the JDBC interfaces for their particular database. An implementation that serves as a reference has been built by Javasoft. It is an ODBC-based driver. SQLJ is a precompiler that takes source code in Java with embedded SQL commands in it and generates JDBC.

Oracle has two different types of JDBC drivers, which are classified as follows:

JDBC OCI	OCI-based driver
JDBC Thin	Pure Java driver

JDBC OCI

The JDBC OCI drivers, pictured in Figure 1-1, are ideal for Java applications and middle-tier servers because of the following reasons:

- The drivers are compatible with all Oracle versions and SQL*Net adapters.
- Java benefits from all OCI features.
- JDBC OCI 8.0 supports Oracle object types.

However, there are a few downsides to using JDBC OCI drivers:

- They are not downloadable to applets.
- SQL*Net installation is required on the client.

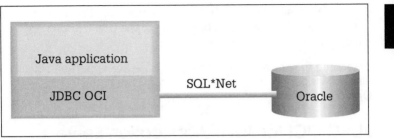

Figure 1-1.   The JDBC OCI driver

The OCI-based driver uses C entry points in the OCI library, whereas the JDBC Thin driver connects to the database directly via Java sockets. The OCI-based drivers are appropriate for use by Java applications, which include the WebServer Java cartridge, or any other Java middle tier. They call OCI directly from Java, providing the highest compatibility with the different versions of the RDBMS. You need the OCI7 driver if you have an Oracle7 installation or the OCI 8 driver if you have an Oracle8 installation.

The JDBC OCI driver is a type 2 driver that uses Java native methods to call the C entry points of the OCI library. Because of the use of Java native methods, the JDBC OCI driver is machine specific.

JDBC OCI requires SLQ*Net 2.3 to be installed on the client side.

NOTE: JDBC OCI cannot be used by Java applets. This is because the Java native methods are architecture dependent and cannot be downloaded. JDBC OCI is designed to be used by Java applications or Java middle tiers such as code running in the Java cartridge of the Oracle Web Application Server.

Being based on OCI, JDBC OCI supports all SQL*Net adapters installed on your system. It can connect to Oracle over IPC, named pipes, TCP/IP, Decnet, etc.

In the next couple of paragraphs, we look at some of the applications that JDBC OCI lends itself to very easily.

JDBC OCI for Java Applications

A Java application can access the relational data in Oracle through JDBC OCI because OCI provides the SQL*Net interface to the

Oracle server (see Figure 1-2). Therefore, traditional client/server applications where Java clients connect to the Oracle server are easily supported.

Extending the above by one more step, the Java application could also access data in non-Oracle databases through the Oracle Open Gateways.

JDBC OCI for Java Application Servers

Java-enabled NCA application servers can access the Oracle database with JDBC. In this scenario, some NCA client can invoke a service provided by a Java application server through the IIOP protocol (see Figure 1-3). The Java application server, in turn, communicates with the Oracle database via JDBC OCI and SQL*Net.

JDBC OCI for the Java Cartridge

Yet another instance where JDBC OCI readily lends itself for use is with Java cartridges (see Figure 1-4). Assume that there is a Web browser that uses the HTTP protocol to talk to Oracle's Web server. In the NCA domain, the Web application server is a cartridge, and it needs to communicate with the Java cartridge. This communication between the two cartridges is facilitated through Inter Cartridge eXchange (ICX). The Java cartridge then communicates with Oracle via JDBC OCI and SQL*Net.

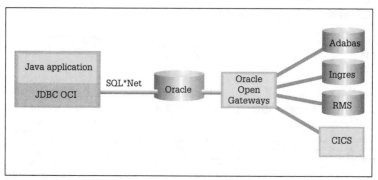

Figure 1-2.   JDBC OCI for Java applications

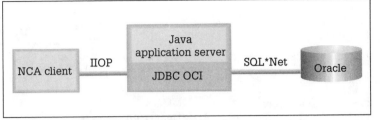

Figure 1-3.   JDBC OCI for Java application servers

JDBC Thin

The JDBC Thin is ideal for Java applets because it is pure Java code—that is, it does not involve the use of OCI (see Figure 1-5). Instead, it uses Java sockets that talk to the database via SQL*Net. The advantages it has are that it can be downloaded with the applet, there is no client installation required, and it needs only 300K of memory. It connects to Oracle Server releases 7.2 and higher. The down side, however, is that it supports only TCP/IP SQL*Net.

The Thin driver is appropriate for use by Java applets that can be downloaded in a Web browser. The Thin driver provides a direct connection from the Web browser to the RDBMS by emulating SQL*Net and TTC (two-task common, the wire protocol used by OCI) on top of Java sockets. This driver works for RDBMS versions 7.2 and above.

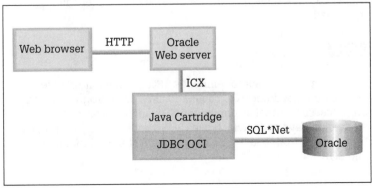

Figure 1-4.   JDBC OCI for the Java cartridge

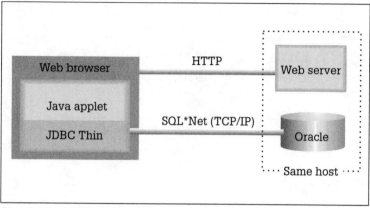

Figure 1-5. JDBC Thin for Java applets

The JDBC Pure Java driver is a type 4 driver: it is 100 percent Java. It connects directly to Oracle on top of Java sockets without the need for an Oracle-specific middle tier. Being Pure Java, the JDBC Pure Java driver is not platform specific. The same distribution works on a broad range of machines that support Java.

In addition to all the appropriate uses of JDBC OCI, the Pure Java driver is appropriate for use by Java applets on the Internet. Being Pure Java, the driver can be downloaded to a Web browser as part of your Java application.

The communication between an applet that uses the Pure Java driver and the Oracle database happens on top of Java TCP/IP sockets. The connection can only be made if the Web browser where the applet is executing allows socket connections to be made.

SQLJ

SQLJ is a preprocessor for embedded SQL in Java. It provides the syntax for embedding SQL commands in a Java program. It is a preprocessor that takes embedded SQL and generates the equivalent Java code, which uses JDBC calls. It is a joint proposal from Oracle, IBM, and Tandem to define a standard for mixing Java and SQL.

There are certain advantages to using SQLJ as opposed to JDBC, which are listed here:

- Easier to use because it is more concise
- Allows for early checking of SQL statements for syntax errors and Java/SQL-type mismatch errors
- Provides strong typing of queries through SQLJ Typed Cursors

How Does SQLJ Work?

SQLJ is basically a precompiler that takes Java code with SQL statements embedded in it and generates Java code with JDBC calls (see Figure 1-6). It does the semantic check of the SQL statements against the database. The generated code compiles and runs like any other Java program.

Java Stored Procedures

Starting from version 8.1, Oracle will have support for Java stored procedures. This implies that there will be a Java Virtual Machine (JVM) within the Oracle Database Server just like the PL/SQL and SQL engines. There will also be a class repository in the database. There will be direct calls from Java to the SQL and PL/SQL engines. With this support for Java, a user has the option of creating stored procedures either in PL/SQL or Java. This does not mean that

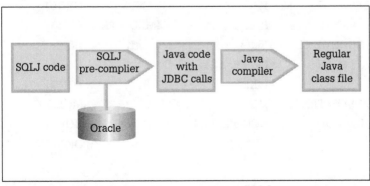

Figure 1-6. Steps involved in processing a SQLJ program

PL/SQL will disappear. In fact, PL/SQL and Java are
complementary. PL/SQL will continue to appeal to SQL
programmers needing procedural extensions. Java stored
procedures will be natural for Java programmers needing
high-performance access to relational data. SQL programmers call
stored procedures in the same way, whether written on PL/SQL or
Java. Java and PL/SQL support seamless interlanguage calls.

SQL Reserved Words and Keywords in Oracle8

The following is a list of the reserved words in Oracle8. You cannot
use reserved words as object identifiers. The words marked with
an asterisk are also ANSI reserved words.

ACCESS	ADD*	ALL*	ALTER*
AND*	ANY*	AS*	ASC*
AUDIT	BETWEEN*	BY*	CHAR*
CHECK*	CLUSTER	COLUMN*	COMMENT
COMPRESS	CONNECT*	CREATE*	CURRENT*
DATE*	DECIMAL*	DEFAULT*	DELETE*
DESC*	DISTINCT*	DROP*	ELSE*
EXCLUSIVE	EXISTS	FILE	FLOAT*
FOR*	FROM*	GRANT*	GROUP*
HAVING*	IDENTIFIED	IMMEDIATE*	IN*
INCREMENT	Index	INITIAL	INSERT*
INTEGER*	INTERSECT*	INTO*	IS*
LEVEL*	LIKE*	LOCK	LONG
MAXEXTENTS	MINUS	MODE	MODIFY
NOAUDIT	NOCOMPRESS	NOT*	NOWAIT
NULL*	NUMBER	OF*	OFFLINE

ON*	ONLINE	OPTION*	OR*
ORDER*	PCTFREE	PRIOR*	PRIVILEGES*
PUBLIC*	RAW	RENAME	RESOURCE
REVOKE*	ROW	ROWID	ROWLABEL
ROWNUM	ROWS*	SELECT*	SESSION*
SET*	SHARE	SIZE*	SMALLINT*
START	SUCCESSFUL	SYNONYM	SYSDATE
TABLE*	THEN*	TO*	TRIGGER
UID	UNION	UNIQUE	UPDATE
USER*	VALIDATE	VALUES*	VARCHAR*
VARCHAR2	VIEW*	WHENEVER*	WHERE*
WITH*			

The following is a list of keywords in Oracle8.

ACCOUNT	ACTIVATE
ADMIN	AFTER
ALL_ROWS	ALLOCATE*
ANALYZE	ARCHIVE
ARCHIVELOG	ARRAY
AT*	AUTHENTICATED
AUTHORIZATION*	AUTOEXTEND
AUTOMATIC	BACKUP
BECOME	BEFORE
BEGIN	BFILE
BITMAP	BLOB
BLOCK	BODY
CACHE	CACHE_INSTANCES
CANCEL	CASCADE*
CAST	CFILE
CHAINED	CHANGE

CHAR_CS

CHARACTER*

CHECKPOINT

CHOOSE

CHUNK

CLEAR

CLOB

CLONE

CLOSE*

CLOSE_CACHED_OPEN_
CURSORS

COALESCE*

COLUMNS

COMMIT*

COMMITTED

COMPATIBILITY

COMPILE

COMPLETE

COMPOSITE_LIMIT

COMPUTE

CONNECT_TIME

CONSTRAINT*

CONSTRAINTS*

CONTENTS

CONTINUE*

CONTROLFILE

CONVERT*

COST

COUNT*

CPU_PER_CALL

CPU_PER_SESSION

CURRENT_SCHEMA

CURRENT_USER

CURSOR*

CYCLE

DANGLING

DATABASE

DATAFILE

DATAFILES

DATAOBJNO

DBA

DEALLOCATE*

DEBUG

DEC*

DECLARE*

DEFERRABLE

DEFERRED

DEGREE

DEREF

DIRECTORY

DISABLE

DISCONNECT

DISMOUNT

DISTRIBUTED

DML

DOUBLE*

DUMP

EACH

ENABLE

END*

ENFORCE

ENTRY	ESCAPE*
ESTIMATE	EVENTS
EXCEPT*	EXCEPTIONS
EXCHANGE	EXCLUDING
EXECUTE*	EXPIRE
EXPLAIN	EXTENT
EXTENTS	EXTERNALLY
FAILED_LOGIN_ATTEMPTS	FALSE
FAST	FIRST_ROWS
FLAGGER	FLUSH
FORCE	FOREIGN*
FREELIST	FREELISTS
FULL	FUNCTION
GLOBAL*	GLOBAL_NAME
GLOBALLY	GROUPS
HASH	HASHKEYS
HEADER	HEAP
IDLE_TIME	IF
INCLUDING	IND_PARTITION
INDEXED	INDICATOR*
INITIALLY	INITRANS
INSTANCE	INSTANCES
INSTEAD	INT*
INTERMEDIATE	ISOLATION*
ISOLATION_LEVEL	KEEP
KEY*	KILL
LAYER	LESS
LIBRARY	LIMIT
LINK	LIST
LOB	LOCAL*
LOG	LOGFILE

LOGGING	LOGICAL_READS_PER_CALL
LOGICAL_READS_PER_SESSION	MANAGE
MASTER	MAX*
MAXARCHLOGS	MAXDATAFILES
MAXINSTANCES	MAXLOGFILES
MAXLOGMEMBERS	MAXSIZE
MAXTRANS	MAXVALUE
MEMBER	MIN*
MINEXTENTS	MINIMUM
MINVALUE	MOUNT
MOVE	MTS_DISPATCHERS
MULTISET	NATIONAL*
NCHAR*	NCHAR_CS
NCLOB	NEEDED
NESTED	NETWORK
NEW	NEXT*
NLS_CALENDAR	NLS_CHARACTERSET
NLS_ISO_CURRENCY	NLS_LANGUAGE
NLS_NUMERIC_CHARACTERS	NLS_SORT
NLS_SPECIAL_CHARS	NLS_TERRITORY
NOARCHIVELOG	NOCACHE
NOCYCLE	NOFORCE
NOLOGGING	NOMAXVALUE
NOMINVALUE	NONE
NOORDER	NOOVERIDE
NOPARALLEL	NORESETLOGS
NOREVERSE	NORMAL
NOSORT	NOTHING
NUMERIC	NVARCHAR2
OBJECT	OBJNO
OBJNO_REUSE	OFF

1

OID	OIDINDEX
OLD	ONLY*
OPCODE	OPEN*
OPTIMAL	OPTIMIZER_GOAL
ORGANIZATION	OVERFLOW
OWN	PACKAGE
PARALLEL	PARTITION
PASSWORD	PASSWORD_GRACE_TIME
PASSWORD_LIFE_TIME	PASSWORD_LOCK_TIME
PASSWORD_REUSE_MAX	PASSWORD_REUSE_TIME
PASSWORD_VERIFY_FUNCTION	PCTINCREASE
PCTTHRESHOLD	PCTUSED
PCTVERSION	PERCENT
PERMANENT	PLAN
PLSQL_DEBUG	POST_TRANSACTION
PRECISION*	PRESERVE*
PRIMARY*	PRIVATE
PRIVATE_SGA	PRIVILEGE
PROCEDURE*	PROFILE
PURGE	QUEUE
QUOTA	RANGE
RBA	READ*
REAL*	REBUILD
RECOVER	RECOVERABLE
RECOVERY	REF
REFERENCES*	REFERENCING
REFRESH	REPLACE
RESET	RESETLOGS
RESIZE	RESTRICTED
RETURN	RETURNING

REUSE	REVERSE
ROLE	ROLES
ROLLBACK*	RULE
SAMPLE	SAVEPOINT
SCAN_INSTANCES	SCHEMA*
SCN	SCOPE
SD_ALL	SD_INHIBIT
SD_SHOW	SEG_BLOCK
SEG_FILE	SEGMENT
SEQUENCE	SERIALIZABLE
SESSION_CACHED_CURSORS	SESSIONS_PER_USER
SHARED	SHARED_POOL
SHRINK	SKIP_UNUSABLE_INDEXES
SNAPSHOT	SOME*
SORT	SPECIFICATION
SPLIT	SQL_TRACE
SQLCODE*	SQLERROR
STANDBY	STATEMENT_ID
STATISTICS	STOP
STORAGE	STORE
STRUCTURE	SUM*
SWITCH	SYSDBA
SYSOPER	SYSTEM
TABLES	TABLESPACE
TABLESPACE_NO	TABNO
TEMPORARY	THAN
THE	THREAD
TIME	TIMESTAMP
TOPLEVEL	TRACE
TRACING	TRANSACTION*
TRANSITIONAL	TRIGGERS

TRUE	TRUNCATE
TX	TYPE
UBA	UNARCHIVED
UNDER	UNDO
UNLIMITED	UNLOCK
UNRECOVERABLE	UNTIL*
UNUSABLE	UNUSED
UPDATABLE	USAGE*
USE	USING*
VALIDATION	VALUE
VARRAY	VARYING
WHEN	WITHOUT
WORK*	WRITE*
XID	

SQL*Plus

SQL*Plus is a program used most popularly by Oracle developers and DBAs in conjunction with the SQL language and PL/SQL, Oracle's procedural extension to SQL. SQL, as we know, is a database language. SQL*Plus allows users to execute anything from simple SQL commands to PL/SQL program units such as stored procedures, functions, packages, etc. In addition, you can also do the following:

- Format, perform calculations on, store, and print query results in the form of reports
- List column definitions for any table
- Access and copy data between SQL databases
- Send messages to and accept input from an end user

SQL*Plus is a basic yet powerful reporting tool that can be used very effectively for the purpose of program development, debugging, and reporting. In order to run SQL*Plus, you need to have installed Oracle server on a machine to which you can connect from SQL*Plus. In addition, you need to have a valid username and password to log on to the Oracle database. It is typically the DBA's (or system administrator's) responsibility to install SQL*Plus and create user accounts.

Using SQL*Plus

In order to log on to SQL*Plus, you would type in the following command at your operating system prompt:

sqlplus *scott/tiger* (assuming *scott/tiger* is your password)

At this point, if everything goes well, you will log on to SQL*Plus as shown below:

```
ORA8 % sqlplus scott/tiger

SQL*Plus: Release 8.0.3.0.0 - Production on Mon Jan 26
17:34:41 1998

(c) Copyright 1997 Oracle Corporation.  All rights reserved.


Connected to:
Oracle8 Enterprise Edition Release 8.0.3.0.0 - Production
With the Partitioning and Objects options
PL/SQL Release 8.0.3.0.0 - Production

SQL>
```

In order to exit from SQL*Plus, you would type **EXIT** (needn't be in uppercase).

```
SQL> exit
Disconnected from Oracle8 Enterprise Edition
Release 8.0.3.0.0 - Production
With the Partitioning and Objects options
PL/SQL Release 8.0.3.0.0 - Production
ORA8 %
```

After you log on to SQL*Plus, you will be prompted with *SQL>*. At this point, you can begin to execute any SQL commands to perform various tasks such as creating tables, querying tables for data, modifying tables, updating tables, creating stored program units, etc. In addition, you could also execute formatting and reporting commands from the SQL> prompt. To get assistance on using commands in SQL*Plus, you could use the online help facility by typing **HELP *command-name***. Once you have entered your command, you can execute it by pressing ENTER. SQL*Plus will processes your command and will return either the results or error messages, if any.

SQL Buffer

The area where SQL*Plus stores your command before executing it is called the *SQL buffer*. The command or block of code remains there until you enter another one, so if you want to edit your command or rerun it, you can do so without retyping it.

Ending a SQL Command

There are three different ways in which you can end a SQL command:

- With a semicolon (;)
- With a forward slash (/) on a line by itself
- With a blank line

Executing a Set of SQL or SQL*Plus Commands

You can execute a set of SQL commands from the SQL*Plus prompt by putting all the commands in a file and saving it with the extension .SQL (the extension need not be in uppercase). You then execute this file by typing either **run *filename*** or **@*filename***. You can execute a PL/SQL block by starting with either DECLARE or BEGIN and terminating it with END, followed by a period (.) by itself on a new line.

System Variables

The SQL*Plus command SET controls many variables—called *system variables*. The behavior of SQL*Plus is governed by the values at which these system variables are set. Many features such as column width, column title, page size, etc., are modifiable by the SET command.

Bind Variables

Bind variables are variables you create in SQL*Plus and then reference in PL/SQL. You can use bind variables for such things as storing error codes, and you can create a bind variable by simply declaring it as follows:

```
VARIABLE var_name    number
```

where the datatype could be any valid SQL datatype and the variable name could be any valid identifier.

Substitution Variables

A *substitution variable* is a user variable name preceded by one or two ampersands (&). When SQL*Plus encounters a substitution variable in a command, it executes the command as if it contained the value in the variable rather than the variable itself. Substitution variables can be used anywhere in SQL and SQL*Plus.

HOST Command

This command allows you to get to the operating system prompt without actually exiting SQL*Plus.

SQL*Plus is a very powerful reporting tool. A very brief overview of this tool has been provided in this appendix. There are several different categories of commands that have not been discussed here as they are beyond the scope of this book. For further details, refer to the *SQL*Plus User's Guide and Reference*.

Part II
Syntax Flowcharts

DDL Commands

ALTER CLUSTER

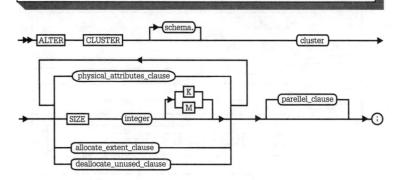

physical_attributes_clause :=

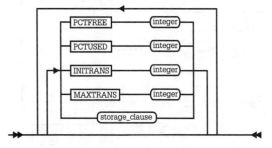

allocate_extent_clause :=

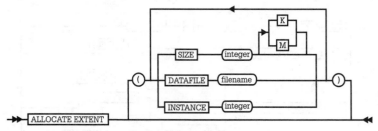

ALTER DATABASE

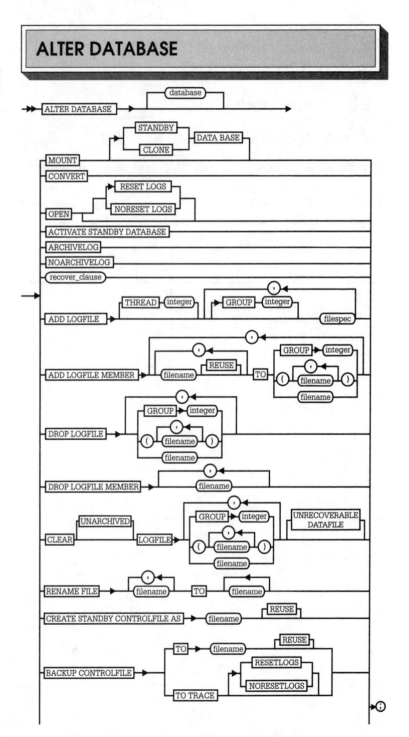

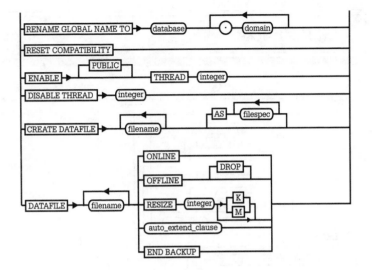

auto_extend_clause :=

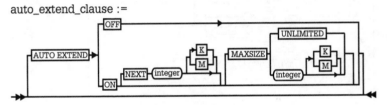

ALTER FUNCTION

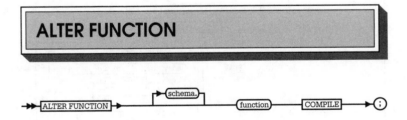

ALTER INDEX

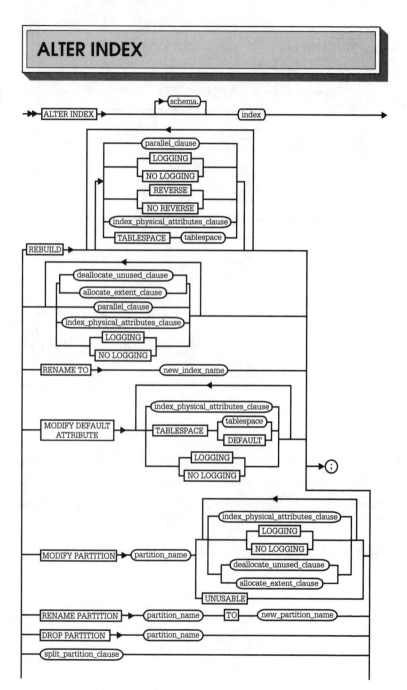

2

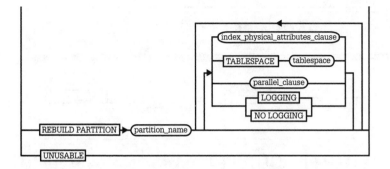

index_physical_attributes_clause ::=

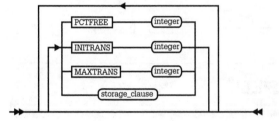

allocate_extent_clause ::=

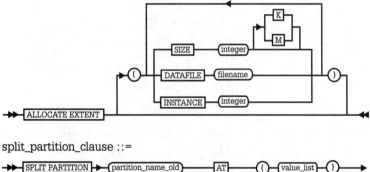

split_partition_clause ::=

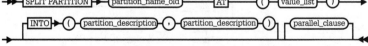

partition_description ::=

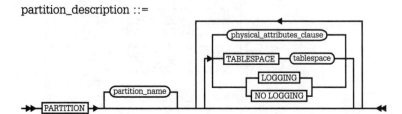

ALTER PACKAGE

ALTER PROCEDURE

ALTER PROFILE

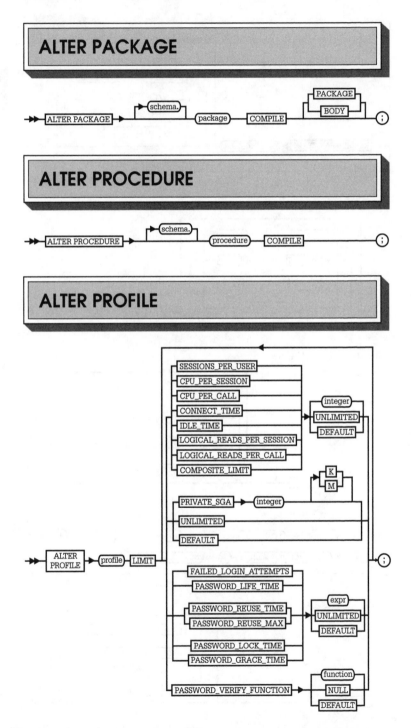

ALTER RESOURCE COST

ALTER ROLE

ALTER ROLLBACK SEGMENT

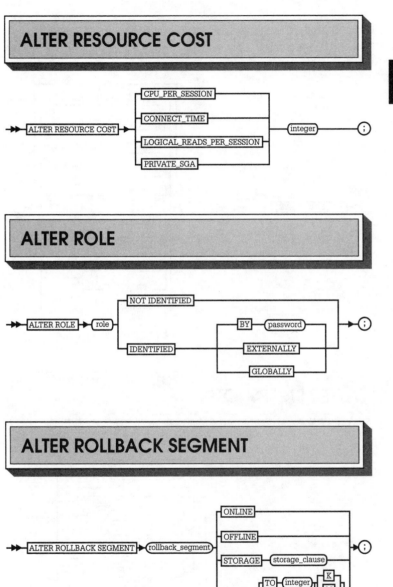

ALTER SEQUENCE

ALTER SNAPSHOT

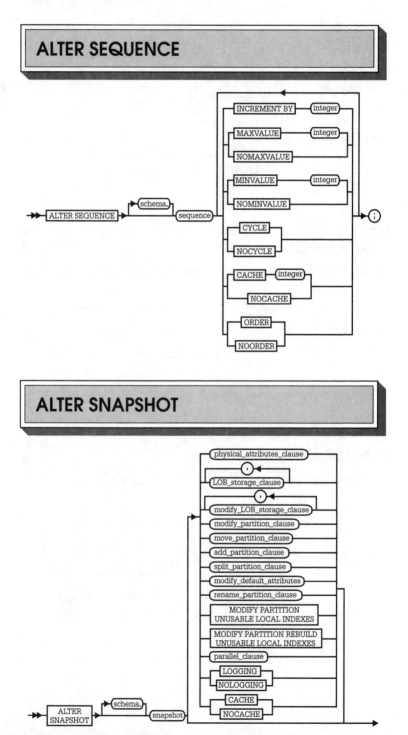

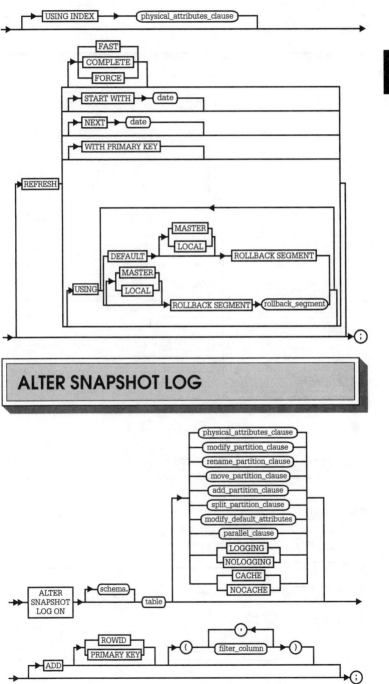

ALTER SNAPSHOT LOG

ALTER TABLE

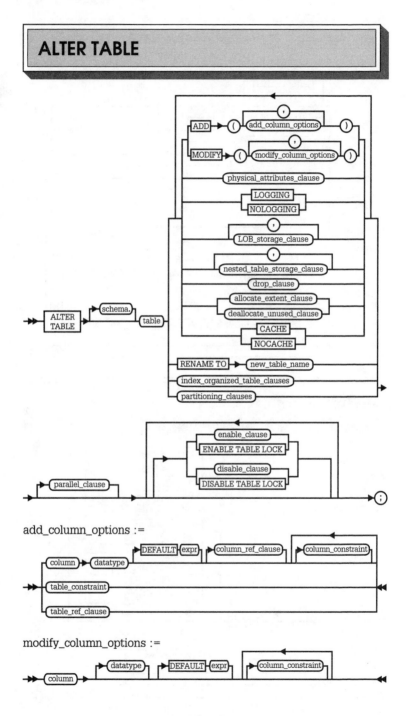

add_column_options :=

modify_column_options :=

column_ref_clause :=

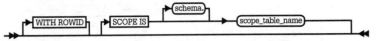

table_ref_clause :=

physical_attributes_clause :=

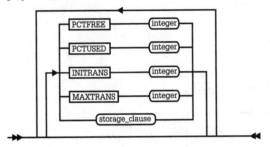

lob_parameters :=

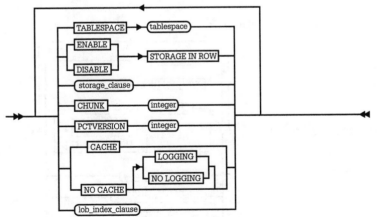

LOB_storage_clause :=

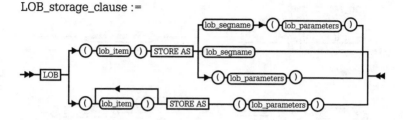

lob_index_clause :=

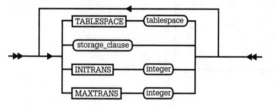

lob_index_parameters :=

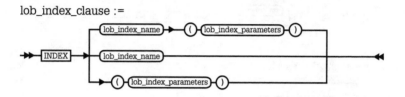

modify_LOB_storage_clause :=

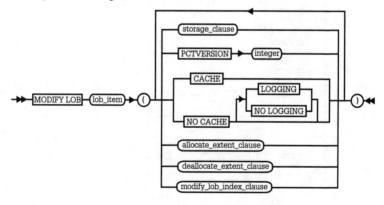

modify_lob_index_clause :=

nested_table_storage_clause :=

allocate_extent_clause :=

index_organized_table_clauses :=

overflow_clause :=

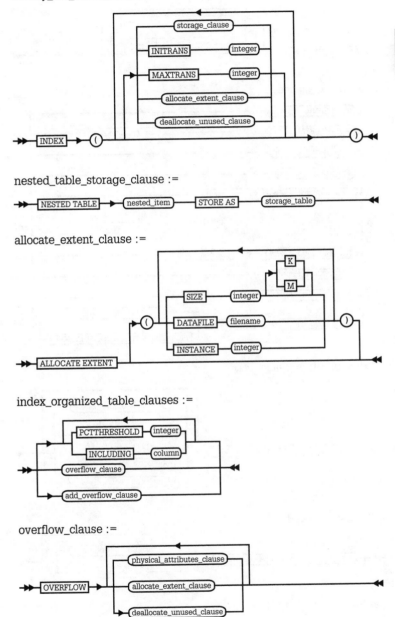

add_overflow_clause :=

partitioning_clause :=

modify_partition_clause :=

move_partition_clause :=

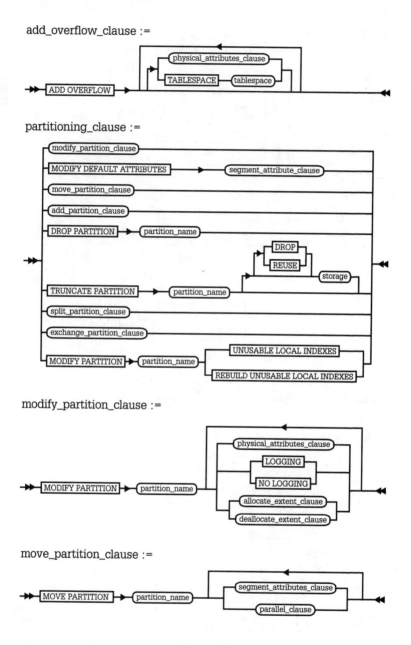

add_partition_clause :=

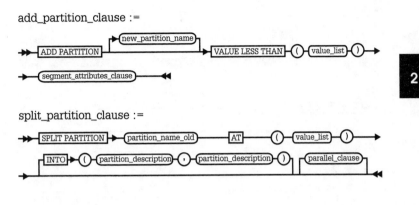

split_partition_clause :=

partition_description :=

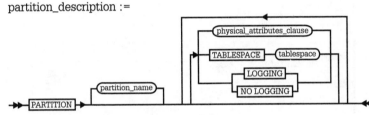

exchange_partition_clause :=

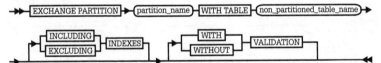

segment_attributes_clause :=

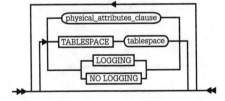

ALTER TABLESPACE

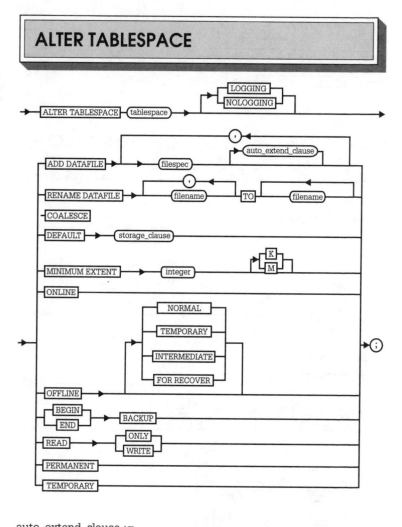

auto_extend_clause :=

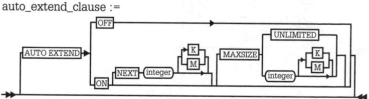

ALTER TRIGGER

ALTER USER

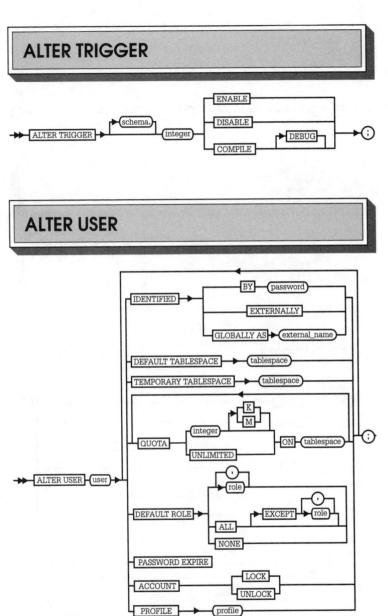

ALTER VIEW

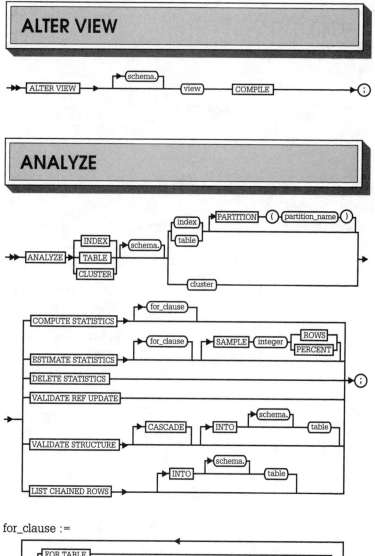

ANALYZE

for_clause :=

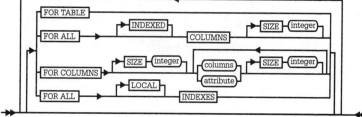

AUDIT (SQL Statements)

AUDIT (Schema Objects)

COMMENT

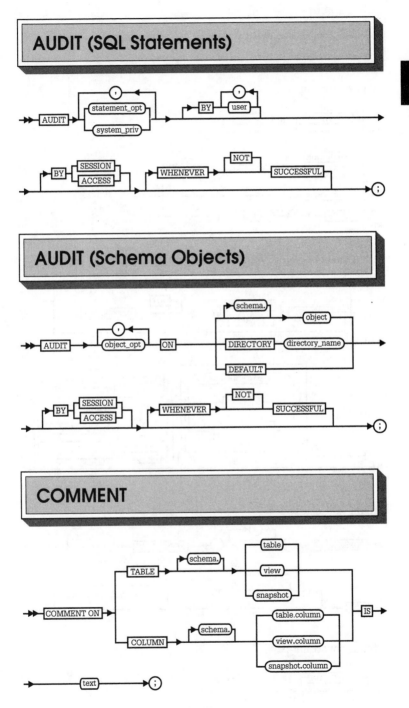

CONSTRAINT

table_constraint :=

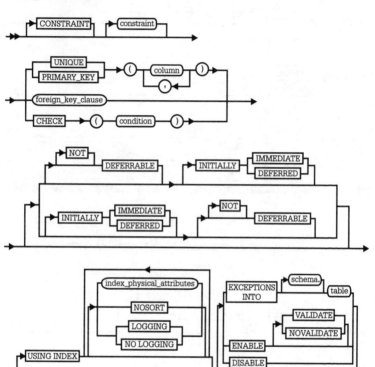

foreign_key_clause :=

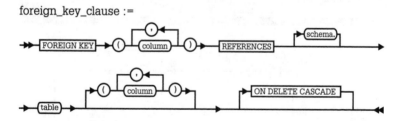

column_constraint :=

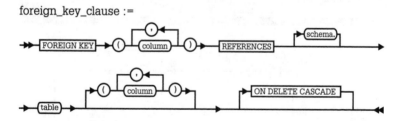

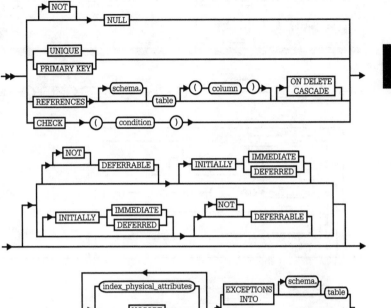

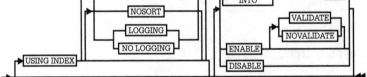

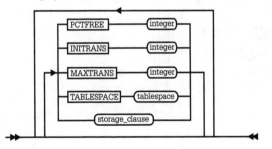

index_physical_attributes :=

CREATE CLUSTER

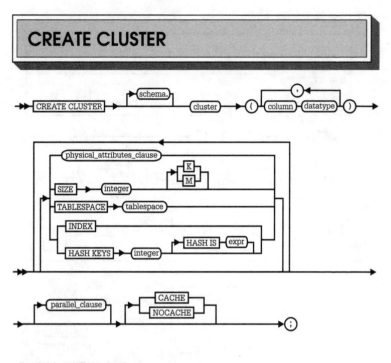

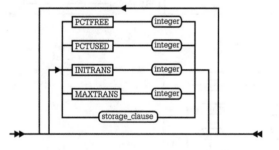

physical_attributes_clause :=

CREATE CONTROLFILE

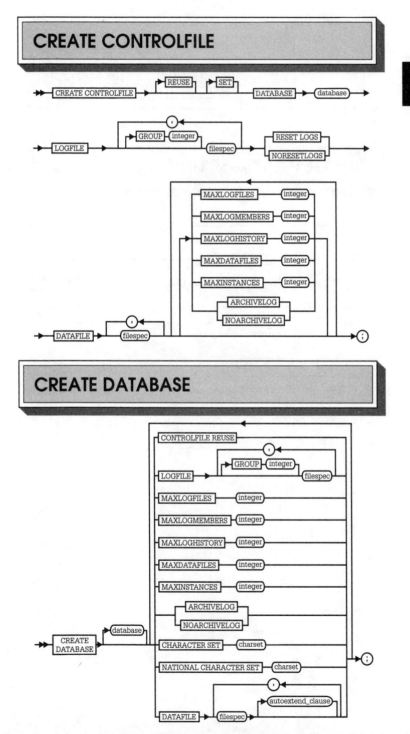

CREATE DATABASE

autoextend_clause :=

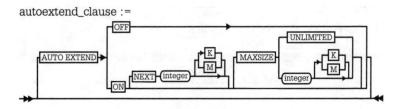

CREATE DATABASE LINK

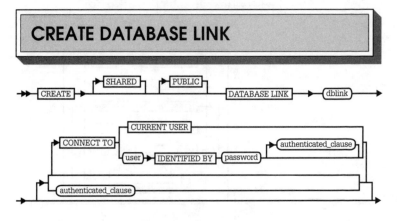

authenticated_clause :=

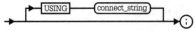

CREATE FUNCTION

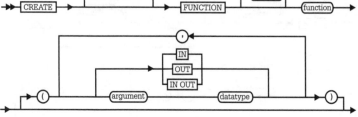

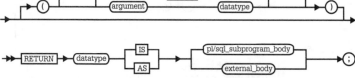

external_body :=

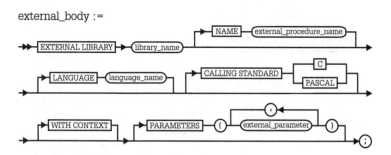

external_parameter :=

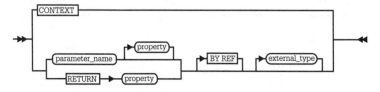

property :=

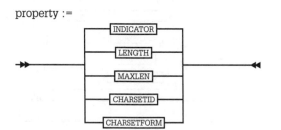

CREATE INDEX

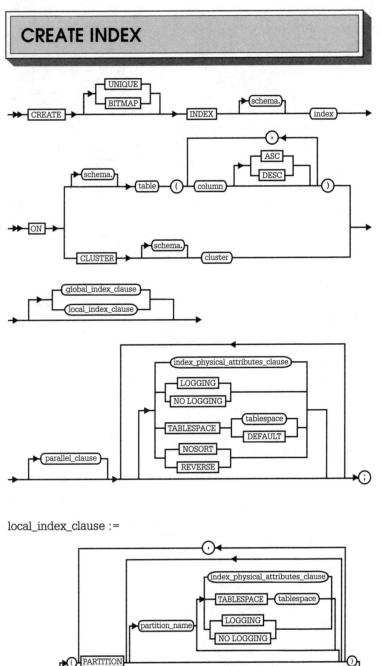

local_index_clause :=

global_index_clause :=

global_partition_clause :=

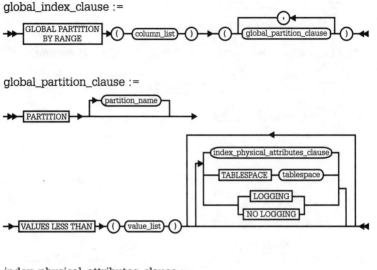

index_physical_attributes_clause :=

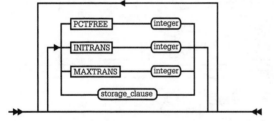

CREATE PACKAGE

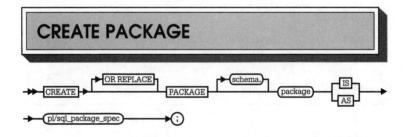

CREATE PACKAGE BODY

CREATE PROCEDURE

external_library :=

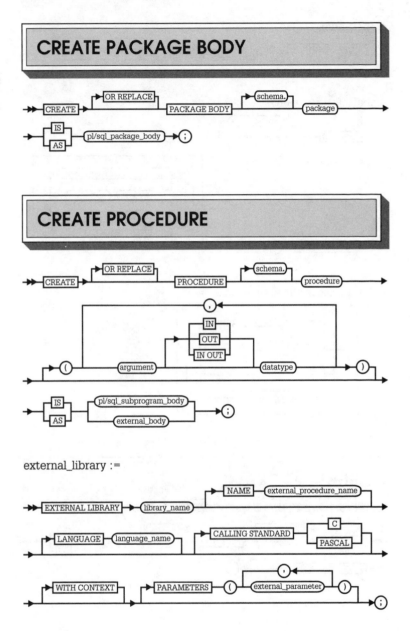

external_parameter :=

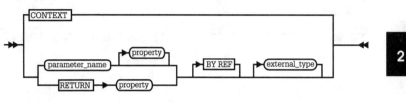

property :=

CREATE PROFILE

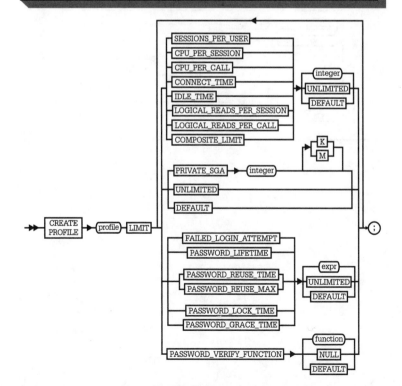

CREATE ROLE

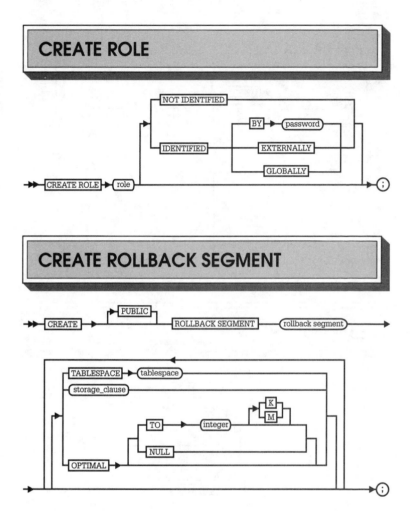

CREATE ROLLBACK SEGMENT

CREATE SCHEMA

CREATE SEQUENCE

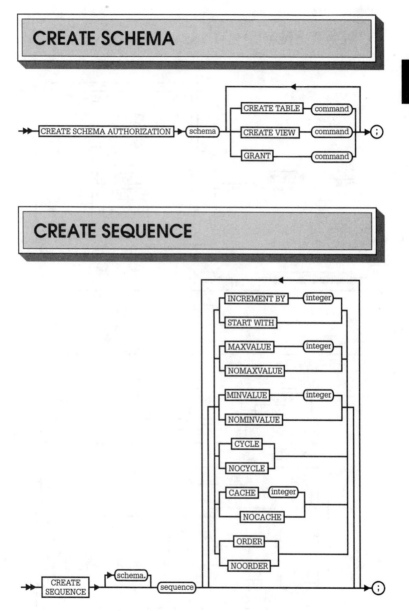

CREATE SNAPSHOT

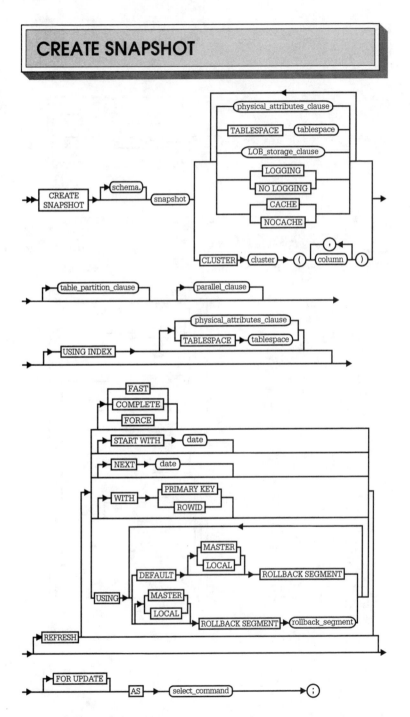

CREATE SNAPSHOT LOG

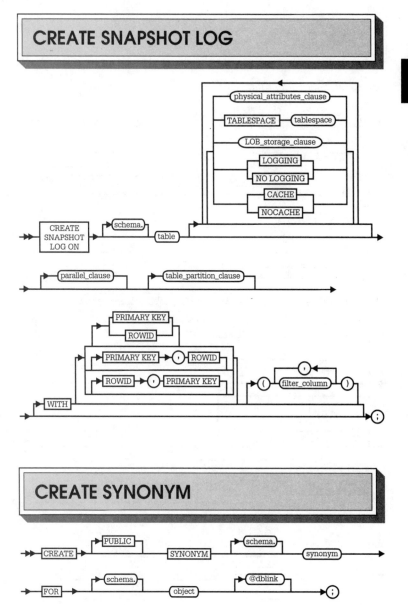

CREATE SYNONYM

CREATE TABLE

relational_table_definition :=

object_table_definition :=

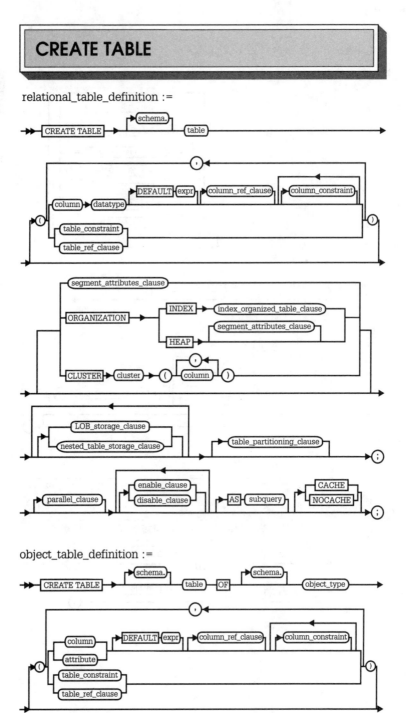

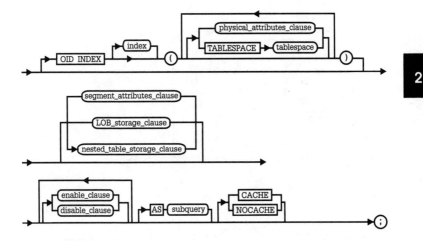

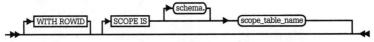

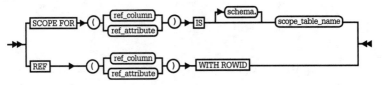

column_ref_clause :=

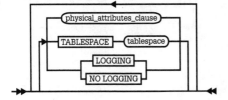

table_ref_clause :=

segment_attributes_clause :=

physical_attribute_clause :=

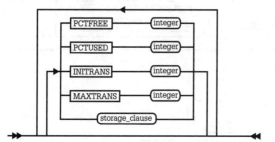

index_organized_table_clause :=

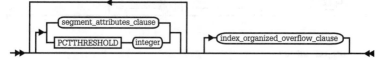

index_organized_overflow_clause :=

LOB_storage_clause :=

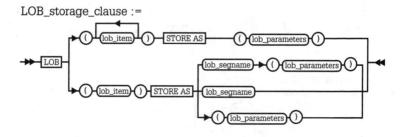

lob_parameters :=

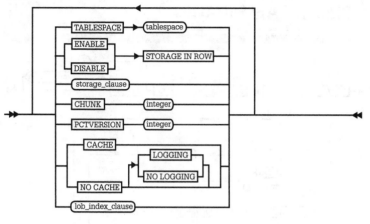

lob_index_clause :=

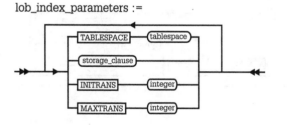

lob_index_parameters :=

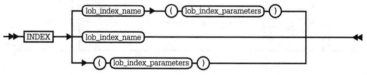

nested_table_storage_clause :=

table_partition_clause :=

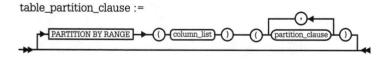

partition_clause :=

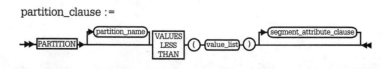

CREATE TABLESPACE

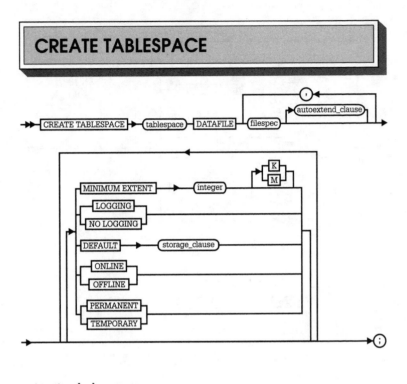

autoextend_clause :=

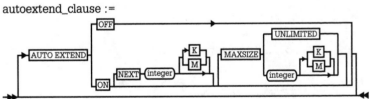

CREATE TRIGGER

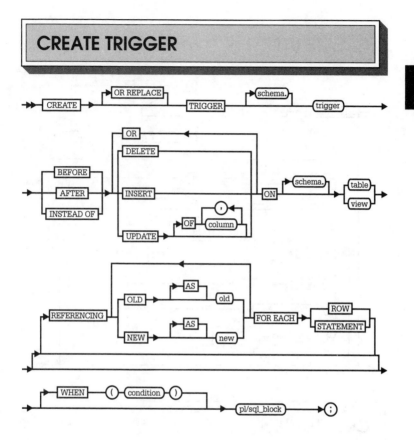

CREATE USER

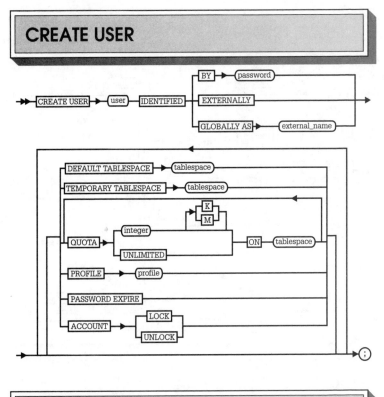

CREATE VIEW

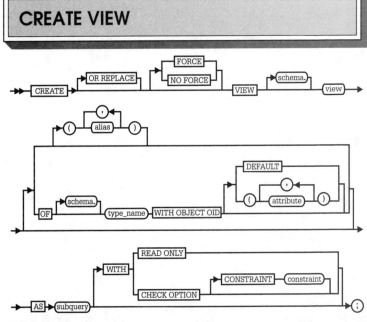

2

DROP

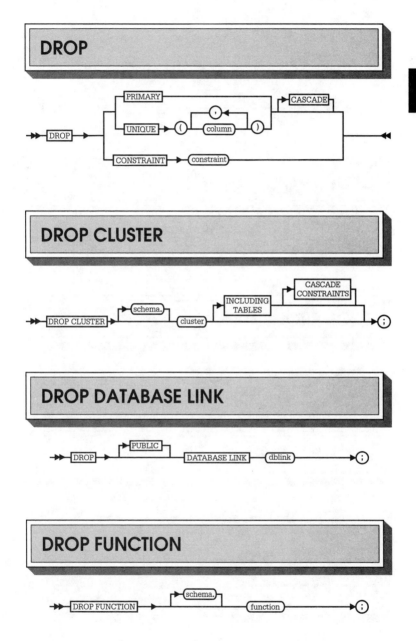

DROP CLUSTER

DROP DATABASE LINK

DROP FUNCTION

DROP INDEX

```
▶▶─ DROP INDEX ─▶─┌─▶ schema. ─┐─── index ──────▶(;)
```

DROP PACKAGE

```
▶▶─ DROP PACKAGE ─▶─┌─▶ BODY ─┐─┌─▶ schema. ─┐── package ──▶(;)
```

DROP PROCEDURE

```
▶▶─ DROP PROCEDURE ─▶─┌─▶ schema. ─┐─── procedure ──────▶(;)
```

DROP PROFILE

```
▶▶─ DROP PROFILE ─▶─ profile ─┌─▶ CASCADE ─┐──────────▶(;)
```

DROP ROLE

```
▶▶─ DROP ROLE ─▶─ role ──▶(;)
```

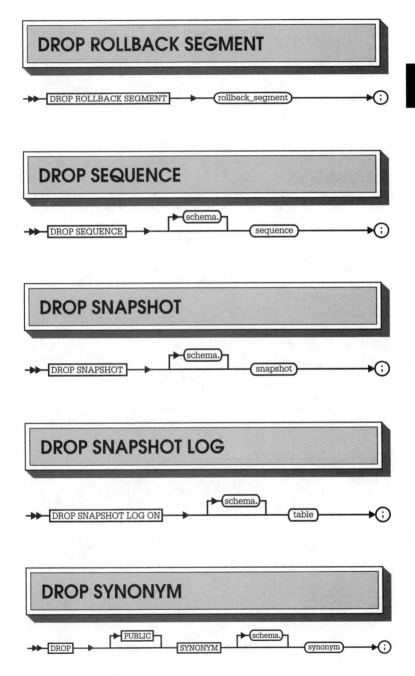

DROP ROLLBACK SEGMENT

▶▶─[DROP ROLLBACK SEGMENT]──▶──(rollback_segment)──────────▶(;)

DROP SEQUENCE

▶▶─[DROP SEQUENCE]──▶──(schema.)──(sequence)──────▶(;)

DROP SNAPSHOT

▶▶─[DROP SNAPSHOT]──▶──(schema.)──(snapshot)──────▶(;)

DROP SNAPSHOT LOG

▶▶─[DROP SNAPSHOT LOG ON]──▶──(schema.)──(table)──────▶(;)

DROP SYNONYM

▶▶─[DROP]──▶──[PUBLIC]──[SYNONYM]──(schema.)──(synonym)──▶(;)

DROP TABLE

▶▶ DROP TABLE → ┌ schema. ┐ table ┌ CASCADE CONSTRAINTS ┐ → (;)

DROP TABLESPACE

▶▶ DROP TABLESPACE → tablespace → ┌ INCLUDING CONTENTS → ┌ CASCADE CONSTRAINTS ┐ ┐ → (;)

DROP TRIGGER

▶▶ DROP TRIGGER → ┌ schema. ┐ trigger → (;)

DROP USER

▶▶ DROP USER → user → ┌ CASCADE ┐ → (;)

DROP VIEW

▶▶ DROP VIEW → ┌ schema. ┐ view → (;)

2

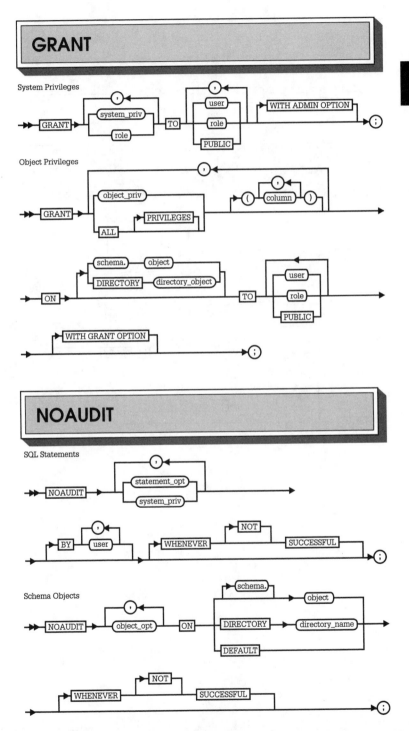

GRANT

System Privileges

Object Privileges

NOAUDIT

SQL Statements

Schema Objects

RENAME

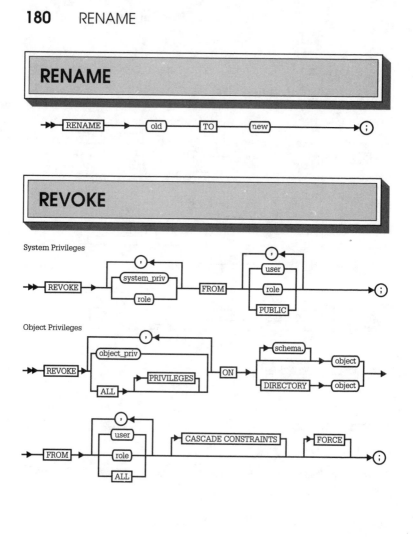

REVOKE

System Privileges

Object Privileges

STORAGE

storage_clause :=

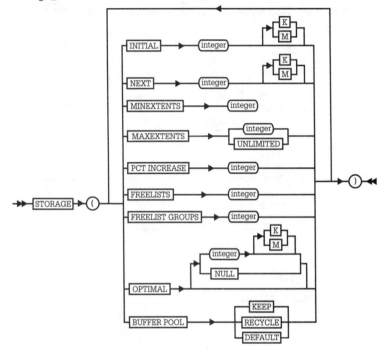

TRUNCATE

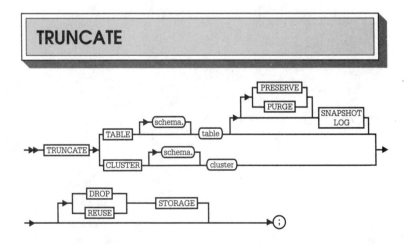

DML Commands

DELETE

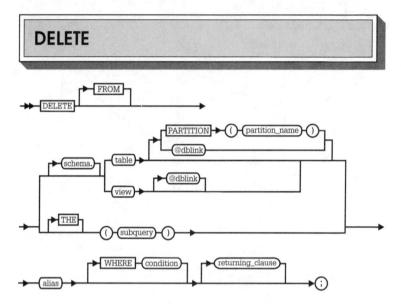

returning_clause :=

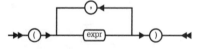

expr_list :=

data_item_list :=

EXPLAIN PLAN

SET STATEMENT_ID=

INSERT

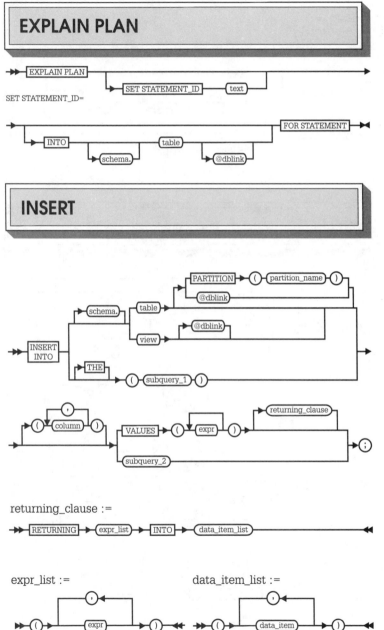

returning_clause :=

expr_list :=

data_item_list :=

LOCK TABLE

SELECT

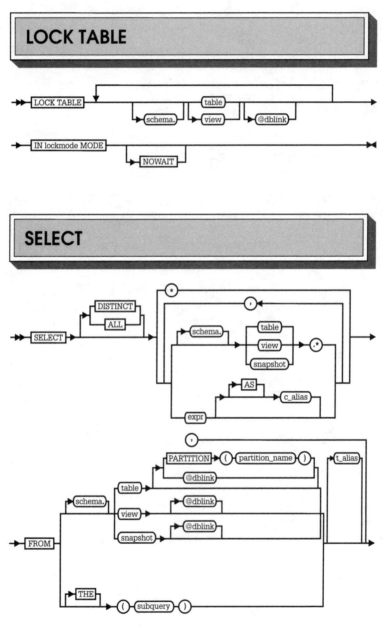

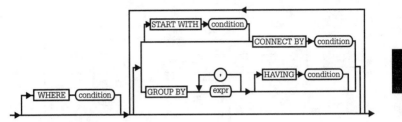

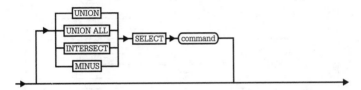

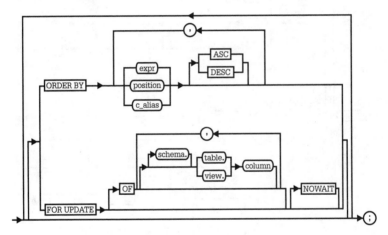

subquery :=

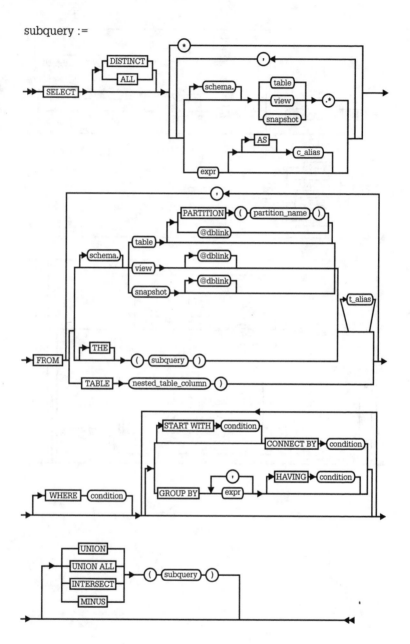

UPDATE

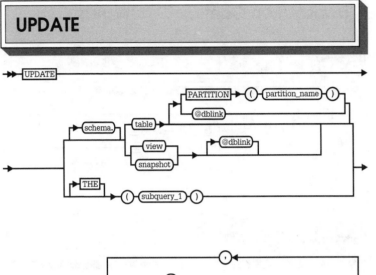

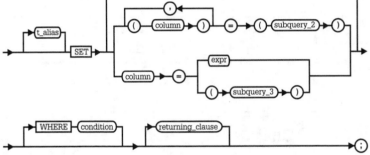

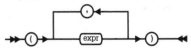

returning_clause :=

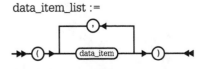

expr_list :=

data_item_list :=

Transaction Control Commands

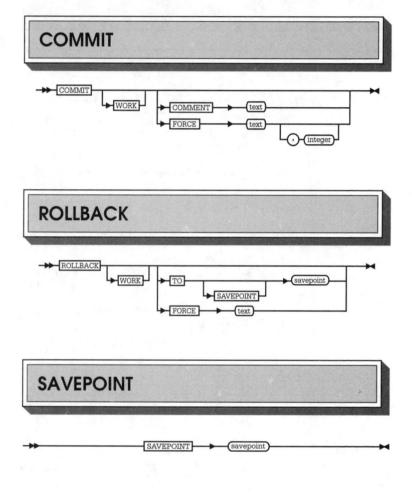

2

SET CONSTRAINTS (Informix)

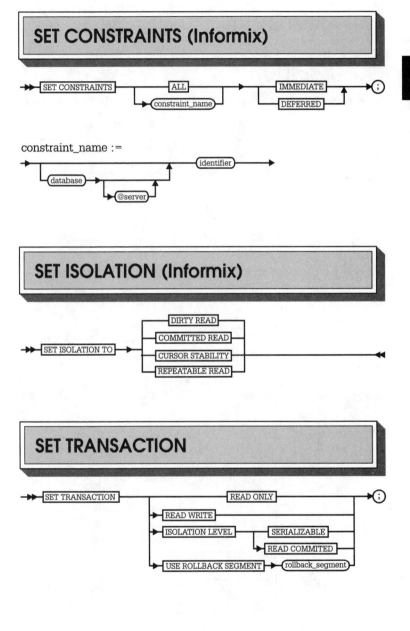

constraint_name :=

Session and System Control Statements

ALTER SESSION

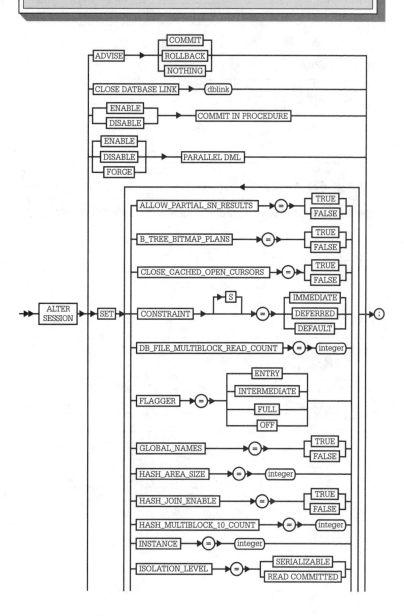

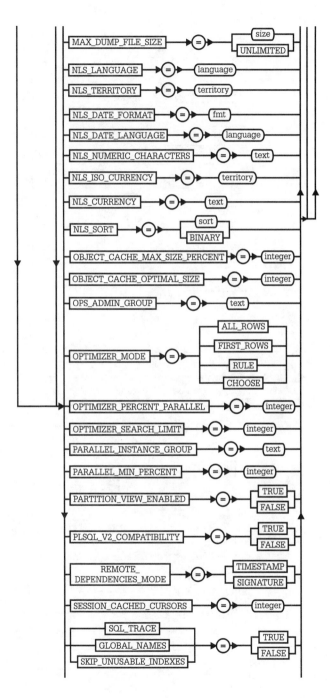

2

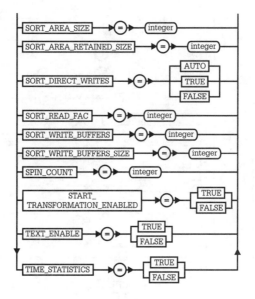

ALTER SYSTEM

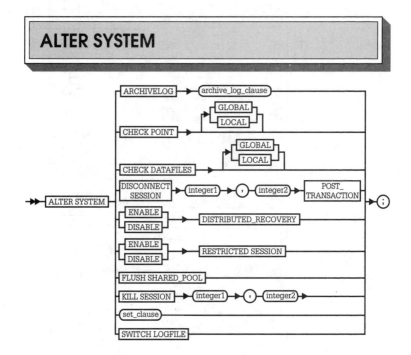

set_clause :=

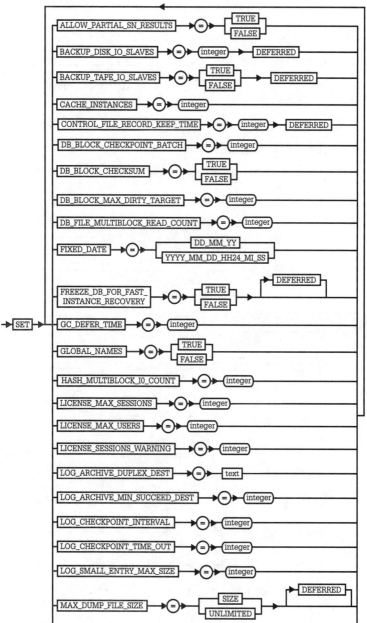

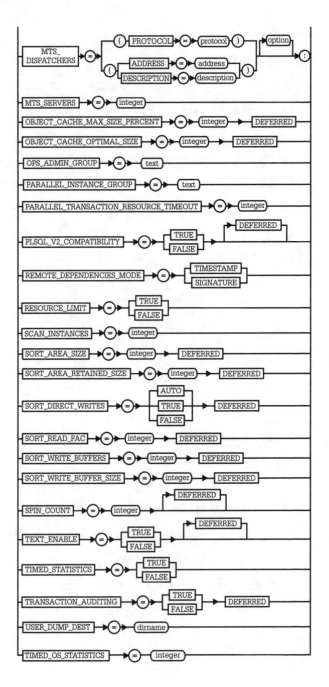

opts_clause :=

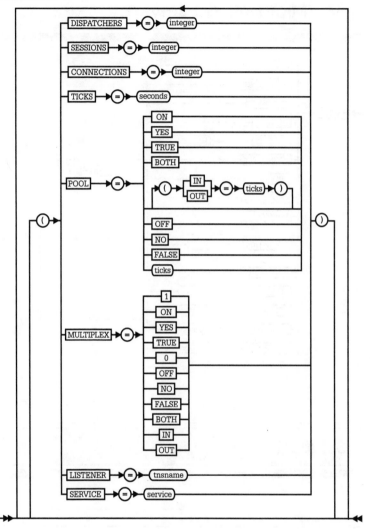

SET (Microsoft SQL Server)

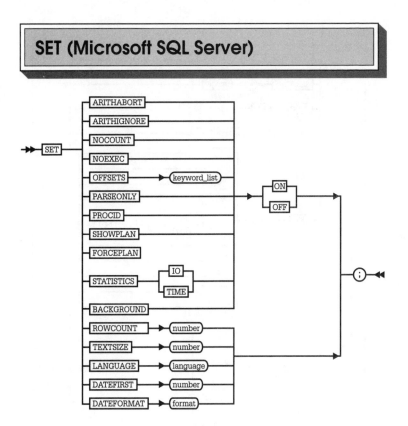

SET ROLE

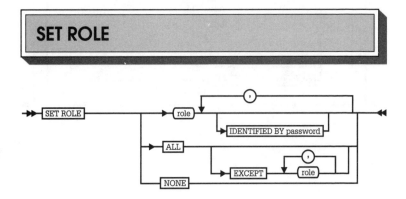

Embedded SQL Statements

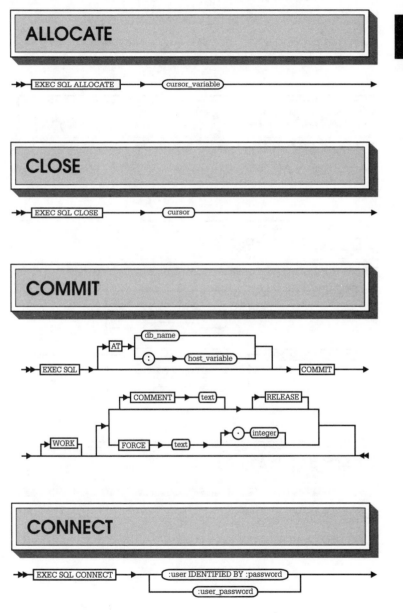

ALLOCATE

➤➤─ EXEC SQL ALLOCATE ──➤── cursor_variable ──────────────────────➤

CLOSE

➤➤─ EXEC SQL CLOSE ──────➤── cursor ──────────────────────────────➤

COMMIT

➤➤─ EXEC SQL ──┬──➤── AT ──┬── db_name ────────┬──➤── COMMIT ──➤
               │   └── : ──➤── host_variable ──┘
               └──────────────────────────────────────┘

  ┌──── COMMENT ──➤── text ────────────┐ ┌──── RELEASE ──┐
──┴──┬── WORK ──┬──┬──────────────────────┴──┬────────────┴──◄◄
     │   │ └── FORCE ──➤── text ──➤── · ──➤── integer ──┘

CONNECT

➤➤─ EXEC SQL CONNECT ──➤──┬── :user IDENTIFIED BY :password ──┬──➤
                          └────── :user_password ─────────────┘

CONTEXT ALLOCATE

CONTEXT USE

DECLARE CURSOR

DECLARE DATABASE

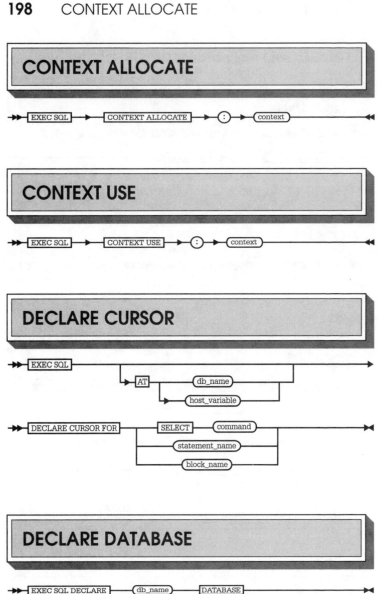

DECLARE STATEMENT

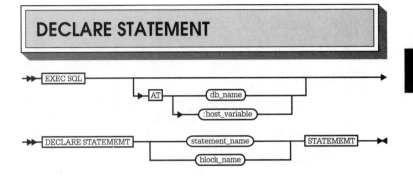

DECLARE TABLE

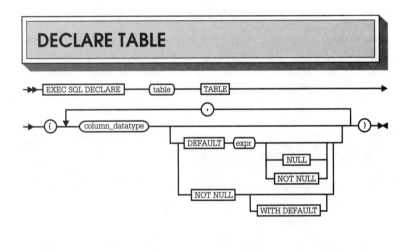

DECLARE TYPE

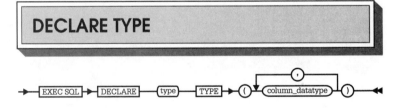

DESCRIBE

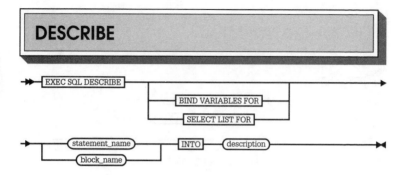

ENABLE THREADS

EXECUTE...END-EXEC

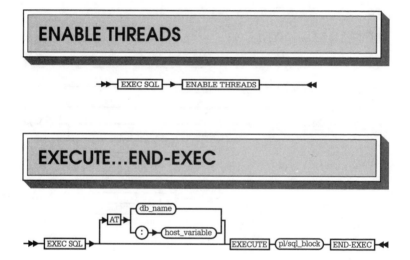

2

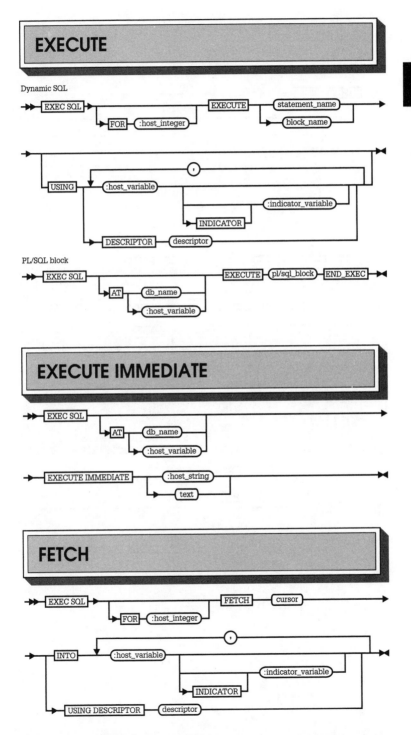

EXECUTE

Dynamic SQL

EXECUTE IMMEDIATE

FETCH

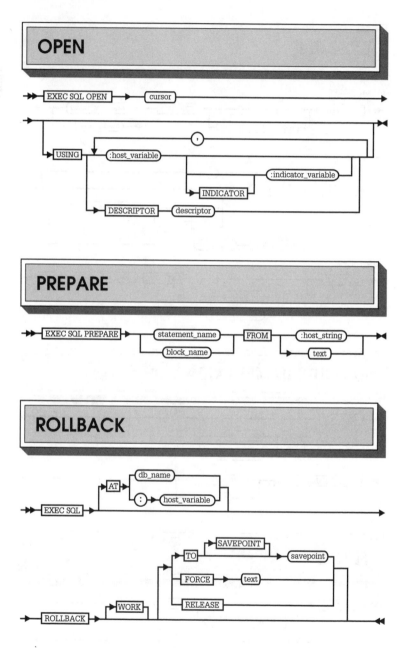

SAVEPOINT

TYPE

VAR

WHENEVER

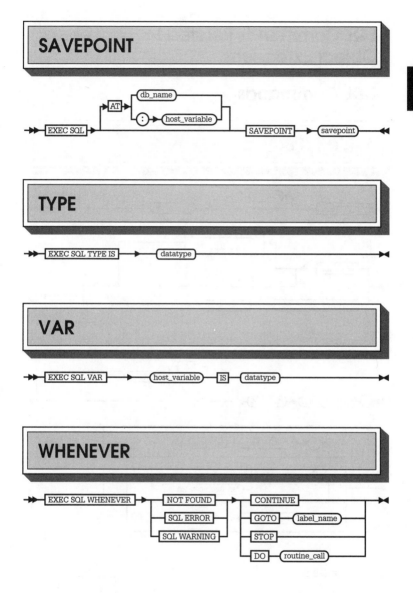

SQL Commands Related to Object Extensions

DDL Commands

ALTER TYPE

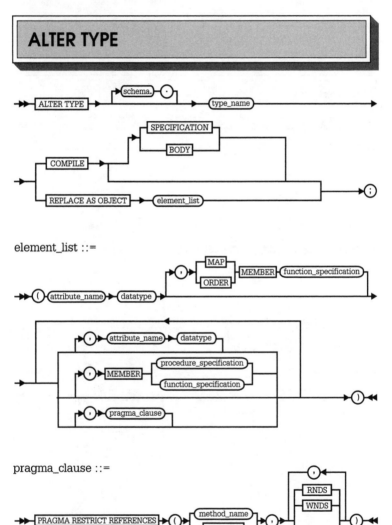

element_list ::=

pragma_clause ::=

CREATE DIRECTORY

CREATE LIBRARY

CREATE TABLE

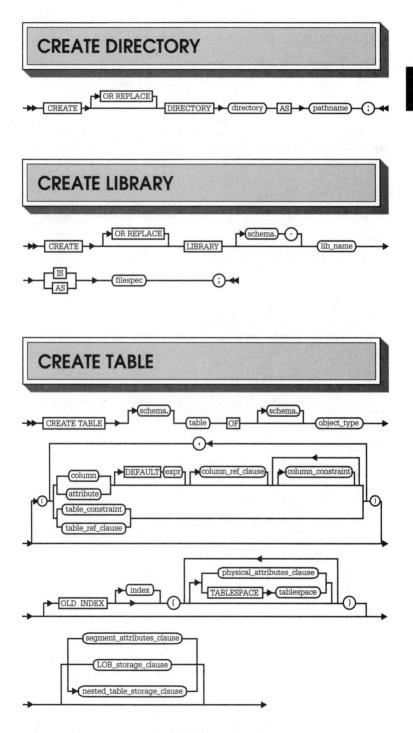

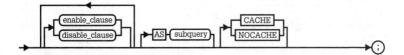

`column_ref_clause :=`

`table_ref_clause :=`

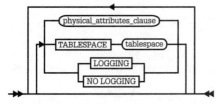

`segment_attributes_clause :=`

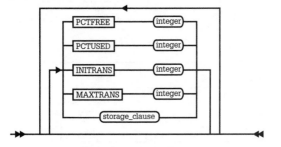

`physical_attributes_clause :=`

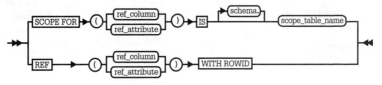

index_organized_table_clause :=

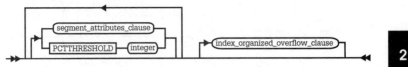

index_organized_overflow_clause :=

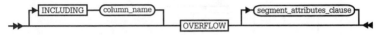

LOB_storage_clause :=

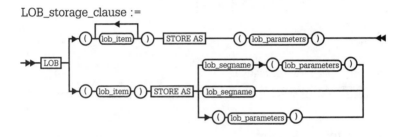

lob_parameters :=

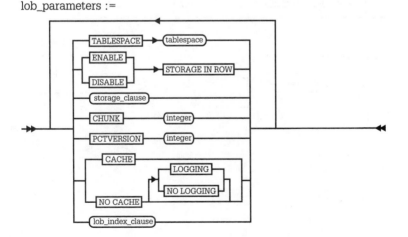

lob_index_clause :=

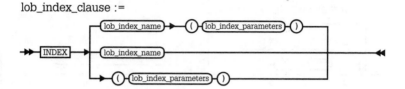

lob_index_parameters :=

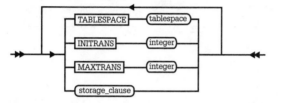

nested_table_storage_clause :=

table_partition_clause :=

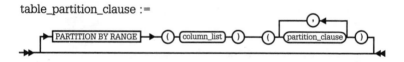

partition_clause :=

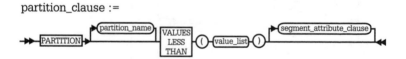

CREATE TYPE

create_incomplete_type :=

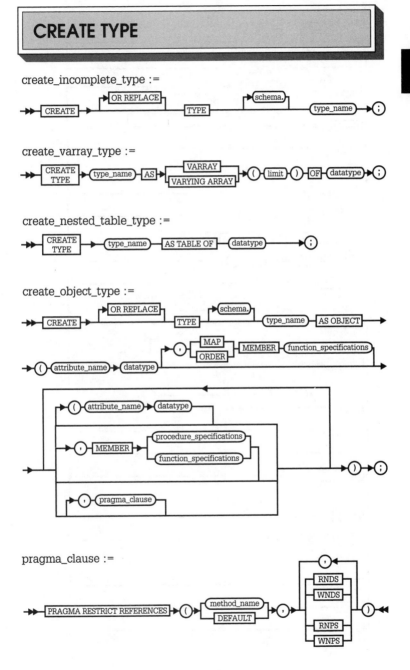

create_varray_type :=

create_nested_table_type :=

create_object_type :=

pragma_clause :=

datatype :=

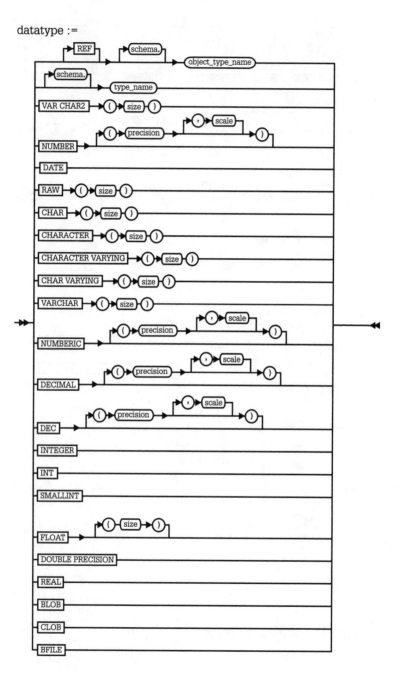

2

CREATE TYPE BODY

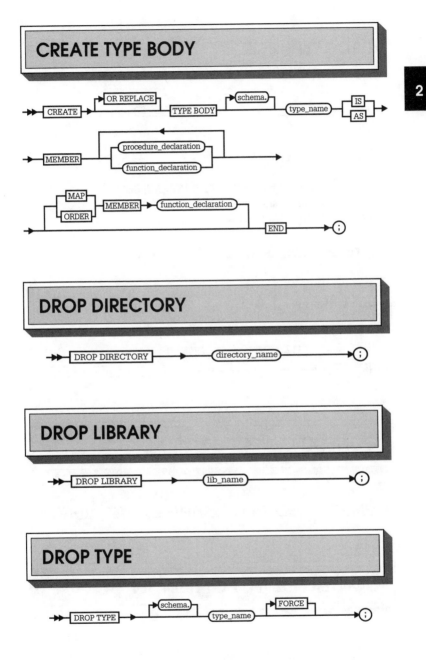

DROP DIRECTORY

DROP LIBRARY

DROP TYPE

DROP TYPE BODY

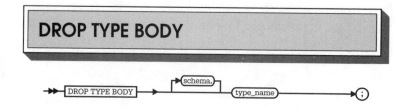

DML Commands

NOTE: Please refer to the DELETE, INSERT, SELECT, and UPDATE commands shown in the previous "DML Commands" section for the drawings of these commands.

Embedded SQL Commands

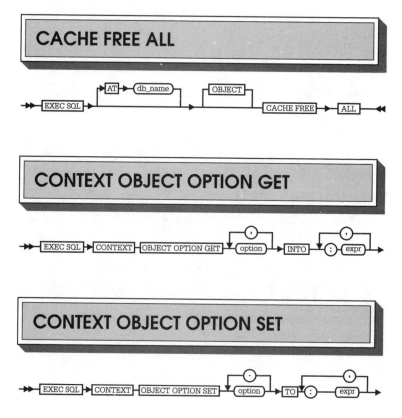

CACHE FREE ALL

CONTEXT OBJECT OPTION GET

CONTEXT OBJECT OPTION SET

FREE

2

OBJECT CREATE

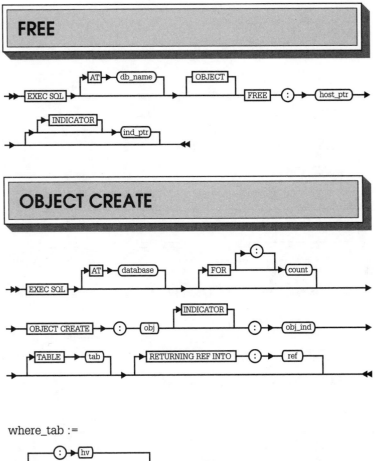

where_tab :=

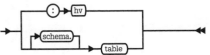

OBJECT DELETE

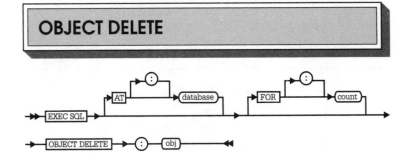

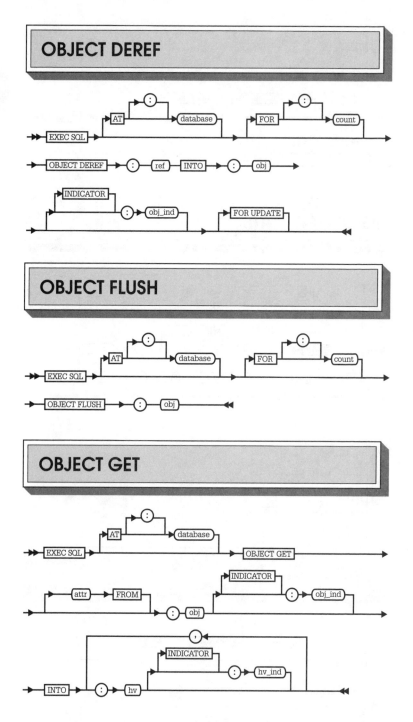

OBJECT DEREF

OBJECT FLUSH

OBJECT GET

2

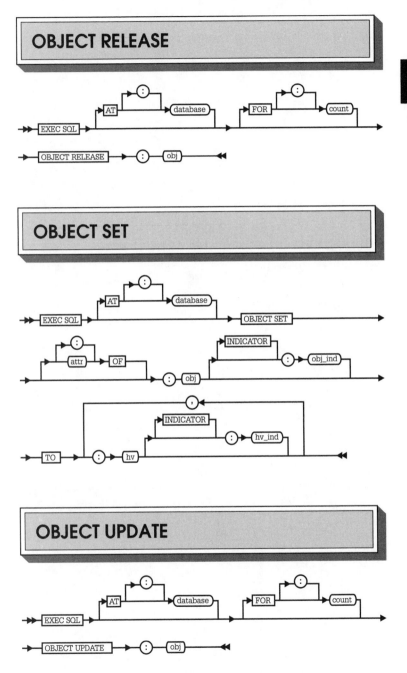

Part III
Keywords and Parameters

This section defines the keywords and parameters for the commands that are illustrated in Part II, the syntax diagram section of the book. Note that Part II and Part III have parallel structure; that is, each command is listed in both parts for easy reference.

3

DDL Commands

ALTER CLUSTER

Schema is the schema containing the cluster.

Cluster is the name of the cluster to be altered.

SIZE is used to set the number of cluster keys stored in the data blocks allocated to the cluster. The SIZE parameter of an indexed cluster can be changed but not that of a hash cluster.

PCTUSED/PCTFREE/INITRANS/MAXTRANS are described under the CREATE TABLE description.

STORAGE changes the storage characteristics for the cluster.

NOTE: The STORAGE clause is discussed in detail towards the end of this section.

ALLOCATE EXTENT explicitly allocates a new extent for the cluster.

SIZE specifies the size of the extent in bytes. The size can be specified in kilobytes or megabytes by using K or M.

DATAFILE specifies one of the data files in the cluster's tablespace to contain the new extent.

INSTANCE makes the new extent available to the specified instance. An instance is identified by INSTANCE_NUMBER, which is the initialization parameter.

DEALLOCATE UNUSED explicitly deallocates unused space at the end of the cluster and makes the freed space available for other segments.

Parallel_clause specifies the degree of parallelism for creating the cluster and the default degree of parallelism for queries on the cluster after it has been created.

ALTER DATABASE

Database identifies the database to be altered. If this is omitted, Oracle alters the database identified by the value of the initialization parameter DB_NAME.

The following options can be used only when the database is not mounted by your instance:

- MOUNT mounts the database.
- STANDBY DATABASE mounts the standby database.
- CLONE DATABASE mounts the clone database.
- CONVERT completes the conversion of the Oracle version 7 data dictionary. This option should be used only when migrating from version 7 to version 8.
- OPEN opens the database, making it available for normal use. A database must be mounted before it is opened. A standby database that has not been activated cannot be opened.
- RESETLOGS resets the current log sequence number to 1 and discards any redo information that was not applied during recovery, guaranteeing that it will never be applied. This option must be used to open the database after performing media recovery with an incomplete recovery using the RECOVER UNTIL clause or with a backup control file. After opening the database with this option, you should perform a complete database backup.

- NORESETLOGS leaves the log sequence number and redo log files in their current state.

- ACTIVATE STANDBY DATABASE changes the state of a standby database to an active database.

The following options can be used only when the database is mounted by your instance in parallel server disabled mode, but not open:

- ARCHIVELOG establishes archivelog mode for redo log file groups. In this mode, the contents of a redo log file group must be archived before the group can be reused. This option prepares for a possible media recovery.

- NOARCHIVELOG establishes noarchivelog mode for redo log files. In this mode, the contents of a redo log file group need not be archived so that the group can be reused. This mode does not prepare for recovery after media failure.

The following options can be used when your instance has the database mounted, open, or closed, and the files involved are not in use:

- *Recover_clause* performs media recovery. The entire database can be recovered only when it is closed. Tablespaces or data files can be recovered even when the database is open, provided the tablespaces or data files to be recovered are offline.

- ADD LOGFILE adds one or more redo log file groups to the specified thread, making them available to the instance that has been assigned the thread. If the THREAD parameter is omitted, then the redo log file group is added to the thread assigned to the instance. Each *filespec* specifies a redo log file group containing one or more members or copies.

- ADD LOGFILE MEMBER adds new members to existing redo log file groups. Each new member is specified by *filename*. If the file already exists, it must be the same size as the other group members and you must specify the REUSE option. If the file does not exist, then Oracle creates a file of the correct size.

You can specify an existing redo log file group in one of these ways:

- GROUP *parameter*   The value of a GROUP parameter that identifies the redo log file can be specified.

- *list of filenames* You can list all the members of the redo log file group. The filenames must be fully specified according to the operating system convention.

DROP LOGFILE drops all members of a redo log file group. A redo log file group cannot be dropped if it needs archiving or if it is currently active. You also cannot drop a redo log file group if doing so would cause the redo thread to contain less than two redo log file groups.

DROP LOGFILE MEMBER drops one or more redo log file members. Each *filename* must fully specify a member. This clause cannot be used to drop all members of a redo log file group that contain valid data.

CLEAR LOGFILE reinitializes an online redo log and, optionally, does not archive the redo log. This clause cannot be used to clear a log needed for media recovery. You must specify UNARCHIVED if you want to reuse a redo log that was not archived. You must specify UNRECOVERABLE DATAFILE if the database has a data file that is offline (not for drop) and if the UNARCHIVED log to be cleared is needed to recover the data file before bringing it back online.

RENAME FILE renames data file or redo log file members. This clause only renames files in the control file. It does not actually rename them on the operating system.

CREATE STANDBY CONTROLFILE creates a control file to be used to maintain a standby database.

BACKUP CONTROLFILE backs up the control file. TO *filename* specifies the file to which the control file is backed up. TO TRACE writes SQL statements to the database trace files rather than making a physical backup of the control file. These SQL commands can be used to start up the database, re-create the control file, and recover and open the database appropriately based on the created control file.

The following options can be used only when your instance has the database open:

- ENABLE, in a parallel server, enables the specified thread of redo log file groups. The thread must have at least two redo log file groups before you can enable it. PUBLIC makes the enabled thread available to any instance that does not explicitly request a specific thread with the initialization parameter THREAD. If the PUBLIC option is omitted, the thread is only available to the instance that explicitly requests it with the initialization parameter THREAD.

- DISABLE disables the specified thread, making it unavailable to all instances.

- RENAME GLOBAL_NAME changes the global name of the database. The *database* is the new database name and can be eight bytes long.

- RESET COMPATIBILITY marks the database to be reset to an earlier version of Oracle when the database is restarted the next time.

The following options can be used when your instance has the database mounted, open, or closed, and the files involved are not in use:

- CREATE DATAFILE creates a new empty data file in place of an old one. This option can be used to re-create a data file that was lost without a backup. The *filename* must identify a file that was once a part of the database.

- DATAFILE changes one of the following for your database:

  - ONLINE brings the data file online.

  - OFFLINE takes the data file offline.

  - DROP takes the data file offline when the database is in the noarchivelog mode.

  - RESIZE attempts to change the size of the data file to the specified absolute size in bytes. You can also use K or M to specify the size in kilobytes or megabytes. There is no default size.

  - AUTOEXTEND enables or disables the automatic extension of a data file:

    - OFF disables AUTOEXTEND if it is turned on. NEXT and MAXSIZE are set to zero.

    - ON enables AUTOEXTEND.

    - NEXT sets the size in bytes of the next increment of disk space to be automatically allocated to the data file when more extents are required. K or M can be used to specify the size.

- MAXSIZE sets the maximum disk space allowed for automatic extension of the data file.
- UNLIMITED sets no limit on allocating disk space to the data file.
- END BACKUP avoids media recovery on database startup after an online tablespace backup is interrupted by a system failure, an instance failure, or SHUTDOWN abort.

ALTER FUNCTION

Schema is the schema containing the function.

Function is the name of the function to be recompiled.

COMPILE causes Oracle to recompile the function. This keyword is required.

ALTER INDEX

Schema is the schema containing the index.

Index is the name of the index to be altered.

The following operations can be performed only on partitioned global indexes (Oracle8):

- Drop partition
- Split partition
- Rename partition
- Rebuild partition
- Modify partition

Partition_name is the name of the index partition to be altered. It must be a partition in an index.

MODIFY DEFAULT ATTRIBUTES is a valid option only for a partitioned index.

PCTFREE/PCTUSED/INITRANS/MAXTRANS change the value of these parameters for a nonpartitioned index, an index partition, or all partitions of a partitioned index, or default values of these parameters for a partitioned index.

Storage_clause changes the storage parameters for a nonpartitioned index, an index partition, or all portions of a partitioned index, or default values of these parameters for a partitioned index.

ALLOCATE EXTENT explicitly allocates a new extent for the index.

SIZE specifies the size of the extent in bytes. The size can be specified in kilobytes or megabytes by using K or M.

DATAFILE specifies one of the data files in the cluster's tablespace to contain the new extent.

INSTANCE makes the new extent available to the specified instance. An instance is identified by INSTANCE_NUMBER, which is the initialization parameter.

DEALLOCATE UNUSED explicitly deallocates unused space at the end of the cluster and makes the freed space available for other segments.

KEEP specifies the number of bytes above the high-water mark that the index will have after deallocation.

REBUILD re-creates an existing index.

REVERSE stores the bytes of the index block in reverse order, excluding the ROWID when the index is rebuilt.

NOREVERSE stores the bytes of the index block without reversing the order when the index is rebuilt.

Parallel_clause specifies that rebuilding the index, or some queries against the index or the index partition, be performed either in serial or parallel execution.

LOGGING/NOLOGGING specify that subsequent SQL*Loader and Direct-Load INSERT operations against a nonpartitioned index, index partition, or all partitions of a partitioned index will be logged (LOGGING) or not logged (NOLOGGING) in the redo log file. These also specify if ALTER INDEX...REBUILD and ALTER INDEX...SPLIT operations will be logged. In NOLOGGING mode, data is modified without redo logging. If the database is run in

ARCHIVELOG mode, media recovery from a backup taken before the LOGGING operation will re-create the index. However, media recovery from a backup taken before the NOLOGGING operation will not re-create the index.

RECOVERABLE option is available only with Oracle7.

UNRECOVERABLE option is also available only in Oracle7.

TABLESPACE specifies the tablespace where the rebuilt index or index partition will be stored, or the default tablespace of a partitioned index.

RENAME renames *index* to *new_index_name*. The *new_index_name* does not include the schema name.

RENAME PARTITION renames index *partition_name* to *new_partition_name*.

MODIFY PARTITION *partition_name* modifies the real physical attributes, logging option, or storage characteristics of index partition *partition_name*.

UNUSABLE marks the index or index partition(s) as unusable. An unusable index must be rebuilt or dropped and re-created before it can be used.

REBUILD PARTITION rebuilds one partition of an index. This option can also be used to move an index partition to another tablespace or to change a create-time physical attribute.

DROP PARTITION removes a partition and the data in it from a partitioned global index.

SPLIT PARTITION splits a global partitioned index into two partitions, adding a new partition to the index. When you split an unusable partition, both the resultant partitions are marked UNUSABLE. The partitions must be rebuilt before using them. Splitting a usable partition results in two partitions populated with index data that are both marked as USABLE.

AT (*value_list*) specifies the new noninclusive upper bound for *split_partition_1*. The *value_list* must compare less than the presplit partition bound for *partition_name_old* and greater than the partition bound for the next lowest partition (if there is one).

INTO describes the two partitions resulting from the split.

PARTITION *partition_name*, PARTITION *partition_name* specifies the names and physical attributes of the two partitions resulting from the split.

ALTER PACKAGE

Schema is the schema containing the package.

Package is the name of the package to be recompiled.

COMPILE recompiles the package specification or package body. This keyword is necessary.

PACKAGE recompiles the package body and specification.

BODY recompiles only the package body. The default option is PACKAGE.

ALTER PROCEDURE

Schema is the schema containing the procedure.

Procedure is the name of the procedure to be recompiled.

COMPILE causes Oracle to recompile the procedure. The COMPILE keyword is required.

ALTER PROFILE

Profile is the name of the profile to be altered.

Integer defines a new limit for a resource in this profile.

In Oracle, the various profiles that can be modified are as follows:

- Sessions per user
- CPUS per sessions

- CPUS per call
- Connect time
- Idle time
- Logical reads per session
- Logical reads per call
- Composite limit
- Private SGA

Changes made to a profile with an ALTER PROFILE statement affect users only in their subsequent sessions.

ALTER RESOURCE COST

Integer is the weight of each resource.

CPU_PER_SESSION is the amount of CPU time used by a session, measured in hundredths of seconds.

CONNECT_TIME is the amount of CPU time used by a session, measured in hundredths of seconds.

LOGICAL_READS_PER_SESSION is the number of data blocks read during a session, including blocks read both from memory and disk.

PRIVATE_SGA is the number of bytes of private space in the System Global Area (SGA) used by a session. This limit applies only if the multithreaded server architecture is being used.

Oracle calculates the total resource cost by multiplying the amount of each resource used in the session by the resource's weight and summing the products for all four resources.

ALTER ROLE

Role is the name of the role to be created. It is recommended that the role contain at least one single-byte character.

NOT IDENTIFIED indicates that this role is authorized by the database and that no password is required to enable the role.

IDENTIFIED indicates that a user has to be authorized by one of the three possible ways before the role is enabled with the SET ROLE command:

- BY *password*   The user must specify the password to Oracle when enabling the role. The password can contain only single-byte characters from the database character set.

- EXTERNALLY   Indicates that the user must be authorized by an external service (most popularly, by the operating system or a third-party service) before enabling the role.

- GLOBALLY   Indicates that the user must be authorized by the Oracle Security Service to use the role before the role is enabled with the SET ROLE command or at the time of logging in to the database.

If both IDENTIFIED and NOT IDENTIFIED options are omitted, the role defaults to NOT IDENTIFIED.

A *role* is a set of privileges that can be granted to users or to other roles. Roles can be used to administer database privileges. Privileges can be added to a role, and the role can then be granted to a user. The user can then enable the role and exercise the privileges granted by the role. A role contains all privileges granted to the role and all privileges of other roles granted to it. A new role is initially empty. Privileges are added to roles through the GRANT command. When a role is created, Oracle grants the role to the user with ADMIN OPTION. ADMIN OPTION allows you to perform the following operations:

- Grant the role to another user or role, unless the role is a global role.

- Revoke the role from another user or role.

- Alter the role to change the authorization needed to access it.

- Drop the role.

Oracle has some predefined roles, namely RESOURCE, CONNECT, DBA, EXP_FULL_DATABASE, IMP_FULL_DATABASE, DELETE_CATALOG_ROLE, EXECUTE_CATALOG_ROLE, and SELECT_CATALOG_ROLE. The RESOURCE, CONNECT, and DBA roles are provided for compatibility with previous versions of Oracle. It is recommended that you create your own roles for database security.

ALTER ROLLBACK SEGMENT

Rollback_segment specifies the name of an existing rollback segment.

ONLINE brings the rollback segment online.

OFFLINE takes the rollback segment offline.

STORAGE changes the rollback segment's storage characteristics. (STORAGE clause is explained in this chapter).

SHRINK attempts to shrink the rollback segment to an optimal or given size.

When a rollback segment is created, it is initially offline. A rollback segment needs to be online in order for it to be available for transactions. The ONLINE option brings the rollback segment online. The OFFLINE option takes the rollback segment offline. If there are no active transactions in the rollback segment, then it is taken offline immediately. Otherwise, the rollback segment is made unavailable for future transactions and becomes offline after all the active transactions are committed or rolled back. The SYSTEM rollback segment cannot be taken offline.

ALTER SEQUENCE

The definitions of the keywords and parameters are exactly identical to the ones for CREATE SEQUENCE.

ALTER SNAPSHOT

Schema is the schema containing the snapshot.

Snapshot is the name of the snapshot to be altered.

Modify_default_attributes specifies new values for the default attributes of a partitioned table.

PCTFREE/PCTUSED/INITRANS/MAXTRANS change the values of these parameters for the internal table used by Oracle to maintain the snapshot's data.

STORAGE changes the storage characteristics of the internal table Oracle uses to maintain the snapshot's data.

LOGGING/NOLOGGING specify the LOGGING attribute. These options are explained in the ALTER TABLE command syntax description.

CACHE/NOCACHE specify that the data will be accessed frequently; therefore, the blocks retrieved for this table are placed at the most recently used end of the LRU list in the buffer cache when a full table scan is performed. All the following clauses pertaining to partitions and LOBs are described in the ALTER TABLE command description:

- *LOB_storage_clause* specifies the LOB storage characteristics.
- *Modify_LOB_storage_clause* modifies the physical attributes of the LOB attribute *lob_item* or the LOB object attribute.
- *Modify_partition_clause* modifies the real physical attributes of a table partition.
- *Move_partition_clause* moves table partition *partition_name* to another segment.
- *Add_partition_clause* adds a new partition *new_partition_name* to the "high" end of a partition table.
- *Split_partition_clause* creates two new partitions, each with a new segment, new physical attributes, and new initial extents.
- *Rename_partition_clause* renames table partition *partition_name* to *new_partition_name*.
- *Parallel_clause* specifies the degree of parallelism for the snapshot. The PARALLEL clause is described in this chapter.

MODIFY PARTITION UNUSABLE LOCAL INDEXES marks all the local index partitions associated with *partition_name* as UNUSABLE.

MODIFY PARTITION REBUILD UNUSABLE LOCAL INDEXES rebuilds the unusable local index partitions associated with *partition_name*.

USING INDEX changes the values of INITRANS, MAXTRANS, and STORAGE parameters for the index used by Oracle to maintain the snapshot's data. If USING INDEX is not specified, then default values are used for the index.

USING MASTER ROLLBACK SEGMENT changes remote master rollback segments used during snapshot refresh.

Rollback_segment is the name of the rollback segment to be used.

DEFAULT specifies that Oracle will determine which rollback segment to use. If you specify DEFAULT, you cannot specify *rollback_segment*.

MASTER specifies the rollback segment to be used at the remote master for the individual snapshot.

LOCAL specifies the rollback segment to be used for the local refresh group that contains the snapshot.

REFRESH changes the mode and times for automatic refreshes.

FAST specifies a fast refresh, or a refresh using the snapshot log associated with the master table.

COMPLETE specifies a complete refresh, or a refresh that re-creates the snapshot during each refresh.

FORCE specifies a fast refresh if one is possible, or complete refresh if a fast refresh is not possible.

If none of the above modes are specified, Oracle uses FORCE by default.

START WITH specifies a date expression for the next automatic refresh time.

NEXT specifies a new date expression for calculating the interval between automatic refreshes.

START WITH and NEXT must evaluate to times in the future.

WITH PRIMARY KEY changes a ROWID snapshot to a primary key snapshot.

Primary key snapshots enable snapshot master tables to be reorganized without impacting the snapshot's ability to continue to fast refresh. The master table must contain an enabled primary key constraint.

ALTER SNAPSHOT LOG

Schema is the schema containing the master table.

Table is the name of the master table associated with the snapshot log to be altered.

ADD changes the snapshot log to also record the primary key values or rowid values when rows in the snapshot master table are updated.

PRIMARY KEY specifies that the primary key values of all rows updated should be recorded in the snapshot log.

ROWID specifies that the rowid values of all rows updated should be recorded in the snapshot log.

Filter_columns are nonprimary key columns referenced by snapshots.

LOGGING/NOLOGGING specify the logging attribute. The ALTER TABLE command has more details on these attributes.

CACHE/NOCACHE specify that the data will be accessed frequently; therefore, the blocks retrieved for this table are placed at the most recently used end of the LRU list in the buffer cache when a full table scan is performed. All the following clauses pertaining to partitions and LOBs are described in the ALTER TABLE command description:

- *LOB_storage_clause* specifies the LOB storage characteristics.

- *Modify_LOB_storage_clause* modifies the physical attributes of the LOB attribute *lob_item* or LOB object attribute.

- *Modify_partition_clause* modifies the real physical attributes of a table partition.

- *Move_partition_clause* moves table partition *partition_name* to another segment.

- *Add_partition_clause* adds a new partition *new_partition_name* to the "high" end of a partition table.

- *Split_partition_clause* creates two new partitions, each with a new segment and new physical attributes, and new initial extents.

- *Rename_partition_clause* renames table partition *partition_name* to *new_partition_name*.
- *Parallel_clause* specifies the degree of parallelism for the snapshot. The PARALLEL clause is described in this section.

MODIFY PARTITION UNUSABLE LOCAL INDEXES marks all the local index partitions associated with *partition_name* as unusable.

MODIFY PARTITION REBUILD UNUSABLE LOCAL INDEXES rebuilds the unusable local index partitions associated with *partition_name*.

ALTER TABLE

Schema is the schema containing the table.

Table is the name of the table to be altered. It could be an index-organized table (IOT), too.

ADD adds a column or an integrity constraint. You cannot add columns to an IOT.

MODIFY modifies the definition of an existing column. If an optional part of the column definition is left out (datatype, default value, column constraint), then these remain unchanged.

Column is the name of the column to be added or modified.

Datatype specifies a datatype for a new column or a new datatype for an existing column. The datatype can be omitted only if the column is designated as part of a foreign key referential integrity constraint. Oracle automatically assigns the column the same datatype as the corresponding column of the referenced key of the referential integrity constraint.

DEFAULT specifies a default value for a new column or a new default for an existing column. Oracle assigns this value to a column if a subsequent INSERT statement omits the value for this column.

Column_constraint adds or removes a NOT NULL constraint to or from an existing column. The CONSTRAINT clause is explained later in this section.

Table_constraint adds an integrity constraint to the table.

MODIFY DEFAULT ATTRIBUTES is a valid option only for partitioned tables (Oracle8) and is used to specify new values for the default attributes of a partitioned table.

PCTFREE/PCTUSED/INITRANS/MAXTRANS change the values of specified parameters for the table, partition, the overflow data segment, or the default characteristics of a partitioned table. These parameters are described in the CREATE TABLE command.

STORAGE changes the storage characteristics of the table, partition, or data overflow segment, or the default characteristics of a partitioned table.

PCTTHRESHOLD specifies the percentage of space reserved in the index block for an IOT table row. Any portion of the row that exceeds the specified threshold is stored in the overflow area. If OVERFLOW is not specified, then the rows exceeding the PCTTHRESHOLD limit are rejected. The value of PCTTHRESHOLD ranges from 0 to 50.

INCLUDING *column_name* specifies a column at which to divide an IOT into index and overflow portions. All columns that follow *column_name* are stored in the overflow data segment. A *column_name* is either the name of the last primary key column or any nonprimary key column.

LOB specifies the LOB storage characteristics (Oracle8).

Lob_item is the LOB column name or LOB object attribute for which you are explicitly defining tablespace and storage characteristics that are different from those of the table.

STORE AS *lob_segment* specifies the name of the LOB data segment. *Lob_segment* cannot be used if more than one *lob_item* is present.

ENABLE STORAGE IN ROW specifies that the LOB value be stored in the row (inline) if its length is less than approximately 4,000 bytes minus system control information. This is the default.

DISABLE STORAGE IN ROW specifies that the LOB value be stored outside the row regardless of its size.

NOTE: Irrespective of the above clauses, the LOB locator is stored in the table row itself. Once STORAGE IN ROW is set, you cannot modify it.

CHUNK *integer* is the unit of LOB value allocation and manipulation. Each unit of LOB storage is a CHUNK, which is calculated as *integer * data block size*. For example, if the integer is 4 and the data block size is 1,024 bytes, then the unit of LOB storage is 4K. The maximum value is limited by the largest Oracle block size, which is 32K.

PCTVERSION integer is the maximum percentage of overall LOB storage space used for creating new versions of the LOB. The default value is 10.

INDEX *lob_index_name* is the name of the LOB index segment. You cannot use *lob_index_name* if more than one *lob_item* is present.

MODIFY LOB(*lob_item*) modifies the physical attributes of the LOB attribute *lob_item* or LOB object attribute.

NESTED TABLE *nested_item* STORE AS *storage_table* specifies *storage_table* as the name of the storage table in which the rows of all the *nested_item* values reside. The *nested_item* is the name of the column or column-qualified attribute whose type is a nested table. The *storage_table* is the name of the storage table. The storage table is modified in the same schema and tablespace as the parent table.

DROP drops an integrity constraint. The DROP clause is described in this chapter.

ALLOCATE EXTENT explicitly allocates a new extent for the table, the partition, the overflow data segment, the LOB data segment, or the LOB index.

SIZE specifies the size of the extent in bytes. The size can be specified in kilobytes or megabytes by using K or M.

DATAFILE specifies one of the data files in the cluster's tablespace to contain the new extent.

INSTANCE makes the new extent available to the specified instance. An instance is identified by INSTANCE_NUMBER, which is the initialization parameter.

DEALLOCATE UNUSED explicitly deallocates unused space at the end of the cluster and makes the freed space available for other segments.

KEEP specifies the number of bytes above the high-water mark that the index will have after deallocation.

OVERFLOW specifies the overflow data segment physical storage attributes to be modified for the index-organized table.

ADD OVERFLOW adds an overflow data segment to the specified IOT.

Enable_clause enables a single integrity constraint on all triggers associated with the table.

ENABLE TABLE LOCK enables DML (data manipulation language) and DDL (data definition language) locks on a table in a parallel server environment.

Disable_clause disables a single integrity constraint on all triggers associated with the table. Another way to enable and disable integrity constraints is through the use of ENABLE and DISABLE keywords in the CONSTRAINT clause. If an integrity constraint is defined but not explicitly enabled or disabled, Oracle automatically enables it.

DISABLE TABLE LOCK disables DML and DDL locks on a table to improve performance in a parallel server environment.

Parallel_clause specifies the degree of parallelism for the table. The PARALLEL clause is described in this chapter. It is not a valid option for IOTs.

CACHE specifies that the data will be accessed frequently; therefore, the blocks retrieved for this table are placed at the most recently used end of the LRU list in the buffer cache when a full table scan is performed. This is not a valid option for IOTs.

NOCACHE specifies that the data is not accessed frequently; therefore, the blocks retrieved for this table are placed at the least recently used end of the LRU list in the buffer cache when a full table scan is performed. For LOBs, the LOB value is either not brought into the buffer cache or brought into the buffer cache and placed at the least recently used end of the LRU list. NOCACHE is not a valid option for index-organized tables.

LOGGING/NOLOGGING specify that subsequent SQL*Loader and Direct-Load INSERT operations against a nonpartitioned index, an index partition, or all partitions of a partitioned index will be logged (LOGGING) or not logged (NOLOGGING) in the redo log file. These also specify if ALTER INDEX...REBUILD and ALTER INDEX...SPLIT operations will be logged. In NOLOGGING mode, data is modified without redo logging. If the database is run in ARCHIVELOG mode, media recovery from a backup taken before the LOGGING operation will re-create the index. However, media recovery from a backup taken before the NOLOGGING operation will not re-create the index.

RENAME TO *new_table_name* renames table to *new_table_name*.

MODIFY PARTITION *partition_name* modifies the real physical attributes, logging option, or storage characteristics of index partition *partition_name*.

RENAME PARTITION *partition_name* to *new_partition_name* renames *partition_name* to *new_partition_name*.

MOVE PARTITION *partition_name* moves table partition *partition_name* to another segment. You can move partition data to another tablespace, recluster data to reduce fragmentation, or change a create-time physical attribute.

ADD PARTITION *new_partition_name* adds a new partition *new_partition_name* to the "high" end of a partition table. You can specify any physical attributes for the partition such as PCTFREE, PCTUSED, INITRANS, MAXTRANS, STORAGE, etc.

VALUES LESS THAN (*value_list*) specifies the upper bound for the new partition. The *value_list* is a comma-separated ordered list of literal values corresponding to *column_list*. The *value_list* must collate greater than the partition bound for the highest existing partition in the table.

DROP PARTITION removes a partition and the data in it from a partitioned global index.

TRUNCATE PARTITION *partition_name* removes all rows from a partition in a table.

DROP STORAGE specifies that the space from the deleted rows be deallocated and made available for use by other SCHEMA objects in the tablespace.

REUSE STORAGE specifies that the space from the deleted rows remain allocated to the partition.

SPLIT PARTITION *partition_name_old* creates two new partitions, each with a new segment and new physical attributes, and new initial extents. The segment associated with old partition is discarded.

AT (*value_list*) specifies the new noninclusive upper bound for *split_partition_1*. The *value_list* must compare less than the presplit partition bound for *partition_name_old* and greater than the partition bound for the next lowest partition (if there is one).

INTO describes the two partitions resulting from the split.

PARTITION *split_partition_1*, PARTITION *split_partition_2* specifies the name and physical attributes of the two partitions resulting from the split.

EXCHANGE PARTITION *partition_name* converts PARTITION *partition_name* into a nonpartitioned table, and a nonpartitioned table into a partition of a partitioned table by exchanging their data (and index) segments.

WITH TABLE *table* specifies the table with which the partition will be exchanged.

INCLUDING INDEXES specifies that the local index partitions be exchanged with the corresponding regular indexes.

EXCLUDING INDEXES specifies that all the local index partitions corresponding to the partition and all regular indexes on the exchanged table are marked as UNUSABLE.

WITH VALIDATION specifies that any rows in the exchanged table that do not collate properly should return an error.

WITHOUT VALIDATION specifies that proper collation of rows in the exchanged table is not checked.

UNUSABLE LOCAL INDEXES marks all the local index partitions associated with *partition_name* as UNUSABLE.

REBUILD UNUSABLE LOCAL INDEXES rebuilds the unusable local index partitions associated with *partition_name*.

ALTER TABLESPACE

Tablespace is the name of the tablespace to be altered.

LOGGING/NOLOGGING specify the logging attribute of all tables, indexes, and partitions within the tablespace. The tablespace-level logging can be overridden by logging specifications at the table, index, and partition levels. When an existing tablespace's logging attributes are changed by the ALTER TABLESPACE command, all tables, indexes, and partitions created after the statement will have the new logging attribute. In NOLOGGING mode, data is modified without redo logging. Therefore, if it is not affordable to lose an object, it is important to take a backup after the NOLOGGING operation. The following operations support NOLOGGING mode:

- DML Direct-Load INSERT (serial or parallel) and Direct Loader (SQL*Loader)
- DDL:
  - CREATE TABLE...AS SELECT
  - CREATE INDEX
  - ALTER INDEX...REBUILD
  - ALTER INDEX...REBUILD PARTITION
  - ALTER INDEX...SPLIT PARTITION
  - ALTER TABLE...SPLIT PARTITION
  - ALTER TABLE...MOVE PARTITION

ADD DATAFILE adds a data file specified by *filespec* to the tablespace.

AUTOEXTEND enables or disables autoextending the size of the data file in the tablespace.

OFF disable AUTOEXTEND if it is ON. NEXT and MAXSIZE are set to zero. These need to be specified again in future ALTER TABLESPACE AUTOEXTEND commands.

ON enables AUTOEXTEND.

NEXT is the size in bytes of the next increment of disk space to be automatically allocated to the data file when more extents are required. The letters K and M can be used to specify the size in kilobytes and megabytes, respectively. The default is in bytes and one data block in size.

MAXSIZE is the maximum disk space allowed for automatic extension of the data file.

UNLIMITED sets no limit on allocating disk space to the data file.

RENAME DATAFILE renames one or more of the tablespace's data files.

COALESCE coalesces all contiguous free extents into larger contiguous extents for each data file in the tablespace.

DEFAULT *storage_clause* specifies the new default storage parameters for objects subsequently created in the tablespace.

MINIMUM EXTENT *integer* controls free space fragmentation in the tablespace by ensuring that every used and/or free extent size in a tablespace is at least as large as, and is a multiple of, *integer*.

ONLINE brings the tablespace online.

OFFLINE takes the tablespace offline.

NORMAL performs a checkpoint for all data files in the tablespace. All of these data files must be online. You must use this option if the database is in the NOARCHIVELOG mode.

TEMPORARY performs a checkpoint for all online data files in the tablespace but does not ensure that all files can be written.

IMMEDIATE does not ensure that tablespace files are available and does not perform a checkpoint. Media recovery must be performed on the tablespace before bringing it back online.

FOR RECOVER takes the production database tablespace in the recovery set offline. The Default is NORMAL.

ALTER TRIGGER

Schema is the schema containing the trigger.

Trigger is the name of the trigger to be altered.

ENABLE enables the trigger.

DISABLE disables the trigger.

COMPILE compiles the trigger.

DEBUG instructs the PL/SQL compiler to generate and store the code for use by the PL/SQL debugger. This option can be used for normal triggers and for INSTEAD OF triggers.

ALTER TRIGGER command can be used to explicitly recompile a trigger that is invalid. Explicit recompilation eliminates the need for implicit runtime recompilation, which improves performance. When an ALTER TRIGGER command is executed, Oracle first recompiles the objects upon which the trigger is dependent, if any of the objects are invalid. If the trigger is recompiled successfully, then the trigger becomes valid; otherwise, an error is returned and the trigger remains invalid.

ALTER USER

The definitions of the keywords and parameters are exactly identical to the ones in the CREATE USER description.

NOTE: The DEFAULT ROLE clause can only contain roles that have been granted directly to the user with a GRANT statement.

ALTER VIEW

Schema is the schema containing the view.

View is the name of the view to be compiled.

COMPILE causes Oracle to recompile the view. This keyword is required.

You would want to explicitly recompile a view after one of the view's base tables has been altered to ensure that the alteration does not affect the view or other objects that depend on it. This command, however, does not change the definition of an existing view. To change the definition, you would use the CREATE VIEW command.

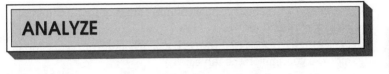

ANALYZE

Attribute specifies the qualified column name of an item in an object.

INDEX identifies an index to be analyzed.

TABLE identifies a table to be analyzed. When you collect statistics for a table, Oracle also collects statistics for all the indexes, provided no FOR clauses are used.

PARTITION *(partition_name)* specifies that statistics will be gathered for *(partition_name)*.

CLUSTER identifies a cluster to be analyzed. When you collect statistics for a cluster, Oracle also collects statistics for all the tables and all their indexes, including the cluster index.

VALIDATE REF UPDATE validates the REFs in the specified table, checks the ROWID part of each REF, compares it with the true ROWID, and corrects if necessary (Oracle8).

COMPUTE STATISTICS computes exact statistics about the analyzed object and stores them in a data dictionary.

ESTIMATE STATISTICS estimates statistics about the analyzed object and stores them in the data dictionary.

SAMPLE specifies the amount of data from the analyzed object that Oracle samples to estimate statistics. The default is 1,064 rows. If more than half the data is specified, then Oracle reads all the data and computes statistics.

ROWS causes Oracle to sample *integer* rows of the table, or cluster or *integer* entries from the index. The *integer* must be > 1.

PERCENT causes Oracle to sample the *integer* percent of the rows from the table or cluster or the *integer* percent of the index entries. The *integer* can range from 1 to 99.

The following clauses are related to histograms and apply only to the ANALYZE TABLE version of this command:

- FOR TABLE collect table statistics for the table.
- FOR ALL COLUMNS collects column statistics for all columns and scalar attributes.
- FOR ALL INDEXED COLUMNS collects column statistics for all indexed columns in the table.
- FOR COLUMNS collects statistics only for the specified columns and scalar object attributes.
- FOR ALL INDEXES results in all indexes associated with the table being analyzed.
- FOR ALL LOCAL INDEXES specifies that all local index partitions be analyzed. The LOCAL keyword has to be specified if the PARTITION*(partition_name)* clause and the INDEX option are specified.
- SIZE specifies the maximum number of partitions in the histogram. The default value is 75, the minimum is 1, and the maximum is 254.

DELETE STATISTICS deletes any statistics about the analyzed object that are currently stored in the data dictionary.

VALIDATE STRUCTURE validates the structure of the analyzed object.

INTO specifies a table into which Oracle lists the ROWIDs of the partitions whose rows do not collate correctly. If this clause is omitted, then the name of the table containing this information is invalid_rows.

CASCADE validates the structure of the indexes associated with the table or cluster.

LIST CHAINED ROWS identifies migrated and chained rows of the analyzed table or cluster. This option cannot be used when analyzing an index.

INTO specifies a table into which the migrated and chained rows are listed. If this clause is omitted, Oracle assumes that the table is named CHAINED_ROWS. To analyze an index-organized table (IOT), you must create a separate chained_rows table for each IOT to accommodate the primary key storage of IOTs.

You cannot estimate or compute statistics for columns of the following types:

- REFs
- VARRAYs
- Nested tables
- LOBs (these are not analyzed)
- LONGs
- Object types

AUDIT (SQL Statements)

Statement_opt chooses specific SQL statements for auditing.

System_priv chooses SQL statements that are authorized by the specified system privilege for auditing.

BY *user* chooses only SQL statements issued by a specified user for auditing.

BY SESSION causes Oracle to write a single record for all SQL statements of the same type issued in the same session.

BY ACCESS causes Oracle to write one record for each audited statement.

The default is BY SESSION for non-DDL statements. For DDL statements, Oracle audits by access regardless of what you specify.

WHENEVER SUCCESSFUL chooses auditing only for statements that succeed.

NOT chooses auditing only for statements that fail or result in errors.

Auditing keeps track of operations performed by database users. The audit information consists of the username, type of operation, object involved in the operation, and date and time of the operation. The records are written to the audit trail. The audit trail can be examined through data dictionary views.

AUDIT (Schema Objects)

object_opt specifies a particular operation for auditing.

Schema is the schema containing the object chosen for auditing.

Object identifies the object chosen for auditing. The object must be one of the following types:

- Table
- View
- Sequence
- Stored procedure, function, or package
- Snapshot
- Library

DIRECTORY *directory_name* identifies the name of the directory on which auditing is being stopped.

BY SESSION means that Oracle writes a single record for all operations of the same type on the same object issued in the same session.

BY ACCESS means that Oracle writes one record for each audited operation.

The default is BY SESSION.

WHENEVER SUCCESSFUL chooses auditing only for SQL statements that complete successfully.

NOT chooses auditing only for SQL statements that fail or result in errors.

If the WHENEVER SUCCESSFUL clause is eliminated, then Oracle audits all SQL statements irrespective of their success or failure.

COMMENT

TABLE specifies the schema and name of the table, view, or snapshot to be commented.

COLUMN is the column to be commented.

IS *text* is the text of the comment.

CONSTRAINT

CONSTRAINT identifies the integrity constraint by the name *constraint*. Oracle stores this name in the data dictionary along with the definition of the integrity constraint. If you omit this identifier, Oracle generates a name with this form: SYS_Cn.

NULL specifies that the column can contain null values.

NOT NULL specifies that a column cannot contain null values. The default is NULL.

UNIQUE designates a column or combination of columns as a unique key. You cannot define UNIQUE constraints on index-organized tables.

PRIMARY KEY designates a column or combination of columns as the table's primary key.

FOREIGN KEY designates a column or combination of columns as the foreign key in a referential integrity constraint.

REFERENCES identifies the primary or unique key that is referenced by a foreign key in a referential integrity constraint.

ON DELETE CASCADE specifies that Oracle maintain referential integrity by automatically removing dependent foreign key values if you remove a referenced primary or unique key value.

CHECK specifies a condition that each row in the table must satisfy.

DEFERRABLE indicates that constraint checking can be deferred until the end of the transaction by using the SET CONSTRAINT(S) command.

NOT DEFERRABLE indicates that this constraint is checked at the end of each DML statement. You cannot defer a NOT DEFERRABLE constraint with the SET CONSTRAINT(S) command. If you do not specify DEFERRABLE or NOT DEFERRABLE, then NOT DEFERRABLE is the default.

INITIALLY IMMEDIATE indicates that at the start of every transaction, the default is to check this constraint at the end of every DML statement. If no INITIALLY clause is specified, INITIALLY IMMEDIATE is the default.

INITIALLY DEFERRED implies that this constraint is DEFERRABLE and specifies that, by default, the constraint is checked only at the end of each transaction.

USING INDEX specifies parameters for the index Oracle uses to enable a UNIQUE or PRIMARY KEY constraint. The name of the index is the same as the name of the constraint. You can choose the values of the INITRANS, MAXTRANS, TABLESPACE, STORAGE, PCTFREE, LOGGING, and NOLOGGING parameters for the index.

NOTE: Use this clause only when enabling UNIQUE and PRIMARY KEY constraints.

NOSORT indicates that the rows are stored in the database in ascending order and therefore Oracle does not have to sort the rows when creating the index.

EXCEPTIONS INTO specifies a table into which Oracle places the ROWIDs of all rows violating the constraint. Note: You must create an appropriate exceptions report table to accept information from the EXCEPTIONS option of the ENABLE clause before enabling the constraint. You can create an exception table by submitting the script UTLEXCPT.SQL, which creates a table named *exceptions*. You can create additional exceptions tables with different names by modifying and resubmitting the script. The EXCEPTIONS INTO

clause is a valid option only when validating a constraint (see the
ENABLE clause) or when enabling a constraint with an ALTER
TABLE command.

ENABLE VALIDATE ensures that all new INSERT, DELETE, and
UPDATE operations on the constrained data comply with the
constraint. It also checks that all old data also obeys the constraint.
An enabled and validated constraint guarantees that all data is and
will continue to be valid. This is the default.

ENABLE NOVALIDATE ensures that all new INSERT, UPDATE,
and DELETE operations on the constrained data comply with the
constraint. Oracle does not verify that existing data in the table
complies with the constraint.

DISABLE disables the integrity constraint. If an integrity constraint
is disabled, Oracle does not enable it. If you do not specify this
option, Oracle automatically enables the integrity constraint.

There are two syntactic formats for the CONSTRAINT clause,
namely:

- *Table_constraint* is part of the table definition. An integrity
  constraint defined with this syntax can impose rules on any
  columns in the table.

- *Column_constraint* is part of the column definition. Usually, an
  integrity constraint defined with this syntax can only impose
  rules on the column on which it is defined.

The NOT NULL constraint specifies that a column cannot contain
null values. This means that every row in the table must contain a
value for the column.

The UNIQUE constraint designates a column or combination of
columns as a unique key. To satisfy a UNIQUE constraint, no
two rows in the table can have the same value for the unique key.
However, the unique key made up of single columns can contain
nulls.

A PRIMARY key constraint designates a column or combination of
columns as the table's primary key. To satisfy a PRIMARY KEY
constraint, both of the following conditions must be true:

- No primary key value can appear in more than one row of
  a table.

- No column that is part of a primary key can contain a null.

A table can have only one primary key.

A referential integrity constraint designates a column or combination of columns as a foreign key and establishes a relationship between that foreign key and a specific primary or unique key, called the reference key. In this relationship, the table containing the foreign key is called the *child* table and the table containing the referenced key is called the *parent* table.

A referential integrity constraint is defined in the child table. A referential integrity constraint definition can include any of the following keywords:

- FOREIGN KEY identifies the column or combination of columns in the child table that makes up the foreign key.

- REFERENCES identifies the parent table and the column or combination of columns that makes up the referenced key.

- ON DELETE CASCADE allows deletion of referenced key values in the parent table that have dependent rows in the child table and causes Oracle to automatically delete dependent rows from the child table to maintain referential integrity.

- The CHECK constraint explicitly defines a condition. The rows in the table must make the condition TRUE or unknown (due to a null).

Enabling a constraint involves locking the table in an EXCLUSIVE mode because while all the old data is being checked for validity, no new data can be entered into the table. Due to this behavior, only one constraint can be enabled at a time.

CREATE CLUSTER

Schema is the schema to contain the cluster.

Cluster is the name of the cluster to be created.

Column is the name of a column in the cluster key.

Datatype is the datatype of a cluster key column. A cluster key column can have any datatype except LONG or LONG RAW.

PCTUSED specifies the limit that Oracle uses to determine when additional rows can be added to a cluster's data blocks.

PCTFREE specifies the space reserved in each of the cluster's data blocks for future expansion.

INITRANS specifies the initial number of concurrent update transactions allocated for data blocks of the cluster. The value of this parameter for a cluster cannot be less than 2 or more than the value of the MAXTRANS parameter.

MAXTRANS specifies the maximum number of concurrent update transactions for any block belonging to the cluster. This value has to be greater than INITRANS and its maximum value is 255.

SIZE specifies the amount of space in bytes to store all the rows with the same cluster key value or the same hash value. Space can be specified in kilobytes or megabytes by using the letters K or M.

TABLESPACE specifies the tablespace in which the cluster is created.

STORAGE specifies how data blocks are allocated to the cluster.

INDEX creates an indexed cluster. In an indexed cluster, rows are stored together based on their cluster key values.

HASHKEYS creates a hash cluster and specifies the number of hash values for a hash cluster.

HASH IS specifies an expression to be used as the hash function for the hash cluster. The expression must do the following:

- Evaluate to a positive value.
- Contain at least one column with referenced columns of any datatype as long as the entire expression evaluates to a number of scale 0.

PARALLEL specifies the degree of parallelism to use when creating the cluster and the default degree of parallelism to use when querying the cluster after creation.

CACHE specifies that the blocks retrieved for this table are placed at the most recently used end of the LRU list in the buffer cache when a full table scan is performed.

NOCACHE specifies that the blocks retrieved for this table are placed at the least recently used end of the LRU list in the buffer cache when a full table scan is performed. This is the default behavior.

CREATE CONTROLFILE

REUSE specifies that existing control files identified by the initialization parameter CONTROL_FILES can be reused, thus ignoring and overwriting any information they may currently contain. If this option is omitted and any of the control files exist, then Oracle returns an error.

SET DATABASE changes the name of the database. The name of a database can be as long as eight bytes.

DATABASE specifies the name of the database. The value of this parameter must be the existing database name established by a previous CREATE DATABASE or CREATE CONTROLFILE statement.

LOGFILE specifies the redo log file groups for your database. You must list all members of all redo log file groups.

RESETLOGS ignores the contents of the files listed in the LOGFILE clause. These files don't have to exist.

NORESETLOGS specifies that all files listed in the LOGFILE clause must be used as they were when the database was last open. These files must exist and must be the current redo log files rather than restored backups.

DATAFILE specifies the data files of the database. You must list all data files. These files must exist.

MAXLOGFILES specifies the maximum number of redo log file groups that can ever be created for the database. Oracle uses this number to determine how much space in the control file to allocate for the names of redo log files. The default and maximum values depend on the operating system.

MAXLOGMEMBERS specifies the maximum number of members, or copies, for a redo log file group. Oracle uses this value to determine how much space in the control file to allocate for the names of the redo log files. The minimum value is 1. The maximum is dependent on the operating system.

MAXLOGHISTORY specifies the maximum number of archived redo log file groups for automatic media recovery of the Oracle8 Parallel Server.

MAXDATAFILES specifies the initial sizing of the data files section of the control file at CREATE DATABASE or CREATE CONTROLFILE time.

MAXINSTANCES specifies the maximum number of instances that can simultaneously have the database mounted and open. This value takes precedence over the value of the initialization parameter INSTANCES. The minimum value is 1.

ARCHIVELOG establishes the mode of archiving the contents of redo log files before reusing them. This option prepares for the possibility of media recovery as well as instance recovery.

NOARCHIVELOG is the default mode chosen by Oracle. After creating the control file, modes can be switched via the ALTER DATABASE command.

CREATE DATABASE

Database is the name of the database to be created and can be up to eight bytes long. Oracle writes this name into the control file. If the database name is omitted from the CREATE DATABASE command, then the name specified by the initialization parameter DB_NAME is used.

CONTROLFILE REUSE reuses existing control files identified by the initialization parameter CONTROL_FILES. This will cause any information currently contained in the control files to be ignored and overwritten. This option is used only for re-creating databases.

LOGFILE specifies one or more files to be used as redo log files. Each *filespec* specifies a redo log file group containing one or more redo log file members or copies.

MAXLOGFILES specifies the maximum number of redo log file groups that can ever be created for the database. The number of redo log file groups accessible to your instance is limited by the initialization parameter LOG_FILES.

MAXLOGMEMBERS specifies the maximum number of members, or copies, for a redo log file group.

MAXLOGHISTORY specifies the maximum number of archived redo log files for automatic media recovery of Oracle with the Parallel Server option.

MAXDATAFILES specifies the initial sizing of the data files section of the control file at CREATE DATABASE or CREATE CONTROLFILE time.

MAXINSTANCES specifies the maximum number of instances that can simultaneously have this database mounted and open. This value takes precedence over the value of the initialization parameter INSTANCES. The minimum value is 1.

ARCHIVELOG establishes archivelog mode for redo log file groups.

NOARCHIVELOG establishes noarchivelog mode for redo log file groups. In this mode, contents of the redo log file group need not be archived before the group can be reused.

CHARACTER SET specifies the character set the database uses to store data. You cannot change the database character set after creating the database.

NATIONAL CHARACTER SET specifies the national character set used to store data in columns specifically defined as NCHAR, NCLOB, or NVARCHAR2. You cannot change the national character set of the database after creating the database.

DATAFILE specifies one or more files to be used as data files. These files become part of the system tablespace.

AUTOEXTEND enables or disables the automatic extension of a data file.

OFF disables autoextend if it is turned on.

ON enables autoextend.

NEXT represents the size in bytes of the next increment of disk space to be automatically allocated to the data file when more extents are required. You can use K or M to specify the size in kilobytes or megabytes, respectively.

MAXSIZE is the maximum disk space allowed for automatic extension of the data file.

UNLIMITED sets no limit on allocating disk space to the data file.

CREATE DATABASE LINK

3

SHARED uses a single network connection to create a public database link that can be shared between multiple users. This option is available only with the multithreaded server configuration.

PUBLIC creates a public database link.

Dblink is the complete or partial name of the database link.

CONNECT TO enables a connection to the remote database.

CURRENT_USER creates a current user database link.

User IDENTIFIED BY *password* is the username and password used to connect to the remote database.

AUTHENTICATED BY *user* IDENTIFIED BY *password* specifies the username and password on the target instance. This clause authenticates the user to the remote database and is required for security.

USING *connect string* specifies the service name of a remote database.

CREATE FUNCTION

OR REPLACE re-creates the function if it already exists. This can be used to change the definition of a function without re-creating, dropping, and regranting object privileges previously granted to the function.

Schema is the schema to contain the function.

Function is the name of the function to be created.

Argument is the name of an argument to the function.

IN specifies that the parameter needs to be assigned a value when the function is being called.

OUT specifies that the function will set the argument's value.

IN OUT specifies that a value for the argument can be supplied by the user and may be set by the function.

Datatype is the datatype of an argument. The datatype cannot specify the length, precision, or scale of an argument.

RETURN *datatype* specifies the datatype of the value returned by the function. This is a required clause for a function definition because every function must return a value.

Pl/sql_subprogram_body is the definition of the function.

AS EXTERNAL identifies an external 3GL function stored in a shared library.

LIBRARY specifies the shared library in which the external function is stored.

Library_name is a PL/SQL identifier.

NAME *external_function_name* specifies the external function to be called.

NOTE: External functions are specific to Oracle8 only.

LANGUAGE specifies the 3GL in which the external function was written. At present, C is the only language that is supported.

CALLING STANDARD specifies the calling standard under which the external function was compiled. The default is C.

PARAMETERS specifies the positions and datatypes of parameters passed to the external function.

WITH CONTEXT specifies that a context pointer will be the first parameter passed to the external function.

CREATE INDEX

UNIQUE specifies that the value of the column (or combination of columns) in the table to be indexed must be unique.

BITMAP specifies that the index is to be created as a bitmap rather than as a B-tree.

Schema is the schema to contain the index.

Index is the name of the index to be created. An index can contain several partitions.

Table is the name of the table for which the index is to be created. If the index is LOCAL, then table must be partitioned.

Column is the name of a column in the table. An index can have up to 32 columns.

ASC/DESC are allowed for DB2 syntax compatibility, although indexes are always created in ascending order.

CLUSTER specifies the cluster for which a cluster index is to be created.

INITRANS/MAXTRANS establish the values for these parameters for the index.

TABLESPACE is the name of the tablespace to hold the index or index partition.

STORAGE establishes the storage characteristics for the index.

PCTFREE is the percentage of space to leave free for updates and insertions within each of the index's data blocks.

NOSORT indicates to Oracle that the rows are stored in the database in ascending order and therefore Oracle does not have to sort the rows when creating the index.

REVERSE stores the bytes of the index block in reverse order, excluding the ROWID.

LOGGING/NOLOGGING specify that the creation of the index will be logged or not logged.

GLOBAL specifies that the partitioning of the index is user defined and is not equipartitioned with the underlying table.

PARTITION BY RANGE specifies that the global index is partitioned on the ranges of values from the columns specified in the *column_list.*

(column_list) is the name of the column(s) of a table on which the index is partitioned. The *column_list* must specify a left prefix of the index column list. There can be a maximum of 32 columns in *column_list.*

LOCAL specifies that the index is range-partitioned on the same columns, with the same number of partitions and the same partition bounds as the table.

PARTITION *partition_name* describes individual partitions.

VALUES LESS THAN *(value_list)* specifies the (noninclusive) upper bound for the current partition in a global index. The *value_list* is a comma-separated, ordered list of literal values corresponding to *column_list* in the PARTITION BY RANGE clause. Always specify MAXVALUE as the *value_list* of the last partition.

PARALLEL specifies the degree of parallelism for creating the index.

CREATE PACKAGE

OR REPLACE re-creates the package specification if it already exists. This can be used to change the specification of an existing package without re-creating, dropping, and regranting object privileges previously granted to the package.

Schema is the schema to contain the package.

Package is the name of the package to be created.

Pl/sql_package_spec is the package specification.

CREATE PACKAGE BODY

OR REPLACE re-creates the package body if it already exists. This can be used to change the body of an existing package without re-creating, dropping, and regranting object privileges previously granted to it.

Schema is the schema to contain the package.

Package is the name of the package to be created.

Pl/sql_package_body is the package body.

CREATE PROCEDURE

OR REPLACE re-creates the procedure if it already exists. This can be used to change the definition of a procedure without re-creating, dropping, and regranting object privileges previously granted to the procedure.

Schema is the schema to contain the procedure.

Procedure is the name of the procedure to be created.

Argument is the name of an argument to the procedure.

IN specifies that the parameter needs to be assigned a value when the procedure is being called.

OUT specifies that the procedure will set the argument's value.

IN OUT specifies that a value for the argument can be supplied by the user and may be set by the procedure.

Datatype is the datatype of an argument. The datatype cannot specify a length, precision, or scale of an argument.

Pl/sql_subprorgam_body is the definition of the procedure.

AS EXTERNAL identifies an external 3GL procedure stored in a shared library.

LIBRARY specifies the shared library in which the external procedure is stored.

Library_name is a PL/SQL identifier.

NAME *external_function_name* specifies the external function to be called.

NOTE: External functions are specific to Oracle8 only.

LANGUAGE specifies the 3GL in which the external function was written. At present, C is the only language that is supported.

CALLING STANDARD specifies the calling standard under which the external function was compiled. The default is C.

PARAMETERS specifies the positions and datatypes of parameters passed to the external function.

WITH CONTEXT specifies that a context pointer will be the first parameter passed to the external function.

CREATE PROFILE

Profile is the name of the profile to be created.

SESSIONS_PER_USER limits a user's *integer* concurrent sessions.

CPU_PER_SESSION limits the CPU time for a session. This value is expressed in hundredths of seconds.

CPU_PER_CALL limits the CPU time for a call. This value is expressed in hundredths of seconds.

CONNECT_TIME limits the total elapsed time for a session. This value is in minutes.

IDLE_TIME limits the period of continuous inactive time during a session. This value is expressed in minutes.

LOGICAL_READS_PER_SESSION limits the number of data block reads in a session, including block reads from memory and disk.

LOGICAL_READS_PER_CALL limits the number of data blocks read for a call to process a SQL statement to *integer* blocks.

PRIVATE_SGA is the number of bytes of private space in the SGA (System Global Area) used by a session. This limit applies only if the multithreaded server architecture is being used.

FAILED_LOGIN_ATTEMPTS specifies the number of failed attempts to log in to the user account before the account is locked.

PASSWORD_LIFE_TIME limits the number of days the same password can be used for authentication.

PASSWORD_REUSE_TIME specifies the number of days before which a password can be reused.

PASSWORD_REUSE_MAX specifies the number of password changes required before the current password can be reused.

PASSWORD_LOCK_TIME specifies the number of days an account will be locked after the specified number of consecutive logins fail.

PASSWORD_GRACE_TIME specifies the number of days after the grace period begins during which a warning is issued and login is allowed.

PASSWORD_VERIFY_FUNCTION allows a PL/SQL password complexity verification script to be passed as an argument to the CREATE PROFILE command.

Function is the name of the password complexity verification routine.

NULL indicates that no password verification is performed.

DEFAULT omits a limit for this resource in this profile.

COMPOSITE_LIMIT limits the total resources cost for a session. (Check the ALTER RESOURCE COST command for more details.)

UNLIMITED indicates that a user assigned this profile can use an unlimited amount of this resource.

DEFAULT omits a limit for this resource in the profile.

CREATE ROLE

Role is the name of the role to be created. It is recommended that the role contain at least one single-byte character.

NOT IDENTIFIED indicates that this role is authorized by the database and that no password is required to enable the role.

IDENTIFIED indicates that a user has to be authorized by one of these three possible ways before the role is enabled with the SET ROLE command:

- BY *password* requires the user to specify the password to Oracle when enabling the role. The password can contain only single-byte characters from the database character set.

- EXTERNALLY indicates that the user must be authorized by an external service (most popularly, by the operating system or a third-party service) before enabling the role.

- GLOBALLY indicates that the user must be authorized by the Oracle Security Service to use the role before the role is enabled with the SET ROLE command or at the time of logging in to the database.

If both IDENTIFIED and NOT IDENTIFIED options are omitted, the role defaults to NOT IDENTIFIED.

CREATE ROLLBACK SEGMENT

PUBLIC specifies that the rollback segment is public and is available to any instance.

Rollback_segment is the name of the rollback segment to be created.

TABLESPACE identifies the tablespace in which the rollback segment is created.

STORAGE specifies the characteristics for the rollback segment.

OPTIMAL specifies an optimal size in bytes for a rollback segment. You can use K or M to specify the size in kilobytes or megabytes, respectively.

NULL specifies no optimal size for the rollback segment, meaning Oracle never deallocates the rollback segment's extents. This is the default behavior.

3

CREATE SCHEMA

Schema is the name of the schema. This must be same as the Oracle username.

CREATE TABLE *command* is a CREATE TABLE statement to be issued as a part of the CREATE SCHEMA command. (Described in detail under CREATE TABLE.)

CREATE VIEW *command* is a CREATE VIEW statement to be issued as a part of the CREATE SCHEMA *command*. (Described in detail under CREATE VIEW.)

GRANT *command* is a GRANT statement to be issued as part of the CREATE SCHEMA statement.

NOTE: The CREATE SCHEMA statement only supports the syntax of commands as defined by standard SQL, not the complex Oracle SQL syntax.

CREATE SEQUENCE

Schema is the name of the schema to create the sequence in.

Sequence is the name of the sequence to be created.

INCREMENT BY specifies the interval between sequence numbers. This number can be positive or negative but not zero.

MINVALUE specifies the sequence's minimum value. This must be greater than or equal to START WITH and less than MAXVALUE.

NOMINVALUE specifies a minimum value of 1 for an ascending sequence or -10^{26} for a descending sequence.

MAXVALUE specifies a maximum value of 10^{27} for an ascending sequence or -1 for a descending sequence.

START WITH specifies the first sequence number to be generated.

CYCLE specifies that the sequence continue to generate values after reaching its maximum or minimum value.

NOCYCLE specifies that the sequence cannot generate more values after reaching its maximum or minimum value. This is the default.

CACHE specifies how many values of the sequence Oracle preallocates and keeps in memory for faster access.

NOCACHE specifies that the values of the sequence are not preallocated.

ORDER guarantees that the sequence numbers are generated in order of request.

NOORDER does not guarantee sequence numbers are generated in order of request.

CREATE SNAPSHOT

Schema is the schema to contain the snapshot.

Snapshot is the name of the snapshot to be created.

PCTFREE/PCTUSED/INITRANS/MAXTRANS establish values for the specified parameters for the internal table Oracle uses to maintain the snapshot's data.

LOB_storage_clause specifies the LOB storage characteristics.

TABLESPACE specifies the tablespace in which the snapshot is to be created.

STORAGE establishes the storage characteristics for the table Oracle uses to maintain the snapshot's data.

CLUSTER creates the snapshot as part of the specified cluster.

Table_partition_clause specifies that the table is partitioned on a specified range of values.

USING INDEX specifies parameters for the index Oracle creates to maintain the snapshot.

ROLLBACK SEGMENT specifies the local snapshot and/or remote master rollback segments to be used during a snapshot refresh.

Rollback_segment is the name of the rollback segment to be used.

DEFAULT specifies that Oracle will choose which rollback segment to use.

MASTER specifies the rollback segment to be used at the remote master for the individual snapshot.

LOCAL specifies the rollback segment to be used for the local refresh group that contains the snapshot.

REFRESH specifies how and when Oracle automatically refreshes the snapshot.

FAST specifies a fast refresh or a refresh using only the updated data stored in the snapshot log associated with the master table.

COMPLETE specifies a complete refresh.

FORCE specifies a fast refresh if one is possible or a complete refresh if a fast refresh is not possible.

START WITH specifies a date expression for the first automatic refresh time.

NEXT specifies a date expression for calculating the interval between automatic refreshes.

WITH PRIMARY KEY specifies that primary key snapshots are to be created. Primary key snapshots allow snapshot master tables to be reorganized without impacting the snapshot's ability to continue a fast refresh.

WITH ROWID specifies that ROWID snapshots are to be created.

FOR UPDATE allows a simple snapshot to be updated.

AS *Select command* specifies the snapshot query.

A *snapshot* is a table that contains the results of a query of one or more tables, often located on a remote database. The tables in the query are called *master tables*. The databases containing the master tables are called the *master databases*. Snapshots are useful in distributed databases.

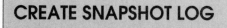

CREATE SNAPSHOT LOG

Schema is the schema containing the snapshot log's master table.

Table is the name of the master table for which the snapshot log is to be created.

WITH specifies whether the snapshot log should record the primary key, ROWID, or both when rows in the master are updated.

PRIMARY KEY specifies that the primary key of all rows updated should be recorded in the snapshot log.

ROWID specifies that the ROWID of all rows updated should be recorded in the snapshot log.

Filter_column is a comma-separated list that specifies the list of filter columns to be recorded in the snapshot log.

PCTFREE/PCTUSED/INITRANS/MAXTRANS establish values for the specified parameters for the snapshot log.

TABLESPACE specifies the tablespace in which the snapshot log is to be created.

STORAGE establishes the storage characteristics for the snapshot log.

LOB_storage_clause specifies the LOB storage characteristics.

Table_partition_clause specifies that the table be partitioned on specified ranges of values.

CREATE SYNONYM

PUBLIC creates a public synonym. Public synonyms are accessible to all users.

Schema is the schema to contain the synonym.

Synonym is the name of the synonym.

FOR identifies the object for which the synonym is being created. The schema object can be one of the following:

- Table
- Object table
- View
- Object view
- Sequence
- Stored procedure, function, or package
- Snapshot
- Synonym

CREATE TABLE

Table is the name of the table to be created.

Column specifies the name of a column in the table. A table can have up to 1,000 columns.

Datatype is the datatype of the column.

DEFAULT specifies a value to be assigned to the column if a subsequent INSERT statement omits a value for the column.

Column_constraint defines an integrity constraint as part of the column definition.

Table_constraint defines an integrity constraint as part of the table definition.

ORGANIZATION INDEX specifies that the table be created as an index-organized table. In an index-organized table, the data rows are held in an index defined on the primary key for the table.

ORGANIZATION HEAP specifies the percentage of space reserved in the index block for an index-organized table row.

PCTTHRESHOLD *integer* specifies the percentage of space reserved in the index block for an index-organized table row. Any portion of the row that exceeds the specified threshold is stored in the area. If OVERFLOW is not specified, then rows exceeding the THRESHOLD limit are rejected.

INCLUDING *column_name* specifies the column at which to divide an index-organized table row into index and overflow portions.

PCTFREE specifies the percentage of space in each of the tables, the object table's OIDINDEX, or partition's data blocks reserved for future updates to the table's rows.

PCTUSED specifies the maximum percentage of used space that Oracle maintains for each data block of the table, object table OIDINDEX, or index-organized table overflow data segment.

INITRANS specifies the initial number of transaction entries allocated within each data block allocated to the table, object table OIDINDEX, partition, LOB index segment, or overflow data segment.

MAXTRANS specifies the maximum number of concurrent transactions that can update a data block allocated to the table, object table OIDINDEX, partition, LOB index segment, or index-organized overflow data segment.

TABLESPACE specifies the tablespace in which Oracle creates the table, object table OIDINDEX, partition, LOB storage, LOB index segment, or index-organized table overflow data segment.

STORAGE specifies the storage characteristics for the table, object table OIDINDEX, partition, LOB storage, LOB index segment, or index-organized table overflow data segment.

OVERFLOW specifies that index-organized table data rows exceeding the specified threshold be placed in the data segment listed in this clause.

LOGGING/NOLOGGING specify that the creation of the table (and any indexes required because of constraints), partition, or LOB storage characteristics will be logged or otherwise in the redo log file.

LOB specifies the LOB storage characteristics.

Lob_item is the LOB column name or LOB object attribute for which you are explicitly defining tablespace and storage characteristics that are different from those of the table.

STORE AS *lob_segname* specifies the name of the LOB data segment.

ENABLE STORAGE IN ROW specifies that the LOB value be stored in the row (inline) if its length is less than 4,000 bytes minus the system control information. This is the default.

DISABLE STORAGE IN ROW specifies that the LOB value be stored outside the row regardless of the length of the LOB value.

NOTE: The LOB locator is always stored in the row regardless of where the LOB value is stored.

CHUNK *integer* is the unit of LOB value allocation and manipulation.

PCTVERSION *integer* is the maximum percentage of overall LOB storage space used for creating new versions of the LOB. The default value is 10.

INDEX *lob_index_name* is the name of the LOB index segment.

CLUSTER specifies that the table is to be part of the cluster.

Parallel_clause specifies the degree of parallelism for creating the table and the default degree of parallelism for queries on the table, once created.

PARTITION BY RANGE specifies that the table be partitioned on ranges of values from *column_list*.

Column_list is an ordered list of columns used to determine into which partition a row should be placed.

PARTITION *partition_name* specifies the physical partition clause.

VALUES LESS THAN specifies the noninclusive upper bound for the current partition.

Value_list is an ordered list of literal values corresponding to *column_list* in the PARTITION BY RANGE clause.

MAXVALUE specifies a maximum value that will always sort higher than any other value, including NULL.

ENABLE enables an integrity constraint.

DISABLE disables an integrity constraint.

AS *subquery* inserts the rows returned by the subquery into the table, upon its creation.

CACHE specifies that the data will be accessed frequently; therefore, blocks retrieved for this table are placed at the most recently used end of the LRU list in the buffer cache when a full table scan is performed.

NOCACHE specifies that the data will not be accessed frequently; therefore, the blocks retrieved for this table are placed at the least recently used end of the LRU list in the buffer cache when a full table scan is performed.

CREATE TABLESPACE

Tablespace is the name of the tablespace to be created.

DATAFILE specifies the data file or files to comprise the tablespace.

MINIMUM EXTENT *integer* controls free space fragmentation in the tablespace by ensuring that every used and/or free extent size in a tablespace is at least as large as, and is a multiple of, *integer*.

AUTOEXTEND enables or disables the automatic extension of data files.

OFF disables autoextend if it is turned on.

ON enables autoextend.

NEXT allows disk space to allocate to the data file when more extents are required.

MAXSIZE allows maximum disk space for allocation to the data file.

UNLIMITED sets no limit on allocating disk space to the data files.

LOGGING/NOLOGGING specify the default logging attributes of all tables, indexes, and partitions within the tablespace. LOGGING is the default.

DEFAULT STORAGE specifies the default storage parameters for all objects created in the tablespace.

ONLINE makes the tablespace available immediately after creation to users who have been granted access to the tablespace.

OFFLINE makes the tablespace unavailable immediately after creation.

PERMANENT specifies that the tablespace will be used to hold permanent objects. This is the default.

TEMPORARY specifies that the tablespace will only be used to hold temporary objects.

CREATE TRIGGER

OR REPLACE re-creates the trigger if it already exists.

Schema is the schema to contain the trigger.

Table is the name of a table or an object table.

View is the name of a view or an object view.

Trigger is the name of the trigger to be created.

BEFORE indicates that the trigger gets fired before executing the triggering statement.

AFTER indicates that the trigger gets fired after executing the triggering statement.

INSTEAD OF indicates the trigger gets fired instead of executing the triggering statement. This is a valid option for views only, not tables.

DELETE indicates that the trigger is fired whenever a DELETE statement removes one or more rows from a table.

INSERT indicates that the trigger is fired whenever an INSERT statement adds one or more rows to a table.

UPDATE OF indicates that the trigger is fired whenever an UPDATE statement changes a value in any column of the table.

ON specifies the schema and object on which the trigger is to be created. The object could be a table or a view.

REFERENCING specifies correlation names. Correlation names can be used in PL/SQL blocks and the WHEN clause of a row trigger to refer specifically to old and new values of the current row.

FOR EACH ROW designates the trigger to be a row-level trigger. This means that the trigger gets executed *n* times, once for each of the rows that are affected.

WHEN specifies the trigger restriction. The trigger restriction is a SQL condition that can only be specified for a row trigger.

Pl/sql_block is the PL/SQL block that gets executed to fire the trigger.

CREATE USER

User is the name of the user to be created.

IDENTIFIED BY *password* denotes that the user must provide a password to log on.

IDENTIFIED EXTERNALLY indicates that Oracle verifies that the operating system username matches the database username specified in the database connection.

IDENTIFIED GLOBALLY AS *external_name* indicates that Oracle permits user access by obtaining the username and required authorizations from the security domain central authority. The *external_name* string denotes the external name of the database user.

DEFAULT TABLESPACE identifies the default tablespace for objects that the user creates.

TEMPORARY TABLESPACE identifies the tablespace for the student's temporary segments.

QUOTA allows the user to allocate space in the tablespace and, optionally, establishes a quota of integer bytes.

PROFILE reassigns the profile named to the user.

PASSWORD EXPIRE causes the user's password to expire.

ACCOUNT LOCK locks the user's account and disables access.

ACCOUNT UNLOCK unlocks the user's account and enables access to the account.

CREATE VIEW

OR REPLACE re-creates the view if it already exists. This option can be used to change the definition of an existing view without dropping, re-creating, and regranting the privileges on objects that must have been granted previously.

FORCE creates the view regardless of whether the view's base tables or the referenced object types exist or the owner of the schema containing the view has privileges on them.

NOFORCE creates the view only if the base tables exist and the owner of the schema containing the view has privileges on them. The default is NOFORCE.

Schema is the schema to create the view in.

View is the name of the view or object view.

Alias is the name for the expression selected by the view query.

OF *object_type* explicitly creates an object view of type *object_type*. The columns of an object view correspond to the top-level attributes of type *object_type*.

WITH OBJECT OID specifies the attributes of the object type that will be used as a key to uniquely identify each row in the object view.

DEFAULT specifies that the intrinsic object identifier of the underlying object table or object view will be used to uniquely identify each row.

Attribute is an attribute of the object type from which the object view is to be created.

AS *subquery* identifies the columns and rows of the table(s) that the view is based on. A view's query can be any SELECT statement without the ORDER BY or FOR UPDATE clauses.

WITH READ ONLY specifies that no DELETE, INSERT, or UPDATE operations can be performed through the view.

WITH CHECK OPTION specifies that the inserts and updates performed through the view must result in rows that the view query can select.

CONSTRAINT is the name assigned to the CHECK OPTION constraint.

DROP

PRIMARY KEY drops the table's PRIMARY KEY constraint.

UNIQUE drops the UNIQUE constraint on the specified columns.

CONSTRAINT drops the integrity constraint named *constraint*.

CASCADE drops all other integrity constraints that depend upon the dropped integrity constraint.

DROP CLUSTER

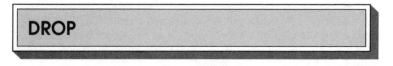

Schema is the schema containing the cluster.

Cluster is the name of the cluster to be dropped.

INCLUDING TABLES drops all tables that belong to the cluster.

CASCADE CONSTRAINTS drops all referential integrity constraints from tables outside the cluster that refer to primary and unique keys in tables of the cluster.

DROP DATABASE LINK

3

PUBLIC must be specified to drop a public database link.

Dblink is the name of the database link to be dropped.

DROP FUNCTION

Schema is the schema containing the function.

Function is the name of the function to be dropped.

DROP INDEX

Schema is the schema containing the index.

Index is the name of the index to be dropped.

DROP PACKAGE

BODY drops only the body of the package. If this keyword is omitted, both the package body and specification are dropped.

Schema is the schema containing the package.

Package is the name of the package to be dropped.

DROP PROCEDURE

Schema is the schema containing the procedure.

Procedure is the name of the procedure to be dropped.

DROP PROFILE

Profile is the name of the profile to be dropped.

CASCADE unassigns the profile from any users to whom it was assigned. Such users get assigned the DEFAULT profile automatically.

DROP ROLE

Role is the role to be dropped.

DROP ROLLBACK SEGMENT

Rollback_segment is the name of the rollback segment to be dropped.

DROP SEQUENCE

Schema is the schema containing the sequence.

Sequence is the name of the sequence to be dropped.

DROP SNAPSHOT

Schema is the name of the schema containing the snapshot.

Snapshot is the name of the snapshot to be dropped.

DROP SNAPSHOT LOG

Schema is the schema containing the snapshot log and its master table.

Table is the name of the master table associated with the snapshot log to be dropped.

DROP SYNONYM

PUBLIC must be specified to drop a public synonym. Schema cannot be specified if PUBLIC is specified.

Schema is the schema containing the synonym.

Synonym is the name of the synonym to be dropped.

DROP TABLE

Schema is the schema containing the table.

Table is the name of the table, object table, or index-organized table to be dropped.

CASCADE CONSTRAINTS drops all referential integrity constraints that refer to primary and unique keys in the dropped table.

DROP TABLESPACE

Tablespace is the name of the tablespace to be dropped.

INCLUDING CONTENTS drops all the contents of the tablespace. This clause needs to be specified to drop a tablespace that contains any database objects.

CASCADE CONSTRAINTS drops all referential integrity constraints from tables outside this clause to drop a tablespace that contains any database objects.

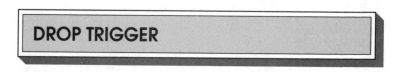

DROP TRIGGER

Schema is the schema containing the trigger.

Trigger is the name of the trigger to be dropped.

DROP USER

User is the user to be dropped.

CASCADE drops all objects in the user's schema before dropping the user.

DROP VIEW

Schema is the schema containing the view.

View is the name of the view to be dropped.

GRANT

System_priv is a system privilege to be granted.

Role is a role to be granted.

TO identifies users or roles to which system privileges and roles are granted.

PUBLIC grants system privileges or roles to all users.

WITH ADMIN OPTION allows the grantee to grant the system privileges or role to other users or roles.

Object_priv is an object privilege to be granted.

ALL PRIVILEGES grants all the privileges for the object that you have been granted with the GRANT OPTION.

Column specifies a table or view column on which privileges are granted.

ON identifies the object on which the privileges are granted.

DIRECTORY *directory_object* identifies a directory object on which privileges are granted by the DBA.

Object identifies the schema object on which the privileges are granted.

TO identifies users or roles to which the object privilege is granted.

PUBLIC grants object privileges to all users.

WITH GRANT OPTION allows the grantee to grant the object privileges to other users and roles.

NOAUDIT

Statement_opt is a statement option for which auditing is stopped.

System_priv is a system privilege for which auditing is stopped.

BY stops auditing only for SQL statements issued by specified users in their subsequent sessions.

WHENEVER SUCCESSFUL stops auditing only for SQL statements that complete successfully.

NOT stops auditing only for statements that result in errors.

RENAME

Old is the current name of an existing table, view, sequence, or private synonym.

New is the new name to be given to the existing object.

REVOKE

System_priv is a system privilege to be revoked.

Role is a role to be revoked.

FROM identifies users and roles from which the privileges or roles are revoked.

PUBLIC revokes the privilege or role from all users.

Object_priv is an object privilege to be revoked.

ALL PRIVILEGES revokes all object privileges that have been granted to the revokee.

ON DIRECTORY *object* identifies a directory object on which privileges are revoked.

ON *object* identifies the object on which the object privileges are revoked.

PUBLIC revokes object privileges from all users.

FROM identifies users and roles from which the object privileges are revoked.

CASCADE CONSTRAINTS drops any referential integrity constraints that the revokee has defined using REFERENCES privileges or the ALL PRIVILEGES option if the revokee has exercised the REFERENCES privileges to define a referential integrity constraint.

FORCE revokes EXECUTE object privileges on user-defined type objects with table dependencies.

STORAGE

INITIAL specifies the size in bytes of the object's first extent. The space is allocated when the schema object is created. You can use K or M to specify the size in kilobytes or megabytes, respectively.

NEXT specifies the size in bytes of the next extent to be allocated to the object. Again, K and M can be used to specify the sizes in kilobytes or megabytes, respectively.

PCTINCREASE specifies the percent by which each extent after the second grows over the previous extent. The default value is 50.

MINEXTENTS specifies the total number of extents to allocate when the object is created. This parameter allows you to allocate a large amount of space when you create an object, even if the space available is not contiguous.

MAXEXTENTS specifies the total number of extents, including the first that Oracle can allocate for the object. The minimum value is 1.

UNLIMITED specifies that the extents should automatically be allocated as needed.

FREELIST GROUPS for schema objects other than tablespace specifies the number of groups of free lists for a table, partition, cluster, or index. The default and minimum value is 1.

FREELISTS specifies (for objects other than tablespaces) the number of groups of free lists for each of the free list groups for the table, partition, cluster, or index. The default and minimum value for this parameter is 1.

OPTIMAL specifies an optimal size in bytes for a rollback segment. This is not applicable to other objects.

NULL specifies no optimal size for the rollback segment, meaning that the rollback segment's extents are never deallocated.

BUFFER_POOL defines a default buffer pool for a schema object. All blocks for the object are stored in the specified cache.

KEEP retains the schema object in memory to avoid I/O operations.

RECYCLE eliminates blocks from memory as soon as they are no longer needed.

DEFAULT always exists for objects not assigned to KEEP or RECYCLE.

TRUNCATE

TABLE specifies the schema and the name of the table to be truncated.

SNAPSHOT LOG specifies whether a snapshot log defined on the table is preserved or purged when the table is truncated.

PRESERVE specifies that any snapshot log should be preserved when the master table is truncated.

PURGE specifies that any snapshot log should be purged when the master table is truncated.

CLUSTER specifies the schema and name of the cluster to be truncated.

DROP STORAGE deallocates the space from the deleted rows from the table or cluster.

REUSE STORAGE leaves the space from the deleted rows allocated to the table or cluster. STORAGE values are not reset to the values when the table or cluster was created.

NOTE: TRUNCATE is different from DELETE in that it is a DDL operation, which means it cannot be rolled back. It is significantly faster because all it does is reset the high-water mark of the table.

DML Commands

DELETE

Schema is the schema containing the table or view. If you omit the schema, Oracle assumes that the table or view is in your own schema.

Table/view is the name of the table from which the rows are to be deleted. If a *view* is specified, rows are deleted from the view's underlying table(s).

dblink is the complete or partial name of a database link to a remote database where the table or view is located. If *dblink* is omitted, the table or view is assumed to be located on the local database.

PARTITION (*partition_name*) specifies partition-level row deletes for table. The *partition_name* is the name of the partition within table targeted for deletes.

Subquery is a subquery from which data is selected for deletion.

Alias is an alias assigned to the table, view, or subquery. Aliases are generally used in DELETE statements with correlated queries.

WHERE deletes only rows that satisfy the condition. The condition can reference the table and can contain a subquery. If *dblink* is omitted, the table or view is assumed to be located on the local database.

RETURNING retrieves the rows affected by the DELETE statement.

Expr is any syntax description. A column expression must be specified in the RETURNING clause for each variable in the *data_item_list*.

INTO indicates that the values of the changed rows are to be stored in the variable(s) specified in *data_item_list*.

EXPLAIN PLAN

SET/STATEMENT_ID specifies the value of the STATEMENT_ID for the rows of the execution plan in the output table. If this clause is omitted, the STATEMENT_ID value defaults to null.

INTO specifies the schema, name, and database containing the output table. This table should exist before you execute the EXPLAIN PLAN command. If you do not specify the *schema*, Oracle assumes that the plan table is in your own schema. The *dblink* can be a complete or partial name of a database link to a remote Oracle database where the output table is located.

FOR statement specifies the SELECT, INSERT, UPDATE, or DELETE statement for which the execution plan is generated.

INSERT

Table/view is the name of the table or view in which to insert the rows. If a view is specified, the rows are inserted into the view's base table.

PARTITION (*partition_name*) specifies partition-level row inserts for *table*. The *partition_name* is the name of the partition within the table targeted for inserts.

Dblink is the complete or partial name of the database link to a remote database where the table or view is located.

Subquery_1 is a subquery that is treated as a view.

Column is a column of the table or view.

VALUES specifies a row of values to be inserted into the table or view. You must specify a value in the VALUES clause for each column in the column list.

Subquery_2 is a subquery that returns rows that are inserted into the table. The select list in this subquery must have the same number of columns as the column list in the INSERT statement.

RETURNING retrieves the rows affected by the INSERT. Only scalar, LOB, ROWID, and REF types can be retrieved.

INTO indicates that the values of the changed rows are to be stored in the variables specified in *data_item_list*.

Data_item_list is a list of PL/SQL or bind variables which stores the retrieved expression value.

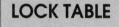

LOCK TABLE

Schema is the schema containing the table or view.

Table/view is the table to be locked. If you specify a view, the view's base tables are locked.

Dblink is a database link to a remote database where the table or view is located. A table or view on a remote database can be locked only if the distributed database option is available.

Lockmode is one of the following:

- ROW SHARE allows concurrent access to the locked table, but prohibits users from locking the entire table for exclusive access. ROW SHARE is synonymous with SHARE UPDATE, which is included for compatibility with earlier versions of Oracle.

- ROW EXCLUSIVE is the same as ROW SHARE, but also prohibits locking in SHARE mode. Row Exclusive locks are automatically obtained when updating, inserting, or deleting.

- SHARE UPDATE; see ROW SHARE.

- SHARE allows concurrent queries but prohibits updates to the locked table.

- SHARE ROW EXCLUSIVE is used to look at a whole table and to allow others to look at rows in the table but to prohibit others from locking the table in SHARE mode or updating rows.

- EXCLUSIVE allows queries on the locked table but prohibits any other activity on it.

NOWAIT specifies that Oracle returns control to you immediately if the specified table is already locked by another user. In this case, Oracle returns a message indicating that the table is already locked by another user. If you omit this clause, Oracle waits until the table is available, locks it, and returns control to you.

SELECT

DISTINCT returns only one copy of each set of duplicate rows selected. Duplicate rows are those with matching values for each expression in the select list.

ALL returns all rows selected, including all copies of duplicates. The default is ALL.

* selects all columns from all tables, views, or snapshots that are listed in the FROM clause.

Table.*/View.*/Snapshot.* selects all columns from the specified table, view, or snapshot. You can use the schema qualifier to select from a table, view, or snapshot in a schema other than your own.

Expr selects an expression. A column name in this list can be qualified only with schema if the table, view, or snapshot containing the column is qualified with schema in the FROM clause.

C_alias provides a different name for the column expression and causes the alias to be used in the column heading. The AS keyword is optional. The alias effectively renames the select list item for the duration of the query. The alias can be used in the ORDER BY clause, but not other clauses in the query.

PARTITION (*partition_name*) specifies partition-level data retrieval. The *partition_name* parameter may be the name of the partition within table from which to retrieve data or a more complicated predicate restricting retrieval to just one partition of the table.

Schema is the schema containing the selected table, view, or snapshot. If you omit *schema*, Oracle assumes the table, view, or snapshot is in your own schema.

Table/view/snapshot is the name of a table, view, or snapshot from which data is selected.

Dblink is the complete or partial name for a database link to a remote database where the table, view, or snapshot is located. If you omit *dblink*, Oracle assumes that the table, view, or snapshot is on the local database.

Subquery is a subquery that is treated in the same manner as a view. Oracle executes the subquery and then uses the resulting rows as a view in the FROM clause. If you apply the keyword THE, the subquery must return a single column value which must be a nested table or an expression that yields a nested table.

T_alias provides a different name for the table, view, snapshot, or subquery for evaluating the query and is most often used in a correlated query. Other references to the table, view, or snapshot throughout the query must refer to the alias.

WHERE restricts the rows selected to those for which the condition is TRUE. If you omit this clause, all rows from the tables, views, or snapshots in the FROM clause are returned.

START WITH ... CONNECT BY returns rows in a hierarchical order.

GROUP BY groups the selected rows based on the value of *expr* for each row, and returns a single row of summary information for each group.

HAVING restricts the groups of rows returned to those groups for which the specified condition is TRUE. If you omit this clause, the summary rows for all groups are returned.

UNION/UNION ALL/INTERSECT/MINUS combine the rows returned by two SELECT statements using a set operation. To reference a column, you must use an alias to name the column. The FOR UPDATE clause cannot be used with these set operators.

ORDER BY orders rows returned by the statement.

Expr orders rows based on their value for *expr*. The expression is based on columns in the select list or columns in the tables, views, or snapshots in the FROM clause.

Position orders rows based on their value for the expression in this position of the select list.

ASC and DESC specify either ascending or descending order. ASC is the default.

FOR UPDATE locks the selected rows.

OF locks the select rows only for a particular table in a join.

NOWAIT returns control to you if the SELECT statement attempts to lock a row that is locked by another user. If you omit this clause, Oracle waits until the row is available and then returns the results of the SELECT statement.

UPDATE

Schema is the schema containing the table or view. If this is omitted, then the table or view is assumed to be in your own schema.

Table/view is the name of the table to be updated. If a view is specified, then the view's base tables are updated.

Dblink is a complete or partial name of a database link to a remote database where the table or view is located.

PARTITION (*partition_name*) specifies partition-level row updates for a table. The *partition_name* is the name of the partition within a table targeted for updates.

Alias provides a different name for the table, view, or subquery to be referenced elsewhere in the statement.

THE informs Oracle that the column value returned by the subquery is a nested table, not a scalar value.

Subquery_1 is a subquery that is treated as a view.

Column is the name of the column of the table or view that is to be updated.

Expr is the new value assigned to the corresponding column.

Subquery_2 is a subquery that returns new values that are assigned to the corresponding columns.

Subquery_3 is a subquery that returns new values that are assigned to the corresponding columns.

WHERE restricts the rows updated to those for which the specified condition is TRUE.

RETURNING retrieves the rows affected by the UPDATE statement.

INTO indicates that the values of the changed rows are to be stored in the variables specified in *data_item_list.*

Transaction Control Commands

3

COMMIT

WORK is supported for compliance with ANSI SQL. COMMIT WORK is the same as COMMIT.

COMMENT specifies a comment to be associated with the current transaction.

Text is a quoted literal up to 50 characters long that is stored in the data dictionary along with the transaction identifier.

FORCE manually commits an in-doubt transaction. The transaction is identified by the 'text' containing its transaction identifier.

Transaction_name is the name of the transaction to BEGIN.

TIP: It is advised that you commit or rollback every transaction before logging out of the database. If you don't commit a transaction and the program halts abnormally, the last uncommitted transaction is rolled back automatically. A normal exit from most Oracle tools (except precompiler programs) causes the transaction to be committed. A normal exit from a precompiler application does not commit the transaction but instead depends on Oracle to rollback the transaction.

TIP: In Microsoft SQL Server, you can nest transactions within one another. In Informix, if you issue a BEGIN WORK statement while you are in the middle of a transaction, you will get an error message.

ROLLBACK

WORK is supported for compliance with ANSI SQL. ROLLBACK WORK is the same as ROLLBACK.

TO rolls back the current transaction to the specified savepoint. If the TO clause is omitted, the entire transaction is rolled back.

FORCE manually commits an in-doubt transaction. The transaction is identified by the 'text' containing its transaction identifier

Save_point is the savepoint to which the transaction rolls back. The savepoint should have been defined earlier by the SAVEPOINT command.

Transaction_name is the name of the transaction to BEGIN.

SAVEPOINT

Savepoint is the name of the savepoint to be created.

Savepoints are used to rollback portions of the current transaction. They are useful in application programs and interactive programs. An application program containing several subprograms can have savepoints after each subprogram; this ensures that work can be rolled back to the point before the start of the subprogram in which the application failed.

NOTE: Savepoints names must be distinct within a given transaction. If you do create two savepoints with the same name, the second savepoint prevails and the first one is erased.

SET CONSTRAINTS (Informix)

IMMEDIATE is the default constraint checking mode. When the SET CONSTRAINTS statement is set to IMMEDIATE, effective checking is turned on and all specified constraints are checked at the end of each INSERT, UPDATE or DELETE statement. If a constraint error occurs, then the statement is not executed.

DEFERRED is used with the SET CONSTRAINTS statement. If set to DEFERRED, effective checking is turned off and all specified constraints are not checked *until* the transaction is committed. If a constraint error occurs, the statement is rolled back.

Database is the name of the database in which the constraint resides.

Owner is the name of the owner of the constraint.

Server is the name of the Informix database server that is home to *database*. The @ sign is a literal character used to introduce database name.

The duration of the SET CONSTRAINTS statements is the transaction in which it is executed. Once a COMMIT WORK or ROLLBACK WORK is executed successfully, the constraint mode reverts to IMMEDIATE.

NOTE: You cannot defer the NOT NULL constraint for a column or set of columns.

SET ISOLATION (Informix)

The database isolation level affects concurrency when rows are retrieved from the database. Informix uses shared locks to support four levels of isolation among processes attempting to access data. The default isolation level is determined at the time of database creation by the database type. The various isolation levels are as follows:

- DIRTY READ is appropriate for tables that are used for queries. This provides zero isolation. With a dirty read isolation level, it is possible for a query to return an uncommitted row that was inserted or modified within a transaction that was subsequently rolled back.

- COMMITTED READ guarantees that every row retrieved is committed in the table at the time that the row is retrieved. No locks are acquired.

- CURSOR STABILITY acquires a shared lock on the selected row. Another process may also acquire a shared lock but no process may acquire an exclusive lock to modify data in the row. The shared lock is released when you fetch another row or when the cursor is closed.

- REPEATABLE READ acquires a shared lock on every row selected during the transaction. Another process also can acquire a shared lock on a selected row during your transaction but no other transaction can modify the selected row during your transaction. The shared locks are released only when the transaction is committed or rolled back.

SET TRANSACTION

READ ONLY establishes the current transaction as a read-only transaction.

READ WRITE establishes the current transaction as a read-write transaction.

ISOLATION LEVEL specifies how transactions containing database modifications are handled.

SERIALIZABLE uses the serializable transaction isolation mode specified in SQL92. That is, if a serializable transaction attempts to execute a DML statement that updates any resource that may have been updated in an uncommitted transaction at the start of the serializable transaction, then the DML statement fails. The COMPATIBLE initialization parameter should be set to 7.3.0 or higher for SERIALIZABLE mode to work.

READ COMMITTED uses the default Oracle transaction behavior. Therefore, if in a transaction there is a DML statement that requires row locks held by another transaction, the DML statement will wait until the row locks are released.

USE ROLLBACK SEGMENT assigns the current transaction to the specified rollback segment. This option also establishes the transaction as a read-write transaction. A READ ONLY transaction does not generate rollback information and hence you cannot specify the USE ROLLBACK SEGMENT clause in a SET TRANSACTION statement.

NOTE: The operations performed by a SET TRANSACTION affect only the current transaction for the user executing the transaction, not for other transactions or other users.

Session and System Control Statements

3

ALTER SESSION

ADVISE sends advice for forcing a distributed transaction to a remote database; the advice options are COMMIT, ROLLBACK, or NOTHING.

CLOSE DATABASE LINK closes the database link dblink, eliminating your session's connection to the remote database. The database link must not be in use by an active transaction or an open cursor.

COMMIT IN PROCEDURE ENABLE permits procedures and functions to issue these statements.

COMMIT IN PROCEDURE DISABLE prohibits procedures and functions from issuing these statements.

PARALLEL DML specifies whether all subsequent DML transactions in the session will be considered for parallel execution. This option can be executed between committed transaction only.

ENABLE enables the session's DML statements to be executed in parallel mode if a parallel hint or parallel clause is specified.

DISABLE executes the session's DML statements serially. This is the default mode.

FORCE forces parallel execution of subsequent DML statements in the session if none of the parallel DML restrictions are violated.

SET sets the following session parameters:

- SQL_TRACE controls the SQL trace facility for your session:
    - TRUE enables the SQL trace facility
    - FALSE disables the SQL trace facility
- GLOBAL_NAMES controls the enforcement of global name resolution for your session:
    - TRUE enables the enforcement of global name resolution.
    - FALSE disables the enforcement of global name resolution.
- SKIP_UNUSABLE_INDEXES controls the use and reporting of tables with unusable indexes or index partitions:
    - TRUE disables error reporting of indexes marked as unusable. Allows inserts, deletes, and updates to tables with unusable indexes or index partitions.
    - FALSE enables error reporting of indexes marked as unusable. Does not allow inserts, deletes, and updates to tables with unusable indexes or index partitions.
- NLS_LANGUAGE changes the language in which Oracle returns error and other messages. This parameter also implicitly specifies new values for the following items:
    - Language for day and month names and abbreviations and spelled values of other elements
    - Sort sequences
    - B.C. and A.D. indicators
    - A.M. and P.M. meridian indicators
- NLS_TERRITORY implicitly specifies new values for these items:
    - Default date format
    - Decimal character and group separators
    - ISO currency symbol
    - First day of the week for D date format element
- NLS_DATE_FORMAT explicitly specifies a new default date format.
- NLS_DATE_LANGUAGE explicitly changes the language for day and month names and abbreviations and spelled values of other date format elements.

- NLS_NUMERIC_CHARACTERS explicitly specifies a new decimal character and group separator. The *text* value must have the following form:
  - *dg*, where *d* is the new decimal character and *g* is the new group separator.
- NLS_ISO_CURRENCY explicitly specifies the territory whose ISO currency symbol should be used.
- NLS_CURRENCY explicitly specifies a new local currency symbol. This symbol cannot exceed ten characters.
- NLS_SORT changes the sequence into which Oracle sorts character values.
- *Sort* specifies the name of a linguistic sort sequence.
- BINARY specifies a binary sort (the default sort for all character sets is binary).
- NLS_CALENDAR explicitly specifies a new calendar type.
- OPTIMIZER_MODE specifies the approach and mode of the optimizer for the session:
  - RULE specifies the rule-based approach
  - ALL_ROWS specifies the cost-base approach and optimizes for best throughput.
  - FIRST_ROWS specifies the cost-based approach and optimizes for best response time.
  - CHOOSE causes the optimizer to choose an optimization approach based on the presence of statistics in the data dictionary.
- FLAGGER specifies FIPS flagging.
  - ENTRY flags for SQL92 Entry level.
  - INTERMEDIATE flags for SQL92 Intermediate level.
  - FULL flags for SQL92 Full level.
  - OFF turns off flagging.
- SESSION_CACHED_CURSORS specifies the size of the session cache for holding frequently used cursors. *Integer* specifies how many cursors can be retained in the cache.
- CLOSE_OPEN_CACHED_CURSORS controls whether cursors opened and cached in memory by PL/SQL are automatically closed at each COMMIT. A value of FALSE signifies that cursors opened by PL/SQL are held open so that subsequent

executions do not have to open a new cursor. A value of TRUE causes open cursors to be closed at each COMMIT or ROLLBACK.

- INSTANCE in a parallel server, accesses database files as if the session were connected to the instance specified by *integer*.

- HASH_JOIN_ENABLED enables or disables the use of hash join operations in queries. The *default* is TRUE, which allows hash joins.

- HASH_AREA_SIZE specifies in bytes the amount of memory to use for hash join operations. The default is twice the value of the SORT_AREA_SIZE initialization parameter.

- HASH_MULTIBLOCK_IO_COUNT specifies the number of data blocks to read and write during a hash join operation. The value multiplied by the DB_BLOCK_SIZE must be < 64Kb. Default value for this parameter is 1.

- REMOTE_DEPENDENCIES_MODE specifies how dependencies of remote stored procedures are handled by the session.

- ISOLATION_LEVEL specifies how transactions containing database modifications are handled.

- SERIALIZABLE uses the serializable transaction isolation mode specified in SQL92. That is, if a serializable transaction attempts to execute a DML statement that updates any resource that may have been updated in an uncommitted transaction at the start of the serializable transaction, then the DML statement fails. The COMPATIBLE initialization parameter should be set to 7.3.0 or higher for SERIALIZABLE mode to work.

- READ COMMITTED uses the default Oracle transaction behavior. Therefore, if in a transaction, there is a DML statement that requires row locks held by another transaction, then the DML statement will wait until the row locks are released.

- CONSTRAINT[S] IMMEDIATE indicates that the conditions specified by the deferrable constraint are checked immediately after each DML statement.

- CONSTRAINT[S] DEFERRED indicates that the conditions specified by the deferrable constraint are checked when the transaction is committed.

- CONSTRAINT[S] DEFAULT restores all constraints at the beginning of each transaction to their initial state of DEFERRED or IMMEDIATE.

- PLSQL_V2_COMPATIBILITY modifies the compile-time behavior of PL/SQL programs to allow language constructs that are illegal in Oracle8 but were legal in Oracle7.

  - TRUE enables Oracle8 PL/SQL programs to execute Oracle7 PL/SQL constructs.

  - FALSE disables illegal Oracle7 PL/SQL constructs. This is the default.

- MAX_DUMP_FILE_SIZE specifies the upper limit of trace dump file size. Specify the maximum size as either a non-negative integer that represents the number of blocks or as UNLIMITED.

SQL Trace   The SQL Trace facility generates performance statistics for the processing of SQL statements. You can enable and disable the SQL trace facility for all sessions on an Oracle instance with the initialization parameter SQL_TRACE. If this parameter is TRUE, then tracing is enabled, and if this parameter is FALSE, then tracing is disabled.

NLS Parameters   Oracle contains support for use in different nations and with different languages. There are several initialization parameters that start with NLS, which control various facets of this feature. You can see the current settings of the various NLS parameters for your session by querying the V$NLS_PARAMETERS view. You can alter them through the ALTER SESSION command.

Optimizing Approach   There are two different strategies that Oracle can use for optimizing a SQL statement:

- Rule-based   The optimizer optimizes a SQL statement based on the indexes and clusters associated with the accessed tables, syntax of the statement, etc.

- Cost-based   The optimizer optimizes a SQL statement by considering the statistics describing the tables, indexes, and clusters accessed by the statement as well as the information considered with the rule-based approach. With the CBO (cost-based optimizer) the optimizer can optimize a SQL statement with one of these goals:

  - Best throughput   The minimal time necessary to return all rows accessed by the statement.

- Best response time   The minimal time necessary to return the first row accessed by the statement.

FIPS Flagging   This causes an error message to be issued whenever a SQL statement is issued that is an extension of the SQL92 standard.

Caching Session Cursors   Performance is greatly affected by reparsing the same SQL statement over and over again. To overcome this, you can set the SESSION_CACHED_CURSORS to store frequently used session cursors in a session cache even if they are closed.

Closing Database Links   A database link allows you to access a remote database in DML statements. When a statement uses a database link, Oracle creates a session for you on the remote database using the database link. The connection remains open until the local session is ended or until the database links for the session exceed the value of OPEN_LINKS (initialization parameter). Database links which are not going to be used in the same session can be closed by using the CLOSE DATABASE LINK clause of the ALTER SESSION command.

Offering Advice for Forcing In-doubt Distributed Transactions The advice is basically used in situations which involve distributed transactions (through database links) that are in an in-doubt state. The ADVICE column of the DBA_2PC_PENDING contains the advice.

Enabling and Disabling Transaction Control in Procedures and Functions   Sometimes, depending on your application, you might want to disallow or allow stored procedures and functions from committing or rolling back transactions. This can be accomplished by the ENABLE/DISABLE clause of the ALTER SESSION command.

ALTER SYSTEM

ENABLE RESTRICTED SESSION allows only users with RESTRICTED SESSION privilege to log on to Oracle.

DISABLE RESTRICTED SESSION reverses the effect of the ENABLE RESTRICTED SESSION option, allowing all users with CREATE SESSION system privilege to log on to Oracle.

FLUSH SHARED POOL clears all data from the shared pool in the System Global Area (SGA).

You can use the following options when your instance has the database mounted, open, or closed:

- CHECKPOINT performs a checkpoint.
- GLOBAL performs a checkpoint for all instances that have opened the database.
- LOCAL performs a checkpoint for the thread of redo log file groups for your instance. If both the above options are omitted, the default is GLOBAL.
- CHECK DATAFILES:
  - GLOBAL verifies that all instances that have opened the database can access all online data files.
  - LOCAL verifies that your instance can access all online data files. GLOBAL is the default option once again.

You can only use the following parameters and options when your instance has the database open:

- RESOURCE_LIMIT controls resource limits.
- TRUE enables resource limits.
- FALSE disables resource limits.
- GLOBAL_NAMES:
  - TRUE enables the enforcement of global names.
  - FALSE disables the enforcement of global names.
- SCAN_INSTANCES specifies the number of instances to participate in parallelized operations in a parallel server (this will become obsolete in the next major release).
- CACHE_INSTANCES specifies the number of instances that will cache a table in a parallel server (this will become obsolete in the next major release).
- MTS_SERVERS specifies a new minimum number of shared server processes.
- MTS_DISPATCHERS specifies a new number of dispatcher processes:
  - *Protocol* is the network protocol of the dispatcher processes.

- *Integer* is the new number of dispatcher processes of the specified protocol.
- LICENSE_MAX_SESSIONS limits the number of sessions on your instance. A value of 0 disables the limit.
- LICENSE_SESSIONS_WARNING establishes a threshold of sessions over which Oracle writes warning messages to the ALERT file for subsequent sessions. A value of 0 disables the limit.
- LICENSE_MAX_USERS limits number of concurrent users on the database. A value of 0 disables the limit.
- REMOTE_DEPENDENCIES_MODE specifies how dependencies of remote stored procedures are handled by the server.
- SWITCH LOGFILE switches redo log file groups.
- ENABLE DISTRIBUTED RECOVERY enables distributed recovery.
- DISABLE DISTRIBUTED RECOVERY disables distributed recovery.
- ARCHIVE LOG manually archives redo log files or enables or disables automatic archiving.
- KILL SESSION terminates a session and any ongoing transactions. You must identify the session with the SID (session id) and SERIAL# from the V$SESSION view.
- DISCONNECT SESSION disconnects the current session by destroying the dedicated server process—or virtual circuit if connection was made via MTS (multithreaded server).
- POST_TRANSACTION allows ongoing transactions to complete before the session is disconnected.
- PLSQL_V2_COMPATIBILITY modifies the compile-time behavior of PL/SQL programs to allow language constructs that are illegal in Oracle8 but were legal in Oracle7.
  - TRUE enables Oracle8 PL/SQL programs to execute Oracle7 PL/SQL constructs.
  - FALSE disallows illegal Oracle7 PL/SQL program constructs.
- MAX_DUMP_FILE_SIZE specifies the trace dump file size upper limit for all user sessions. Specify the maximum *size* as either a non-negative integer that represents the number of blocks or UNLIMITED. If UNLIMITED is specified, no upper limit is imposed.

Restricting Logons   By default, anyone with a valid userid and password can log on to the database. When the system is altered with the ENABLE RESTRICTED SESSION option, then only users having RESTRICTED SESSION privileges can log on to the database.

Shared Pool   The FLUSH_SHARED_POOL option of the ALTER SYSTEM command clears the shared pool in the System Global Area (SGA). The shared pool has the cached data dictionary information and the shared SQL and PL/SQL areas for SQL statements, stored procedures, functions, packages, or triggers that are currently being executed, or for SQL statements for which all rows have not yet been fetched.

Checkpointing   The CHECKPOINT clause of the ALTER SYSTEM command explicitly forces Oracle to perform a checkpoint. A checkpoint can be forced to ensure that all the changes made by committed transactions are written to disks.

Resource Limits   When an Oracle instance is started, resource limits are enabled or disabled based on the value of the initialization parameter called RESOURCE_LIMIT. An alter system command with the RESOURCE_LIMIT option allows you to enable or disable resource limits for a subsequent session.

Global Name Resolution   There is an initialization parameter in Oracle called GLOBAL_NAMES that determines whether global name resolution for remote objects will be imposed. This parameter can be modified subsequently by the ALTER SYSTEM command.

Multithreaded Server Processes   Based on the values for MTS_SERVERS and MTS_DISPATCHERS, Oracle creates shared server processes and dispatcher processes when the instance is started. The MTS_SERVERS parameter specifies the initial and minimum number of shared server processes. Depending on the load, Oracle may automatically start more shared server processes up to a maximum of MTS_MAX_SERVERS value. The MTS_DISPATCHER parameter specifies one or more network protocols and the number of dispatcher processes for each protocol. The ALTER SYSTEM command can be used to create additional shared server processes, to terminate existing shared server processes, to create more dispatcher processes, and to terminate existing dispatcher processes.

Licensing Limits   Concurrent usage licensing and named user licensing limits are enforced by Oracle through the

LICENSE_MAX_SESSIONS, LICENSE_MAX_USERS, and LICENSE_SESSIONS_WARNING initialization parameters. These can be altered by the ALTER SYSTEM command.

SET (Microsoft SQL Server)

The following are query processing options:

- PARSEONLY causes SQL server to parse the query for syntactic and semantic correctness only, without optimizing, compiling, or executing it.

- NOEXEC performs all the steps through compilation but does not execute the query. It is often used with the SHOWPLAN option to determine the execution plan generated for a query.

- SHOWPLAN reveals the query execution plan generated by SQL Server's cost-based optimizer.

- FORCEPLAN forces SQL server to process joins in the same order in which tables appear in the FROM clause.

- BACKGROUND option puts tasks generated by subsequent statements in the background and breaks the connection to the workstation.

- NOCOUNT   If this option is set to ON, the message displayed at the end of each statement execution does not appear.

- SET ROWCOUNT *number* option is used to specify the maximum number of rows the server should process.

The following are statistics options:

- STATISTICS IO displays several pieces of useful information such as the number of table scans, the number of logical accesses (cache reads), the number of physical reads (disk I/Os), and the total number of pages written including log page writes.

- STATISTICS TIME displays time in milliseconds for parsing, compiling, and executing queries.

The following are exception handling options:

- ARITHABORT   When this option is set to ON, the query processing is aborted if either a divide by zero or an overflow condition occurs during execution.

- ARITHIGNORE   When this option is set to ON, a NULL is returned when either a divide by zero or an overflow exception occurs. No error message is returned.

NOTE: Both these options cannot be set to ON simultaneously. The default setting is with both the options set to OFF, which causes SQL server to return an error message and a NULL.

3

The following are result interpretation options:

- OFFSETS   This option is used in application programs to return the position, relative to the beginning of the query, of the specified SQL construct in the command buffer.

- PROCID   Setting this option returns the ID of the stored procedure to the application before it returns any rows generated as a result of the stored procedure.

The following are language options:

- LANGUAGE *language* option sets the language in which the server will display messages. The language must be installed on the server. The default is *us_english.*

- DATEFIRST *number* option sets the first weekday to a number from 1 to 7. The default for *us_english* is 1 (Sunday).

- DATEFORMAT *format* option sets the order of the date parts for entering *datetime* data. The default for *us_english* is *mdy* (month, day, year).

SET ROLE

Role is a role to be enabled for the current session.

Password is the password for the role.

ALL EXCEPT enables all roles granted to you except those listed in the EXCEPT clause. Roles in the EXCEPT clause must be roles granted to you directly, not through a role. This option cannot be used to enable roles that have a password.

NONE disables all roles for the current session.

A privilege domain is established when you start your session by enabling your default roles. Your default privilege domain contains all privileges granted explicitly to you and all privileges in the privilege domains of your default roles.

The SET ROLE command can be used to enable or disable either of the following roles:

- Roles that have been granted to you directly
- Roles that have been granted to you through other roles

You cannot use the SET ROLE command to enable roles that you have not been granted directly or through other roles.

Your current privilege domain is also changed in the following cases:

- If you are granted a privilege
- If one of your privileges is revoked
- If one of your enabled roles is revoked
- If the privilege domain of one of your enabled roles is changed

Embedded SQL Statements

ALLOCATE

Dbname is a null-terminated string containing the database connection name, as established previously in a CONNECT statement. If omitted, or if an empty string, the default database connection is assumed.

Cursor_variable is the cursor variable to be allocated.

Host_ptr is a pointer to a host structure generated by the Object Type Translator (specific to Oracle8 only) for object types.

CLOSE

Cursor is a cursor to be closed.

Cursor_variable is a cursor variable to be closed.

COMMIT

AT identifies the database to which the COMMIT statement is issued. The database can be identified by one of these:

- *Db_name* is a database identifier declared in a previous DECLARE DATABASE statement.
- :*host_variable* is a host variable whose value is a *db_name*.

If this clause is omitted, the COMMIT is issued at the default database.

WORK is supported for standard SQL compliance only.

COMMENT specifies a comment to be associated with the current transaction. The 'text' is a quoted literal stored in the data dictionary view DBA_2PC_PENDING along with the transaction ID if the transaction becomes in-doubt.

RELEASE frees all resources and disconnects the application from the database server.

FORCE manually commits an in-doubt distributed transaction.

CONNECT

:*user*/:*password* specifies the username and password separately.

:*user_password* is a single host variable containing the username and password separated by a slash (/).

AT identifies the database to which the connection is made. The database can be identified either by *db_name*, which is a database identifier declared in a previous DECLARE DATABASE statement, or by *:host_variable*, which is a host variable whose value is a previously declared *db_name*.

USING specifies the database specification string used to connect to a non-default database. If this clause is omitted, you connect to the default database.

ALTER AUTHORIZATION changes the password

:new_password is the new password.

CONTEXT ALLOCATE

Context is the allocated runtime context for which the memory is to be deallocated.

CONTEXT USE

Context is the allocated runtime context to use for subsequent executable SQL statements that follow it.

DECLARE CURSOR

AT identifies the database on which the cursor is declared. The database can be identified by either *db_name*, which is a database identifier declared in a previous DECLARE DATABASE statement, or a *:host_variable* whose value is a previously declared database. If this is omitted, the cursor is declared on the default database.

Cursor is the name of the cursor to be declared.

SELECT *command* is a SELECT statement to be associated with the cursor.

Statement_name or *block_name* identifies a SQL statement or PL/SQL block to be associated with the cursor. The *statement_name* or *block_name* must have been previously declared in a DECLARE STATEMENT statement.

DECLARE DATABASE

Db_name is the identifier established for the non-default database.

DECLARE STATEMENT

AT identifies the database on which the SQL statement or PL/SQL block is declared. The database can be identified by either *db_name*, which is a database identifier declared in a previous DECLARE DATABASE statement, or a *:host_variable* whose value is a *db_name*.

Statement_name or *block_name* is the declared identifier for the statement.

DECLARE TABLE

Table is the name of the declared table.

Column is a column of the table.

Datatype is the datatype of a column.

DEFAULT specifies the default value of a column.

Expr is any expression usable as a default column value in a CREATE TABLE statement.

NULL specifies that a column can contain nulls.

NOT NULL specifies that a column cannot contain nulls.

WITH DEFAULT is supported for compatibility with IBM DB2 database.

DECLARE TYPE

Type is the name of the declared type.

Column is a column.

Datatype is the datatype of the column.

DESCRIBE

BIND VARIABLES initializes the descriptor to hold information about the input variable for the SQL statement or PL/SQL block.

SELECT LIST FOR initializes the descriptor to hold information about the select list of a SELECT statement. (This is the default.)

Statement_name or *block_name* identifies a SQL statement or PL/SQL block previously prepared with a PREPARE statement.

Descriptor is the name of the descriptor to be initialized.

ENABLE THREADS

There are no keywords or parameters for this command.

EXECUTE...END-EXEC

AT identifies the database on which the PL/SQL block is executed. The database can be identified by either *db_name*, which is a database identifier declared in a previous DECLARE DATABASE statement, or :*host_variable*, whose value is a previously declared *db_name*. If this clause is omitted, the PL/SQL block is executed on the default database.

Pl/sql_block is the PL/SQL block to be executed.

END-EXEC must appear after the embedded PL/SQL block, regardless of the programming language used by the precompiler, and it must be terminated by the C/C++ statement terminator, ";".

3

EXECUTE

FOR :*host_integer* limits the number of times the statement is executed when the USING clause contains array host variables. If this clause is omitted, the statement is executed once for each component of the smallest array.

Statement_id is a precompiler identifier associated with the SQL statement or PL/SQL block to be executed. The EXEC SQL PREPARE statement is used to associate the precompiler identifier with the statement or PL/SQL block.

USING specifies a list of host variables with optional indicator variables that are substituted as input variables into the statement to be executed. The host and indicator variables should be either all scalars or all arrays.

EXECUTE IMMEDIATE

AT identifies the database on which the SQL statement or PL/SQL block is executed. The database can be identified by either *db_name*, which is a database identifier declared in a previous DECLARE DATABASE statement, or :*host_variable*, whose value is a previously declared *db_name*. If this clause is omitted, the statement or block is executed on the default database.

Text is a quoted text literal containing the SQL statement or PL/SQL block to be executed. The SQL statement can only be INSERT, UPDATE, or DELETE.

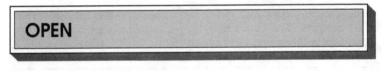

FETCH

FOR *:host_integer* limits the number of rows fetched if you are using array host variables. If this clause is omitted, then the number of rows fetched matches the size of the smallest array.

Cursor is a cursor that is declared by a DECLARE CURSOR statement. The FETCH statement returns one of the rows selected by the query associated with the cursor.

:Cursor_variable is a cursor variable allocated by an ALLOCATE statement. The FETCH statement returns one of the rows selected by the query associated with the cursor variable.

INTO specifies a list of host variables and optional indicator variables into which data is fetched.

USING specifies the descriptor referenced in a previous DESCRIBE statement. This clause is to be used only with dynamic embedded SQL, method 4. Also, this clause cannot be used with a cursor variable.

OPEN

Cursor is the cursor to be opened.

USING specifies the host variables to be substituted into the WHERE clause of the associated query.

:Host_variable specifies a host variable to be substituted into the WHERE clause of the associated query.

DESCRIPTOR specifies a descriptor that describes the host variables to be substituted into the WHERE clause of the associated query. The descriptor must be initialized in a previous DESCRIBE statement.

PREPARE

Statement_id is the identifier to be associated with the prepared SQL statement or PL/SQL block. If this identifier was previously assigned to another statement or block, the prior assignment is superseded.

:Host_string is a host variable whose value is the text of a SQL statement or PL/SQL block to be prepared.

Text is a string literal containing a SQL statement or PL/SQL block to be prepared.

Select_command is a select command.

ROLLBACK

WORK is optional and is provided for ANSI compatibility.

TO rolls back the current transaction to the specified savepoint. If this clause is omitted, the entire transaction is rolled back.

FORCE manually rolls back an in-doubt distributed transaction. The transaction is identified by the text containing its local or global transaction ID. The transaction IDs can be found in the DBA_2PC_PENDING view in Oracle.

RELEASE frees all resources and disconnects the application from the database server. This clause is not allowed with SAVEPOINT and FORCE clauses.

SAVEPOINT

AT identifies the database on which the SQL statement or PL/SQL block is executed. The database can be identified by either *db_name*, which is a database identifier declared in a previous DECLARE DATABASE statement, or *:host_variable*, whose value is a previously declared *db_name*. If this clause is omitted, the statement or block is executed on the default database.

Savepoint is the name of the savepoint to be created.

TYPE

Type is the user-defined datatype to be equivalenced with an Oracle datatype.

Datatype is an Oracle external datatype recognized by the precompilers. The datatype may include length, precision, or scale.

REFERENCE makes the equivalenced type a pointer type.

VAR

Host_variable is the host variable to be assigned an Oracle external datatype.

Dtype is an external datatype recognized by the precompilers. The datatype may include a length, precision, or scale. This external datatype is assigned to the *host_variable*.

Len is the length of the datatype.

Prec is its precision.

Scale is its scale.

Size is the size (in bytes) of a buffer in the runtime library used to perform conversion between character sets of the *host_variable*.

WHENEVER

NOT FOUND identifies any exception condition that returns an error code of +1403 (Oracle) to SQLCODE (or a +100 code when MODE=ANSI).

SQLERROR identifies a condition that results in a negative return code.

SQLWARNING identifies a non-fatal warning condition.

CONTINUE indicates that the program should progress to the next statement.

GOTO indicates that the program should branch to the statement named by the label.

STOP stops the program execution.

DO indicates that the program should call a function that is named *routine*.

DO BREAK performs a break statement from a loop when the condition is met.

DO CONTINUE performs a continue statement from a loop when the condition is met.

SQL Commands Related to Object Extensions

DDL Commands

ALTER TYPE

Schema is the schema to contain the type. If the schema is omitted, the type is created in the current user's schema.

Type_name is the name of the object type, nested table type, or a VARRAY type.

COMPILE compiles the object type specification and body. If, however, you specify the keyword SPECIFICATION or BODY, the corresponding part gets compiled.

REPLACE adds new member methods.

Attribute_name is the name of the attribute of an object.

MEMBER specifies a function or a procedure associated with the object type.

Procedure_specification is the specification of a method that is a procedure.

Function_specification is the specification of a method that is a function.

PRAGMA RESTRICT_REFERENCES is a compiler directive that sets the purity level of functions. The various purity levels are

- WNDS (Writes No Database State)—that is, it does not modify any database tables.
- RNDS (Reads No Database State)—that is, it does not query database tables.
- WNPS (Writes No Package State)—that is, it does not modify package variables.
- RNPS (Reads No Package State)—that is, it does not reference package variables.

Method_name is the name of the MEMBER function whose purity level is being specified.

CREATE DIRECTORY

OR REPLACE re-creates the directory database object if it already exists.

Directory is the name of the directory object to be created. The maximum length of the name of the directory is 30 bytes.

Path_name is the full path name of the operating system directory on the server where the files are located.

NOTE: A directory object specifies an alias name for a directory on the server's file system where external binary file LOBs (BFILEs) are located. The directory name can be used when referring to BFILEs in your applications instead of hard-coding the operating system path name.

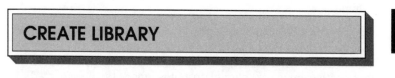

CREATE LIBRARY

OR REPLACE re-creates the library if it already exists. You can use this option to change the definition of an existing library without dropping and re-creating it.

Libname is the name of the library that will be referenced in SQL and PL/SQL.

Filespec is a non-zero length string that is the name of the operating system library.

CREATE TABLE

OF *object_type* explicitly creates an object table of type *object_type*. The object table columns correspond to the attributes of the object type. Since this is an object table, each row has a unique object identifier (OID) that is system-generated.

Attribute specifies the qualified column name of an item in an object. The attributes of an object type can have standard SQL datatypes and also be other object types, REF *object_type*, VARRAYs, and nested tables.

WITH ROWID stores the ROWID and REF in the column or attribute.

SCOPE IS *scope_table_name* restricts the scope of the column REF values to *scope_table_name*. The *scope_table_name* is the name of the object table in which instances of the object reside. There can only be one scope table per REF column.

SCOPE FOR *(ref_column_name)* IS *scope_table_name* restricts the scope of the REF values in *ref_column_value* to *scope_table_name*.

REF *(ref_column_name)* is a reference to a row in an object table.

OIDINDEX specifies an index on the hidden object identifier column and/or the storage specification for the index.

Index is the name of the index on the hidden object identifier column.

NESTED TABLE *nested_item* STORE AS *storage_table* specifies *storage_table* as the name of the storage table in which rows of all *nested_item* values reside. This clause is essential when creating a table with columns or column attributes whose type is a nested table. The *storage_table* is the name of the storage table that is created in the same schema and tablespace as the parent table. The *nested_item* is the name of a column or a column-qualified attribute whose type is a nested table.

CREATE TYPE

OR REPLACE re-creates the type if it already exists. The definition of an existing type can be changed without dropping it.

Schema is the schema to contain the object type.

Type_name is the name of an object type, nested table type, or VARRAY type.

AS OBJECT creates the type as a user-defined object type. Object types have attributes and methods.

AS TABLE creates a named nested table type of the given *datatype*. Datatype could either be a scalar datatype or an object type.

AS VARRAY *(limit)* creates the type as an array of variable length up to a maximum length determined by the value of *limit*.

OF *datatype* is any Oracle built-in datatype or library type. LONG, LONG RAW, and ROWID are invalid datatypes.

REF *object_type_name* associates an instance of a source type with an instance of the target object.

Type_name is the name of the user-defined object type, nested table type, or VARRAY type.

Attribute_name is the name of an attribute of an object.

MEMBER is a keyword used to specify a function or a procedure associated with an object type.

CREATE TYPE BODY

3

OR REPLACE re-creates the type body if it already exists. This option can be used to change the definition of a type body without dropping the type body.

Schema is the schema to contain the type body.

Type_name is the name of an object type.

MEMBER gives the actual body for a method procedure or a method function associated with the object type specification.

Procedure_declaration is the declaration of a procedure.

Function_declaration is the declaration of a function.

MAP MEMBER *function_declaration* declares a MAP member function.

ORDER MEMBER *function_declaration* declares an ORDER member function.

DROP DIRECTORY

Directory_name is the name of the directory database object to be dropped.

DROP LIBRARY

Libname is the name of the external procedure library being dropped.

DROP TYPE

Type_name is the name of the object, VARRAY, or nested table type to be dropped. You can only drop types with no type or table dependencies.

FORCE drops a type that references another type.

DROP TYPE BODY

Type_name is the name of the object type body to be dropped.

DML Commands

DELETE

THE informs Oracle that the column value returned by the subquery is a nested table.

Subquery is a subquery from which data is selected for deletion.

Alias is an alias assigned to the table, view, or subquery. Aliases are generally used with correlated subqueries in DELETE statements.

WHERE deletes only rows satisfying the condition.

RETURNING retrieves the rows affected by the DELETE statement. Only scalar, LOB, ROWID, and REF types can be retrieved.

INSERT

THE informs Oracle that the column value returned by the subquery is a nested table, not a scalar value.

Subquery_1 is a subquery that is treated as a view.

Subquery_2 is a subquery that returns rows that are inserted into the table. The select list in this subquery must have the same number of columns as the column list in the INSERT statement.

RETURNING retrieves the rows affected by the INSERT. Only scalar, LOB, ROWID, and REF types can be retrieved.

INTO indicates that the values of the changed rows are to be stored in the variables specified in data_item_list.

Data_item_list is a list of PL/SQL or bind variables which stores the retrieved expression value.

SELECT

DISTINCT returns only one copy of each set of duplicate rows selected.

ALL returns all rows selected, including all copies of duplicates. This is the default.

Table., View.* snapshot.** selects all columns from all tables, views, or snapshots listed in the FROM clause.

PARTITION *(partition_name)* specifies partition-level data retrieval. The *partition_name* is the name of the partition within *table* from which to retrieve data.

C_alias provides a different name for the column expression and causes the alias to be used in the column heading.

Schema is the schema containing the selected table, view, or snapshot.

Table, view, snapshot is the name of the table, view, or snapshot from which the data is selected.

Dblink is the complete or partial name for a database link to a remote database where the table, view, or snapshot is located.

Subquery is a subquery that is treated in the same manner as a view.

THE informs Oracle that the column value returned by the subquery is a nested table, not a scalar value. A subquery prefixed by THE is called a flattened subquery.

T_alias provides a different name for a table, view, or snapshot, or subquery for evaluating the query and is used most frequently in a correlated query.

WHERE restricts the rows selected to those for which the condition is TRUE.

START WITH CONNECT BY returns rows in a hierarchical order.

GROUP BY groups the selected rows based on the value of the expression for each row and returns a single row of summary information for each group.

HAVING restricts the groups of rows returned to those groups for which the specified condition is true.

UNION/UNION ALL/ INTERSECT/ MINUS combines the rows retrieved by two SELECT statements using a set operation.

NOTE: Results of queries that use the MULTISET or the THE keyword cannot be combined with these set operators.

ORDER BY orders rows returned by the SELECT command.

FOR UPDATE locks the selected rows.

NOTE: It cannot be used with the CURSOR operator.

OF locks the selected rows for a particular table in a join.

NOWAIT returns control to you if the SELECT statement attempts to lock a row that is already locked by a different user. If this clause is omitted, then Oracle waits until the row is available.

UPDATE

Schema is the schema containing the table or view.

Table/view is the name of the table to be updated. If a view is specified, then the view's base table is updated.

Dblink is the complete or partial name of a database link to a remote database where the table or view is located.

PARTITION *(partition_name)* specifies partition-level row updates for a table. The *partition_name* is the name of the partition within the table targeted for updates.

Alias provides a different name for the table, view, or subquery to be referenced elsewhere in the statement.

THE informs Oracle that the column value returned by the subquery is a nested table, not a scalar value.

Subquery_1 is a subquery that Oracle treats in the same manner as a view.

Column is the name of a column in the table or view that is to be updated. Only columns whose names appear in the column list get updated.

Expr is the new value assigned to the corresponding column.

Subquery_2 is a subquery that returns new values that are assigned to the corresponding columns.

Subquery_3 is a subquery that returns new values that are assigned to the corresponding columns.

WHERE restricts the number of rows updated to those for which the specified condition is TRUE.

RETURNING retrieves the rows affected by the UPDATE statement. Only scalar, LOB, ROWID, and REF types can be retrieved.

INTO indicates that the values of the changed rows are to be stored in the variable(s) specified in the *data_item_list*.

Data_item is a PL/SQL variable or bind variable that stores the retrieved *expr* value.

Embedded SQL Commands

CACHE FREE ALL

Db_name is a null-terminated string containing the database connection name, as established previously in a CONNECT statement. If this is omitted, the default database connection is assumed.

CONTEXT OBJECT OPTION GET

Option can be either DATEFORMAT (format for date conversion) or DATELANG (language for conversion).

Expr is the output of type STRING, VARCHAR, or CHARZ, in the same order as option list.

CONTEXT OBJECT OPTION SET

Option can be either DATEFORMAT (format for Date conversion) or DATELANG (language for Date conversion).

Expr is the input of type STRING, VARCHAR, or CHARZ in the same order as the option list.

FREE

Dbname is a null-terminated string containing the database connection name, as established previously in a CONNECT statement. If this is omitted, then the default database connection is assumed.

Host_ptr is a pointer to a host structure generated by the Object Type Translator (OTT) for an object type in the object cache.

OBJECT CREATE

Obj (OUT) is the object instance host variable that must be a pointer to a structure generated by the OTT. This variable is used to determine the referenceable object that is created in the object cache.

Obj_ind (OUT) is a pointer to the OTT-generated indicator structure. Its type must match that of the object instance host variable.

Tab(IN) clause is used to create persistent objects. The table name can be specified as a host variable, *hv*, or as an undeclared SQL identifier.

Hv(IN) is a host variable specifying a table. If a host variable is used, it must not be an array. It is case-sensitive.

Table(IN) is an undeclared SQL identifier that is case-sensitive.

Ref(OUT) is the reference host variable that must be a pointer to the OTT-generated reference type. The type of *ref* must match that of the object instance host variable.

OBJECT DELETE

There are no new keywords or parameters for this command.

OBJECT DEREF

There are no new keywords or parameters for this command.

OBJECT FLUSH

Ref (IN) is the object reference variable, which must be a pointer to the OTT-generated reference type. This variable (or array of variables) is dereferenced, returning a pointer to the corresponding object in the object cache.

Obj(OUT) is the object instance host variable, which must be a pointer to an OTT-generated structure. Its type must match that of the object reference host variable.

Obj_ind (OUT) is the object instance indicator variable, which must be a pointer to the OTT-generated indicator structure. Its type must match that of the object reference indicator variable.

FOR UPDATE   If this clause is present, an exclusive lock is obtained for the corresponding object in the server.

OBJECT GET

Attr is an identifier that specifies which attributes of the object will be retrieved. The first attribute in the list is paired with the first host variable in the list, and so on. The attribute must represent a base type such as OCIString, OCINumber, OCIRef, or OCIDate.

Obj (IN) specifies the object that serves as the source for the attribute retrieval. The bind variable *obj* must not be an array.

Hv (OUT) is the bind variable used to hold output from the OBJECT GET statement. It can be an int, float, double, one-dimensional char array, or structure containing those types. The statement returns the converted attribute value in this host variable.

Hv_ind (OUT) is the associated indicator variable for the attribute value.

OBJECT RELEASE

There are no specific keywords or parameters for this command.

OBJECT SET

Attr is an identifier that specifies which attributes of the object will be retrieved. The first attribute in the list is paired with the first host variable in the list, and so on. The attribute must represent a base type such as OCIString, OCINumber, OCIRef, or OCIDate.

Obj (IN/OUT) specifies the object to be updated. The bind variable *obj* must not be an array.

Obj_ind (IN/OUT) is the parallel indicator structure that will be updated. It must be a pointer to an OTT-generated indicator structure.

Hv (IN) is the bind variable used as input to the OBJECT SET statement. It can be an int, float, double, one-dimensional char array, or structure containing those types. The statement returns the converted attribute value in this host variable.

Hv_ind (IN) is the associated indicator variable used as an input to the OBJECT SET statement.

OBJECT UPDATE

There are no keywords or parameters specifically for this command.

INDEX

325